Aug 3 1993

SWEET
REPRIEVE

May 3, 1991

Brada & Janan;

Since were not going to see you for a while I thought better send this to you.

Your support and love has meant so much to us during this journey. Mom or I couldn't have gotten this far without your caring.

It's so exciting to begin the 3rd year with the best blood tests in 15 yrs. We certainly hope it continues.

Love
Dad & Mom

SWEET

One Couple's Journey to
the Frontiers of Medicine

REPRIEVE

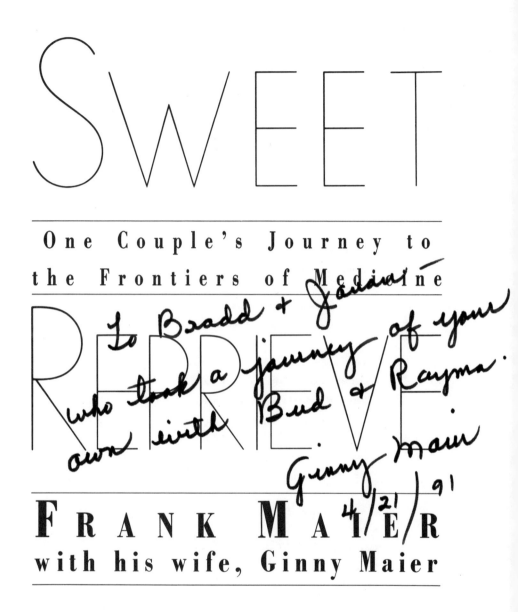

To Bradd + Jordaine
who took a journey of your
own with Bud + Rayma.

Ginny Maier
4/21/91

FRANK MAIER
with his wife, Ginny Maier

CROWN PUBLISHERS, INC.
NEW YORK

Grateful acknowledgment is made to the C. M.
Paula Company for permission to reprint previously
published material. Copyright owned by the C. M.
Paula Company. All rights reserved.

Copyright © 1991 by the Estate of Frank Maier

Published by Crown Publishers, Inc., 201 East 50th Street,
New York, New York 10022. Member of the Crown Publishing
Group.

CROWN is a trademark of Crown Publishers, Inc.

Manufactured in the United States of America

Library of Congress Cataloging-in-Publication Data

Maier, Frank.
    Sweet Reprieve : one couple's journey to the frontiers of medicine / by
Frank Maier. — 1st ed.
        p.   cm.
    1. Maier, Frank—Health.   2. Liver Transplantation—Patients—
United States—Biography.   Journalists—United States—
Biography.   4. Married people—United States—Biography.
I. Title.
RD546.M27   1991
362.1'97556—dc20   90-48761
                                                                          CIP

ISBN 0-517-58161-2

10 9 8 7 6 5 4 3 2 1

Book design by Deborah Kerner

First Edition

FOR GINNY RYAN MAIER
AND MICHAEL,
KATIE,
DANIEL,
AND HEIDI

"The best thing
you can ever do
for your children
is to love their mother."
THE REV. THEODORE M. HESBURGH, C.S.C.

CONTENTS

ACKNOWLEDGMENTS

The characters in this book are all real people we encountered in a journey we never planned to take. It is Ginny's and my hope that you will enjoy meeting them, just as we did.

But there are other people who are not properly thanked within these pages for what they have done for us. Ever so inadaquately, we thank them here.

A special thanks to my agent, Rollene Saal, for her encouragement right from the start; and to my editors Arlene Friedman and Joyce Engelson for their enthusiasm and judgment right to the finish.

I would not be here to write this book were it not for the care and skills of many medical professionals whose names I never will know. I give special thanks to nurses everywhere, those underappreciated, underpaid men and women who care for the ailing and the hurting among us. I thank the nurses at Northwest Community Hospital in my hometown of Arlington Heights, Illinois, particularly those in the Intensive Care Unit and the Endoscopy Department, for keeping me alive until the Liver Transplant Team at Mayo Clinic and the nurses at Station 53 at Rochester Methodist Hospital could give me new life.

To my editors at *Newsweek* magazine we acknowledge a special debt. In an age when most employers value the "bottom line" more than loyalty, they walked that extra mile with us.

Everyone who has undergone an organ transplant or received a tissue graft, anyone who suffers from chronic disease on which research is being done, owes an unpayable debt to those generous families who, despite their own pain, magnanimously offer a priceless gift from the body of their loved ones. I express my gratitude to the particular family that gave me such a gift and, on behalf of all transplant recipients, to every donor family.

Finally, Ginny and I always will remember the courage and example shown by those fellow pilgrims we met along the way who did not make it to the end of the journey: Walter, Sally, Michael, Janet, Paul, Mary Ann, Molly, Dee, and Neil.

May God hold them gently in the palms of His hands.

SWEET
REPRIEVE

PROLOGUE

This is what it's like to die. A nurse cutting off my T-shirt, the blue and white one that says "Ixtapa 84." Someone else slapping my right hand. A doctor pushing a tube up my nose and saying, "Swallow. Swallow." The slapping stops; then a stinging jab in the hand. Everything looks jerky and grainy, like an old movie. And somewhere off in the fog a woman's voice, like a phonograph winding down, is saying, "Blood pressure ninety over zero." I feel the sap oozing from my body, but I can't stop it. Will someone please tell Ginny to call the office and say I won't be in today?

I died for the first time at 9:37 in the morning on the Wednesday before Easter in 1986. It wasn't at all like I had expected. On the ambulance ride to the hospital, I chattered like a schoolboy on a field trip, even suggesting to the driver how he could avoid a detour on Cleveland Avenue. Like the Duke of Windsor, I deigned to ask the paramedic who was taping the IV line to my arm whether he liked his work. Everything seemed white to me, like we were driving through a snow storm. I felt it was my duty to comfort the two ambulance attendants. So I didn't tell them about the cold envelope that was starting to form around my body, like someone slowly pulling a sheet over me. I remember thinking: "If I'm dying, why am I so calm?"

On that spring day when I nearly bled to death for the first time, neither my wife, Ginny, nor I could possibly imagine what awaited us down the road or how we would change during our unexpected journey. At the time, the doctors in the emergency room didn't think I would last the night. Had I known what lay ahead in the next fourteen months, maybe I would have given up right then: three more serious hemorrhages; the stopping of my heart on one of the 125 days I spent in hospital beds; the 165 units of blood (each transfusion worrying about AIDS despite the doctors' smiling reassurances); finally a grueling ten-hour liver transplant that, for now, has postponed my death.

Ginny and I have lived through a medical adventure, a story that only a few people in the entire history of the world have experienced. In the next decade, many more people will follow that same path because of the explosive development of transplant medicine. Our story is about dying and coming back to life, about having a second chance at life.

If you will sit down with me for a while, I would like to tell you our story. I would like you to learn how Ginny and I have come to hold life in a new way, gently, the way you cup water in your hands.

Part One

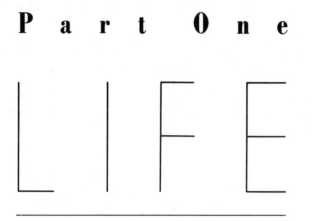

LIFE

1

ON TOP OF THE WORLD

Something wasn't quite right. Maybe it was the car, a rented Oldsmobile instead of my little Chevette, which was in the shop for repairs. The morning rush-hour traffic on the Kennedy Expressway was whisking along at a brisk 55 miles an hour toward the sun-sparkled buildings of Chicago's Loop. For some reason I felt uneasy in the middle lane with cars surging on either side of me. I looked for an opening and eased into the far left lane where I could nestle up comfortably to the retaining wall.

That's when and where life changed for me. At ten minutes before nine on a bright June morning in 1984, where the inbound Kennedy merges with the Edens Expressway, I learned in the space of ten seconds what I should have known from fifty years of living: that life is as fragile and uncertain as your next breath.

Without warning, the outside world began twirling in my head. I could not tell right from left, up from down. My foot fumbled for the brake peddle, but kept slipping off. I tried to steer straight and bring the car to a gradual stop, but I had no sense of direction. My eyes were spinning; horns were blaring; brakes were screeching. The car jolted into a guardrail and, like an exhausted animal, came to a panting stop. A young doctor stopped his car and ran back to me. He thought I had suffered a heart attack. My eyes had stopped spinning, but my heart pounded, my stomach ached, and my body shivered in fresh sweat. "You could have gotten killed," the doctor said, an observation that needed no planting in my imagination.

I was more embarrassed than frightened. Making a scene always did that to me. I assured him that I had not suffered a heart attack, that it probably was my eyes. That was it. I needed to get my eyes checked. I wished he would leave. Then maybe the passing cars would speed up and people would stop staring. At last he left, but only after making me promise to drive immediately to my doctor's office. I got out, walked around to inspect the crumpled right front fender, and did the only thing I ever seemed capable of doing when discombobulated by an automobile: I scratched my head.

The motor was still running, though the fender was bent away from the tire like a harelip. I figured it could limp to the nearest Hertz office, and from there I could taxi to work. I felt weak in the arms and a bit light-headed. But a busy day lay ahead, and I considered myself as fit as any other out-of-shape male with half a century on the odometer.

When I finally reached my office, I phoned Ginny to tell her of my misadventure, only to find her steaming mad. The workmen who were hired to lay carpeting in a bedroom that morning could not do it because the baseboard had not dried from paint Ginny had applied two days earlier.

"I'm so mad," she fumed. "I'll never get that room back together."

"When I tell you what happened to me, the wet baseboard won't seem all that important," I said proudly. "You nearly became a widow today."

At the time, I secretly enjoyed dumping on Ginny the news of my narrow escape on the expressway, a marital one-up-manship on my part—contrasting my close brush with death to her mundane problems with the carpet layers.

How could I know then that the incident on the expressway that morning was an early warning sign that I was seriously ill, that I was, in fact, starting to die? But at that time, death was not real for us, just a story to be told at the next dinner party.

Someone once said that life is what happens to us while we are making other plans. Well, death is much the same. It was not a convenient time to die. If anything, 1984 was a vintage year for mild-mannered reporter Frank Magner Maier. I had one of the best jobs in journalism, Midwest bureau chief for *Newsweek* magazine. For someone who dreamed of being a reporter when other kids were fantasizing about being shortstops, it was the pinnacle of success.

Working for *Newsweek* was a long throw from my first job as a $1.25-an-hour, one-man sports department at a tiny Midwestern daily newspaper. Although I figured to have another fifteen years in the business, I already had a stash of adventures to tell my grandchildren. I had done everything from playing chess with a 419-pound flagpole sitter named "Little John" atop his perch one Christmas Eve to interviewing the families of the nurses slaughtered by Richard Speck and the friends of the boys buried in John Wayne Gacy's basement.

Many times I had been on the fringes of historic events, including sitting just across the aisle from Bobby Kennedy on his campaign plane over Indiana on April 4, 1968, when aides told him that Martin Luther King Jr. had just been shot in Memphis.

Looking back, I now realize how much of my working life was spent in the shadow of violence and death. Only two months after I had seen Kennedy's ashen face on that airplane, I sat at my typewriter at the *Chicago Daily News* taking dictation from reporters covering his own funeral at St. Patrick's Cathedral in New York.

As a police reporter in Rockford, I led a schizophrenic life: at night I prowled the streets one jump behind the squad cars and emergency vehicles; during the day I took my children to the swings in the park like any other young father. To this day, I can see vividly every street corner, tavern, or rancid apartment in Rockford where I witnessed or reconstructed a tale of death or violence for readers to scan at their breakfast tables.

I can still see the two detectives using a curling iron to search for bullet fragments in the gelatinous pool of purple blood from a woman shot by her boyfriend in a beauty parlor. The toddler floating face down in the flooded field north of town and the little boy in a skeleton mask lying dead in the street on a rainy Halloween night. The college kid in his softball uniform sprawled on the highway, his life snuffed out in a head-on crash with a drunk driver.

Nothing in my childhood had prepared me for what I experienced daily as a young newspaper reporter. I grew up in a large, Depression-era home, benevolently presided over by parents and grandparents who tolerated a lot of confusion but absolutely no violence, verbal or physical, from my three sisters, my brother, or myself. Life in Oak Park, Illinois, for me at least, was like growing up on Walton's Mountain—only with Chicago right next door. The most violence I experienced growing up was when my two older sisters painted my fingernails bright red as I slept the night before I was to be an altar boy at the seven o'clock Mass.

As a reporter, I learned to cope with death and violence by growing a callus around my emotions, the way homicide detectives or emergency room attendants do. I dealt with death by never calling it by its right name. As a police reporter, I learned early in my career to keep my language impersonal. When you called the city desk to report that a pregnant teenager had jumped from a rooftop, you said, "I've got a leaper." The more of a pro you were, the more bored and detached you tried to sound when dictating a story from the police squad room to the rewrite desk. When a young father was killed in a car crash, you transformed him on the spot into a nonbeing, a "fatal." You asked rewrite, "Do you want me to dictate the fatal or come in and write it?"

I look back with a mixture of disbelief and sadness at the image of my younger self aggressively extracting names, facts, and details from people too stunned by disaster or disarmed by agony to realize what was going on. A police reporter engages in a brutal trade. How could that little boy I once was become so hard? I guess I did it by building separate rooms in my heart—a warm cozy room for the hours with my family and friends, and a cold, windowless compartment for the brutal hours on the job.

The higher I climbed on the journalistic ladder, the more sophisticated and mammoth the evil I encountered. Instead of recording in four-inch impersonal summaries the agonies suffered by victims of car crashes, murders, and drownings, I graduated to documenting for larger audiences violence on a grander scale—assassinations, horrible plane crashes, mass murders, tornadoes, and floods.

I will never forget the long night in the summer of 1966 when I wandered all over Austin, Texas, waking people up and talking to cops in an attempt to reconstruct the last hours of Charles Whitman,

8

former altar boy and Eagle Scout, before he stabbed his pretty young wife to death and then climbed to the top of Texas University Tower with a six-mm bolt-action rifle and methodically slaughtered fifteen and wounded thirty-three strangers strolling across campus.

I remember my nauseous fatigue as I walked through the rubble of downtown Richmond, Indiana, the morning after it was devastated by a gas explosion.

Even when assigned to a political story, I could not escape the shadow of death. In the midst of the 1966 Illinois senate race between the late Senator Paul Douglas and business executive Charles H. Percy, a home invader brutally murdered one of Percy's daughters, Valerie. Instead of reporting the colorful political battle between the crusty old Douglas and his energetic young opponent, I ended up joining the team of reporters trying to piece together her brutal murder.

When I became bureau chief in Chicago for *Newsweek,* my working day became less brutish. I was part-reporter and part-regional editor, able to assign the gut-wrenching stories to younger reporters and pluck the more cerebral or pastoral assignments for myself. As a city boy, I became fascinated with small towns and farms. I remember feeling like a character in a Normal Rockwell painting when I spent a day with a teacher and children in a one-room school north of Bismarck, North Dakota. Then a John Wayne Gacy would appear and I would be dragged back into the violent cruel world I knew as a young reporter.

For the most part, as I reached my personal half-century mark, I was pretty pleased with myself and the way life was working out for Ginny and me. Compared to many people, we were sitting on top of the world. We were about to reap some benefits from marrying young. Our oldest children, Michael and Katie, were out of college and working. Our youngest, Daniel and Heidi, were nearing the finish line without towing too much college debt behind them.

That summer of 1984 I was preparing to cover the Democratic National Convention in San Francisco. Then Ginny and I were going to tour the wine country with two of our oldest friends, Paul and Mary Kearney, who had moved to California a decade earlier. After that, to use up vacation time I had accumulated while working the previous year on *Newsweek*'s fiftieth anniversary special issue, I planned to fulfill a long-standing promise to take the former Ginny Ryan to Ireland to see the land of her ancestors.

Like other national publications and broadcast networks, *Newsweek* always puts on a full-court press at events like the Olympics or national political conventions. 1984 in San Francisco was no exception. I was part of a vast army of *Newsweek* editors, reporters, photographers, and torch-bearers descending on the city. I ended up having little to do except enjoy the fine restaurants and follow the high-jinks, or low-jinks, of the Chicago delegates. Only later did I realize that it was just as well for *Newsweek*'s millions of readers that I had no important reportorial chores at that convention. After looking through my disjointed journal entries and recalling what I can of that week, I realize that my mind was not functioning properly. It was like a misfiring engine, bursts of energy followed by frightening blanks.

I remember—if that's the correct word—a luncheon *Newsweek* threw for Colorado Senator Gary Hart and his wife, Lee. He was then considered an up-and-comer with a possible shot at the vice presidential nomination or—who knows?—the presidential nomination four years down the road. It was one of a series of luncheons that *Newsweek*, like other major publications, hosts during conventions to pass idle hours and expose the editors to real live politicians.

I was among the designated questioners for the Hart lunch. Our top editors and Katharine Graham, head of the Washington Post Co., which owns *Newsweek*, were there. As the lunch progressed and the *Newsweek* ers peppered Hart with questions, some ponderous and some fluffy, I realized that I was having a hard time following the ball back and forth across the conversational net. I was expected to toss in a few questions—from the vantage point of the Heartland, don't you know. Instead, I broke into a fearful sweat when I realized that, despite decades of experience bracing everybody from aldermen to archbishops, I could not frame a single intelligible question.

Incredible as it sounds, I never told anyone—least of all Ginny— about my confusion. Nor did I bring up the daily nosebleeds or the chronic fatigue that accompanied me like my shadow throughout each day. Like generations of stalwart Maiers before me, I figured what I didn't know couldn't hurt me. And somewhere in my early years, maybe from my father, I had acquired the notion that it was noble and manly to suffer in silence.

Later that summer, after an uneventful tour of the wine country and just before our journey to Ireland, I had still another warning. By trade I am a general assignment reporter, a passing breed in this era of specialization. For three decades, I have been a scribe-of-all trades, a generalist who might cover an ax murder one day and a Baptist convention the next. For someone with a lot of curiosity and a short attention span, being a general assignment reporter is a job only a benevolent God would design. The late summer of 1984 brought me an assignment that I knew came nonstop from Paradise.

The Chicago Cubs—on whose behalf I had wasted the prayers of my youth—were leading their division of the National League as the season dwindled down. It appeared that the most consistently inept franchise in baseball might actually win the pennant, a feat the Cubs had not accomplished since 1945, when I was twelve years old. Our editors in New York benignly blessed my proposal that we do a story on the surprising Cubs. I felt like a kid hired to work in a candy store. Though I had been a reporter in Chicago for almost two decades, first for the *Daily News* and then for *Newsweek,* I had never covered a Cubs game. I couldn't wait to get my press credentials for the "Friendly Confines" of Wrigley Field, where I could banter with the players around the batting cage and even sit in the dugout before games.

As I prepped for the story, rummaging through ancient files on past Cubs glories, a buzzer went off in my brain—maybe a reporter's early warning signal. There are two cardinal rules of my trade—at least as I had been trained by a string of gruff city editors: never blow your deadline and never promise more than you can deliver. What if I wasn't up physically to the job? What if I had an attack of vertigo while strolling through the team locker room? Or my brain switched off while interviewing Ryne Sandberg? Front-page swagger wouldn't save me then. And what if my thoughts turned to mush while I was organizing and writing the story for telexing to New York?

I went to my friend and deputy bureau chief, the always depend-able John McCormick. "John, why don't we both work on the Cubs piece?" (I shudder to think of the entry in my heavenly records: "Bureau chief protects his ass while trying to look like nice sharing guy. Five demerits.")

As it turned out, I did need John's help in reporting the piece and making the deadline. And I nearly paid dearly for my fuzzy-headedness. On our first day at the ballpark, to my delight, I spotted the Cubs hero of my generation, the immortal Ernie Banks. He was there to compete in an old-timer's game before the Cubs played their regular opponent. One way or another, I was determined to get a few words of Ernie Banks's sunny wisdom into the story.

It took patience because Ernie kept signing autographs for fans stacked next to the dugout. Finally he turned his smiling attention my way and invited me to run with him to the old locker room along the left field foul line. I began trotting like a schoolboy beside the great Ernie Banks, notebook flapping and ballpoint poised for action. Suddenly somebody yelled, "Look out!" I froze. A whizzing white cannonball flashed by my ear. I had just missed having my head drilled by a fastball from Rick Sutcliffe, who was warming up in the bull pen. "You don't want to do that," clucked Ernie as I staggered to safety.

McCormick and I later had a good laugh at my near fatal beaning by the star Cubs pitcher. "What a way to go," I said.

In truth, there would be times in the next three years when getting taken out by a Sutcliffe fastball would have seemed not at all a bad way to go.

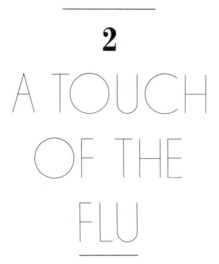

2

A TOUCH OF THE FLU

Some people never get around to executing a will because they have an atavistic sense that doing so makes them walking targets. They are convinced that speeding cab drivers and deadly microbes have them in their sights even as they emerge from the lawyer's office. Most men I know, excluding a few lovable hypochondriacs, have this same superstitious dread when it comes to illness and doctors. I certainly fit that category. Had I not been born a Catholic, I would have been a custom-made prospect for Christian Scientist recruiters.

So determined was I to avoid contact with medical practitioners that I even developed my own all-purpose diagnosis that fit any symptoms of any ailment: "a touch of the flu." It covered everything from the sniffles to appendicitis. One time, when I jammed a finger while charging up the stairs to quiet two brawling children, Ginny showed her contempt for my diagnostic skills. As I held the throbbing finger under the cold water faucet, she commented: "Looks like it has a touch of the flu."

The former Ginny Ryan did not share my aversion to doctors. Consequently, after my near fatal spinout on the Kennedy Expressway, she made appointments for physical and eye examinations. I learned of them much like a little boy does. On the morning of the appointments, she stuffed a reminder note in my shirt pocket. "Be there, Frankie," she said. Whenever she called me "Frankie," I knew to pay attention.

After seeing an internist, an opthalmologist, and an ear, nose, and throat specialist, I managed to convince myself that the vertigo, nosebleeds, and general fatigue were nothing to get particularly alarmed about—certainly not signs of any serious illness. The eyes were fine, and the dizziness was probably caused by an imbalance of fluids in my inner ear. As for the nosebleeds, I was advised to get a humidifier for the bedroom. The internist found no change in the status of a leaky heart valve that dated to my two bouts of rheumatic fever as a teenager.

The only warning sign—and I didn't get the impression it was anything more than a blinking sign—was that blood tests showed a slight elevation of my liver enzymes. But that was enough of a concern for the internist to tell me to abstain from alcohol and avoid aerosol sprays or chemicals like cleaning fluids and degreasers, all substances that can damage the liver.

I never bothered to tell any of the doctors about my occasional lapses of concentration or episodes of confusion. I'm not sure today whether that was out of stupidity, male stubborness, or simple fear of what the symptoms might be disguising. Patients, I came to learn, can be very selective in what they tell their doctors.

That September, Ginny and I flew to Ireland, where we spent two weeks driving through the countryside, studiously avoiding all the well-known attractions. Although I felt some anxiety about having another dizzy spell, I did all the driving. Ginny is too much of a talker and gawker for those narrow, winding Irish roads. Also, she has a real problem telling left from right, a handicap when driving on the unfamiliar left side of the road. We had a grand time, even finding the cottage where four of her father's unmarried cousins, Sean, Mary, Jerry, and Kitty, lived in rustic tranquillity. We found them fairly close to where an old man suggested they might be— "doon the second boreen on ye left jes nort of Dunohill." He called it "Dun-ole."

We also located the tiny village of Castlemagner, a mythical place in my father's family history where, so our side of the story goes, the British chased off the Magner family in about 1760. My unusual middle name—Magner—traces back through my father's mother (she was a Ryan too) to this Irish "castle." We found the stone ruins of my castle on the edge of the village. It now serves as a shelter for dairy cows belonging to a neighboring farmer. Ginny climbed a barbed wire fence to retrieve a piece of rock from my ancestral castle, in the process ripping her new Gloria Vanderbilt stretch jeans. "That's the last castle I ever sack for you," she said.

I probably am the only person of my background and profession who spent two weeks in Ireland and had only two pints of beer. But I was wary enough of my general health to follow the doctor's heeding about alcohol. But the trip was not without incident for me—though I never told Ginny about it until we were flying home. While sitting on a bench as Ginny strolled through shops in the quaint, thatched-roofed town of Adare, I suddenly lost all sense of self. It was as if my spirit was sliding out of my body. I thought I was dying. Fearing I would faint, I slumped over on the bench so as not to fall. All I could think of was poor Ginny having to get tangled up in red tape to get my body back home. What I experienced sounds much like the panic attacks that afflict some people, a sudden sensation that they are losing control of themselves and are about to die. My distress lasted only a few minutes. By the time Ginny surfaced from the shops, I was sitting up again, convinced that it was just a "touch of the flu."

As happened so often in our marriage, Ginny decided to take things into her own hands. She knew I would not, or could not, admit that something was seriously wrong with me. In fact, I discovered that she already had taken action before we left on vacation. Through her brother, John, a Chicago urologist (she calls him the "family plumber"), Ginny made an appointment for me at the celebrated Mayo Clinic in Rochester, Minnesota. The confirmation letter from Mayo was waiting when we returned from Ireland. I made my token protests: I had been away from work too long; there was a presidential campaign going on; I had new, young reporters assigned to the bureau who needed my attention.

"In my opinion, I can put this off until after the election," I said. Ginny didn't bother arguing. "You're entitled to your opinion," she said, "but both you and I know that your opinion is wrong."

Before I knew it, we were driving through the gold and tan hills of southern Minnesota toward the Mayo Clinic. I thought I would appease Ginny and at the same time get an oil and lube job on my fifty-year-old frame. Even with all the warnings I had experienced, I still had no inkling of how our lives would be changed by what we would learn from Mayo's experts.

Some people call Mayo Clinic "the Lourdes of medicine," a citadel of hope that looms like a shimmering City of Oz above the farm fields of Minnesota. Every year some 300,000 pilgrims come to Mayo from all over the world, some for routine physicals, but many because they have run out of hope that anyone can cure their serious or mystifying illnesses. Mayo consists of an ever-expanding complex of buildings in the heart of Rochester, connected by underground walkways to protect staff and patients from harsh Minnesota winters.

Most of the doctoring takes place in the nineteen-story clinic building on an out-patient basis. (I was intrigued to note that this citadel of science had bowed to superstition and omitted a thirteenth floor.) But Mayo also includes two hospitals, Rochester Methodist and St. Mary's, plus two satellite clinics opened in the late 1980s in Jacksonville, Florida, and Scottsdale, Arizona. About 950 of medicine's most skilled physicians and researchers and about 14,000 supporting staffers work for the nonprofit Mayo Foundation. All are salaried employees, their incomes not dependent on how many patients they see, how many procedures they perform, or how many medical breakthroughs they achieve.

Teamwork has been the motto of Mayo ever since William Worrall Mayo, an English-born, five-foot, four-inch frontier doctor, set up practice in "the little town on the edge of nowhere" after the Civil War. Its development into the world's largest and oldest group practice of medicine dates from 1883, when a tornado devastated Rochester. Without a hospital, old Dr. Mayo and his two physician sons, William and Charles (known to generations of clinic patients as "Dr. Will and Dr. Charlie"), began treating the scores of injured in hotels, private homes, and even the local dance hall.

The mother superior of the Sisters of St. Francis opened up the convent as a temporary hospital. Later, the nuns, who had been a teaching order, offered to build a local hospital and provide nursing care if the three Mayos would be the staff physicians. The famed Mayo Clinic resulted from this ecumenical venture of three doctors

16

who were devoted followers of John Wesley, the founder of Method-
ism, and nuns who were inspired by the spirit of the popular Catholic saint, Francis of Assisi.

Over the years, the clinic in the northern prairies became famous
worldwide for its surgical successes and research breakthroughs. It
also served as a model for diagnosing illnesses and treating patients
using a multidiscipline, team approach. Mayo physicians are not
expected to know all the answers, but they are expected to know who
among their colleagues might have the best answer to a particular
patient's problem, and call him—or increasingly her—in for consul-
tation.

When I checked in at the clinic, I was given a paper wallet
containing a thick pack of cards listing my scheduled tests and
examinations for the next four days. The entire town of Rochester
seemed to be populated by men and women carrying these "Mayo
Passports," which not only give time and place of appointments, but
also instructions about fasting or other preparation prior to tests.
The records I brought from home, along with the rapidly accumulating test results from Mayo, always were waiting when I showed up
for any appointment, having been shuttled through the conveyor
systems that run like arteries and veins throughout the medical
complex.

Because my known physical problem was the leaky aortic valve
in my heart, I was assigned a cardiologist as my primary doctor. Dr.
Titus Evans, a thin, soft-spoken native Iowan, with baby-soft skin
and a careless, off-the-rack way of dressing, was not exactly what
I had imagined a Mayo physician would be. My reporter's imagination expected a stern-visaged man, perhaps with European goatee
and rimless spectacles, wearing a starched white lab coat. Instead
I found that Dr. Evans, like all Mayo physicians, wore a suit, not
a lab coat. He looked more like the owner of a hardware store in
Cedar Rapids and president of the Rotary than a cardiologist at a
world-renowned medical mecca.

I discovered another thing about Mayo's system of doing business. Dr. Evans did not seem to be operating under any time
pressure. In fact, as he meticulously reviewed my medical history
and then conducted the most thorough physical examination of my
life, I began to feel uneasy, that I was taking up too much of his

time, that there must be scores of fuming patients waiting outside.

Unlike doctors in my previous experience, he asked me all sorts of questions about my family and my work. No doctor had ever asked what I did for a living—I could have been a mob hitman or a rich playboy for all they knew. None had ever seemed interested in what personal or professional stresses I faced in my daily life.

To my amazement, Dr. Evans also seemed willing to talk a bit about himself, something I never expected a doctor would feel secure enough to do with a patient. The doctors I had known always maintained a certain professional distance, perhaps a way of pre- serving the mystique of their omniscience. It wasn't as if Dr. Evans and I carried on a buddy-buddy conversation, but it certainly was the conversation of one adult with another adult—not the parent to child monologues I had come to expect from doctors. I can't recall what brought it up, but at one point he even told me that his mother had been killed in an automobile accident. I had arrived at Mayo expecting to get swallowed up in the medical equivalent of the Pentagon. Instead, meeting Dr. Evans was just like visiting a coun- try doctor's office. All he lacked was a rolltop desk and a little black bag.

Dr. Evans discovered that, in addition to my leaky aortic valve, I had a problem with a second valve in my heart, the mitral valve. Two of these little trapdoors that regulate the flow of blood through my heart were not shutting properly. If the condition worsened, they could be replaced sometime by artificial valves in a relatively routine procedure, he said. To supplement the x-ray and blood test results that already were in my traveling file, he ordered an echocardiogram of my heart. He then made some phone calls (I was impressed that he didn't have to look up the numbers) and soon had me scheduled to see a neurologist, opthalmologist, and a gastroenterologist.

The neurologist found that I suffered from something called "lab- yrinthine vertigo," which explained, but did not cure, the head- spinning. He also gave a name—"tinnitus"—to the constant screeching in my ears that I had come to ignore, like people do who live next to the train tracks. The ophthalmologist could find nothing else to add to my dossier. Halfway through my visit to Mayo, I was satisfied that the medical experts would confirm what I already knew: that I was basically in sound shape and that my few imperfections could easily be remedied—maybe by taking off a few pounds or "slowing down" or making some other token changes in my life-style.

But my sap-happy outlook collapsed after I was examined by the gastroenterologist, Dr. Jorge Rakela, who was even more soft-spoken than Dr. Evans. A native of Santiago, Chile, with trim dark beard and eyeglasses, he looked like a casting director's idea of a medical expert. He began in a lighthearted manner, talking about Chicago and how much he loved to visit there, but turned quite serious as the interview and exam progressed. I began to feel anxious for the first time.

After reviewing my blood tests, Dr. Rakela seemed almost apologetic when he said I would have to undergo a liver biopsy. Never in my life had I faced any kind of surgery—no matter how minor. I never even had my tonsils out, an operation that was fairly routine for children of my generation. The prospect of a doctor punching a long needle through my rib cage and snipping out a small piece of my liver for microscopic scrutiny left me looking for the exit. But there was no escaping, not with Ginny on the scene. My panic over a relatively minor procedure like a liver biopsy now seems childish. Compared to what was down the road for me, it was like having my fingernails trimmed.

Dr. Rakela's manner was grim when Ginny and I sat down with him at week's end to review the pathologist's report on the liver biopsy. It contained all sorts of polysyllabic words and medical shoptalk like "piecemeal necrosis" and "fibrosis," and something called "scattered Councilman bodies." I was beginning to fear that the report was not going to meet my rose-colored expectations. When translated into lay-talk by the kindly Dr. Rakela, it added up to my death sentence.

All I remember was Ginny's squeezing my arm, my face flushing, and my stomach going cold as Dr. Rakela explained what it meant. He never looked at us, but kept his eyes on the report even though he was not reading from it. I had chronic active hepatitis, caused by a virus so elusive that it was called by an alias, "Non-A, Non-B Hepatitis." Scientists have since isolated it and dubbed it "Hepatitis C."

In simple terms, hepatitis means inflammation of the liver, and it is one of the most widespread afflictions in the world. More than a half million Americans are infected by some type of hepatitis each year, according to estimates by the federal Centers for Disease Control. There are three main types of viral hepatitis: A, B, and C. (Before being isolated in 1988, this viral invader was known only by the fingerprints it left behind, thus the alias "Non-A, Non-B Hepatitis.")

Hepatitis A, the most common and the least dangerous, is usually spread by contaminated food or water. A person can become quite ill with this type of hepatitis, but seldom does it cause serious complications.

On the other hand, Hepatitis B, which can be transmitted from mother to child or through sexual contact, blood transfusions, or contaminated needles, can be deadly. It often evolves into a chronic disease and can lead to cancer of the liver. In some Third World countries, it is estimated that more than 70 percent of the population is infected with the Hepatitis B virus. Although there is a vaccine that now can protect high-risk people like nurses and doctors, HBV remains a serious worldwide menace.

My form of hepatitis, chronic HCV, has been one of the perplexing, long-standing mysteries of medicine. For decades, it was diagnosed by the elimination method, not by direct isolation of the virus. Its method of passing from one individual to another also has been difficult to trace, though one route is known to be via blood transfusions. Since, at the time, I never had received a transfusion, the cause of my hepatitis was labeled "idiopathic." That's doctor talk for "We don't know."

Sometime in my past, the hepatitis virus had invaded my body like a thief in the night. Quietly and undetected, it relentlessly ravaged my liver, the powerhouse and detox station of the body, an organ as vital as the brain or the heart. As this chronic hepatitis methodically chewed up my liver cells, it left behind permanent layers of scar tissue called "cirrhosis," a condition often caused by alcohol abuse, but also caused by congenital defects in the liver, exposure to toxins, or, as in my case, chronic viral attack.

If you get cirrhosis from alcohol abuse, your chances of recovery can be bright, provided you stop drinking in time. The liver has a talent for regeneration under certain conditions. But if cirrhosis develops from chronic active hepatitis, your outlook is poor.

In my case, the prognosis was not poor. It was bad. Down the road I faced life-threatening hemorrhages and the steady deterioration of all the other vital organs of my body, including my brain. Once the liver has been damaged, every other organ of the body is compromised. The solemn Dr. Rakela also informed me that there was no effective cure for my disease, or for most serious liver ailments.

When I realized what Dr. Rakela was saying, I finally asked him the bottom-line question and got the bottom-line answer: no one can predict how quickly my condition would deteriorate. But I had at best seven or eight years to live.

All I could think of as Ginny and I drove silently back to Chicago was: "Kiss those golden years good-bye."

3

MY LITTLE ENGINE THAT COULDN'T

After the initial shock of being told that I had a chronic and terminal illness, I determined to learn more about my liver and the disease that was killing me. For someone with a college degree and work experience that exposed me to a wide range of information, I was terribly ignorant when it came to the workings of my own body. I knew nothing about my liver—what it does, where it is located, or why it is so important in keeping a person healthy and alive.

In my journal entry the day after Dr. Jorge Rakela told me I harbored this smoldering hepatitis, I didn't even know how to spell the word. The first time I wrote *hepatitus;* later I spelled it *hepatitas.* Ginny, who can come up with at least three ways to spell any word in the English language, was not concerned with how to spell my problem. I wanted to understand my disease; she wanted to fight it.

In a way, our different reactions to my illness reflected one of the basic differences in our personalities. Except on the job, when I could be as aggressive as needed to get a story, I was the passive partner in our marriage. I never liked confrontation; I never liked to get involved. Ginny always was more combative, whether negotiating with a sales clerk or demanding that the city fathers install a stop sign near a playground.

First thing she did after our return from Mayo was to drag me to a large bookstore in Chicago where we spent an hour rummaging through the health and medicine section. Beside the diet and "how-to" health books, we found a number of medical textbooks that we could understand—at least up to a point. For the information we needed to mine from them, we did not want to pay their hefty price tag. So we jotted down the most promising titles—including a number of nursing manuals and textbooks—and headed for the public library.

As it turned out, we could have skipped the bookstore and gone straight to the library in our hometown of Arlington Heights. Starting with encyclopedias and working our way through medical books and research journals, we gradually began to understand what the liver did, what hepatitis could do to this vital organ, and—most discouraging—how little doctors knew about treating serious liver disease. One of the most helpful books was a small volume that listed the commonly used medical vocabulary, including many Latin and Greek words or roots that are used in "doctor-talk" to describe illnesses, body parts, or functions.

Watching Ginny struggling to make sense of the medical jargon in the reference books and furiously taking notes like an overachieving grad student, I could not help but smile. Although she always has been street-smart and an avid reader of magazines and newspapers, she never enjoyed academic endeavor—as I always have. But because she could clearly see the practical goal of our research, she threw herself into the medical research with the energy she normally reserved for practical tasks like gardening, tearing down paneling, or changing a furnace filter. Also, maybe because her brother was a doctor or because she was a mother of four children, she had a much better grasp of fundamental medical facts and principles than I did.

But our research did not come easy. By then I was so chronically fatigued that I could not always decifer what I was reading. It was tough for both of us. I remember one afternoon at the library when Ginny slammed closed a thick medical book on clinical gastroenterology and wearily mumbled, "I wish I had paid more attention in freshman Latin."

Between "cramming" at the library and reading brochures from the American Liver Foundation, we gradually started to understand the formidable enemy that seemed already to have defeated us. Since Mayo's experts had said there was no effective treatment for my disease, I considered all this research an intellectual exercise. But for Ginny it was preparing for battle—even if it seemed destined to end, at best, with an orderly, dignified surrender.

At that point in our journey, she was the only one on the home team who thought we had a fighting chance. For my part, I sidestepped the classical stages that Dr. Elisabeth Kubler-Ross and other thanatologists have identified in terminal patients: denial, anger, bargaining, depression, and, finally, acceptance. Always one to avoid ugly or embarrassing confrontations, I jumped right to acceptance. I was dying. That's not news. Everybody is dying. From the day you're born, you're dying.

I did not realize it then, but I had not really adjusted to my new circumstances. If anything, I acted like a steelworker on the girder of a skyscraper under construction. I would be okay as long as I didn't look down. Besides, it just wasn't my style to follow Dylan Thomas's poetic counsel and "rage against the dying of the light."

My outward acceptance of my fate had little relationship to my professed religious convictions. If anything, it stemmed more from pride, which I had been taught as a boy to regard as the root of all sin. I was determined to stay in control of my dying, to go out with dignity, without whine or whimper. By acceptance, I was not surrendering to God and saying, "Thy will be done." It was more like, "I want *my* will to be done, and it's this: I don't want to embarrass myself before my family and friends."

Besides, as proof that a tiny seed of hope always remains rooted deep within us, I convinced myself that my chances of getting killed by a bus were probably just as great as getting killed by a tiny hepatitis virus. And hadn't Dr. Rakela said I might have seven years, depending on how my disease progressed? A lot can happen in seven years. We were soon to discover that a lot can happen in less time than that.

Under Ginny's prodding I learned about the liver, the body's most overworked and underrated organ, a gland as vital for life as the more popular and sentimentalized heart. No one ever composed a song about the liver or set aside a special day to celebrate it. We associate the heart with love; if we associate the liver with anything, it's indigestion.

The liver is a hard-working "blue collar" organ that never gets the credit it deserves. You never know how important it is until it starts to malfunction. I didn't even know how big it was or exactly where it was located. For some reason I thought it was about the size of the appendix and was wedged somewhere into the stomach cavity, maybe down near the intestines. If I was ignorant, other people I knew had even less knowledge of the liver. One college-educated friend, upon hearing that I had liver disease, shook his head in relief and said, "good thing you've got two of them." Another friend, also a bright person on most matters, asked if I was going to begin dialysis treatment, also confusing the liver with the kidneys.

The liver is the largest internal organ of the body and, after the brain, the most complicated. In an adult it weighs about three pounds and is shaped somewhat like an underinflated football. A healthy liver is soft, easily bruised, and deep red, almost chocolate colored. It nestles behind the right rib cage for protection from injury. Whereas the heart is the body's pumping station, the liver is its refinery and detox station.

No one knows exactly how many functions the liver performs, though hepatologists—liver specialists—estimate that it does more than 500 major jobs. Among its galaxy of duties: it detoxes drugs and poisons that would damage the body, converts food into chemicals vital for life, regulates blood clotting, and stores energy-producing elements like glucose. It also produces bile, the thick greenish-yellow fluid that allows us to digest food, and urea, the body's main waste product, which eventually is excreted by the kidneys as urine. When the liver isn't working, every other organ of the body is affected.

Although the heart has received better publicity and has been considered by many cultures to be the very dwelling place of the soul, it wasn't always that way. The ancient Babylonians thought that the liver was the focal point of the soul and used cut-up animal livers to foretell the future. The liver also was prominent in Greek mythology. The gods punished Prometheus for giving men the gift of fire by sending an eagle to peck out his liver each night. It would grow back during the day, only to be pecked out again the next night. Anyone who suffers from serious liver disease can empathize with old Prometheus. The myth not only shows that the ancients knew the importance of the liver, but that they had a primordial knowledge of physiology.

Despite its complexity and the wide variety of functions it performs, the liver is unique in its ability to grow new cells, to regenerate itself. But not if it has been shrunken, hardened, and scarred by cirrhosis, as was my case. The chronic inflammation caused by the hepatitis virus had damaged my liver beyond salvage.

I also learned from material sent to me by the American Liver Foundation that about 25 million men, women, and children in this country suffer from some form of liver, bile duct, or gallbladder disease, an astonishing one out of every ten Americans. An estimated 30,000 die every year from one of the 100 different liver diseases that have been identified.

By early 1985, I had stopped driving because I still experienced the violent twirling episodes about once a month. I took the train to the *Newsweek* bureau in Chicago each workday, and I still taught a four-hour class in news writing at Northwestern University's Medill School of Journalism, a part-time job that I greatly enjoyed and had performed every Monday afternoon for seven years. I tried to shrug off the deep fatigue that fell over me even as I rose in the morning after ten hours of fretful sleep. As much as I clung to some kind of denial, I couldn't ignore my deteriorating health.

My nose bled constantly, a condition I now realize was caused by the failure of the liver's blood clotting mechanism. My nostrils seemed always clogged with pebbles of dried blood. An eye, ear, and throat specialist recommended I get a humidifier for the bedroom. He also told me to sniff a lubricating mixture of water, baking soda, salt, and sugar at least three times a day. It didn't stop the nose bleeds, but it helped flush out the clotted blood so I could breathe freely for a time.

I also became aware of intermittent pain behind my left ear. How long it was there before I added it to my list of daily complaints, I really cannot say. But, ever true to my code of not acknowledging weakness until it can no longer be ignored, I didn't immediately tell

Ginny about it. She needed some respite from my woes. Despite my stout-fellow, stiff-upper-lip manner, inside I was beginning to feel sorry for old Frank Maier—actually, I was beginning to think of myself in a different age bracket. Increasingly I saw myself as a little boy, a hurting little boy at that. Little boys can feel awfully sorry for themselves.

On Saturday, March 2, 1985, I wrote in my journal: "It seems so long since a day passed without my being aware of some whistling and clanking in the old frame. I wish I could forget about the heart being too big and having leaky valves, my liver harboring the hepatitis, my head spinning, and my nose draining blood. From this day on, I will think about the outside world, about other people's hurts. The worst prison is one without windows. The most frightful sentence would be to spend the rest of my days in a room with mirrors for walls. I will fight to break out of that confinement. No mirrors for me!"

I was already starting to sense what I later would come to know: that the worst part of being chronically ill and facing certain death is not the pain or the fear, it's the threat of retreating into yourself. The greatest danger facing me wasn't chronic active hepatitis, it was a more deadly virus, one that can ruin your very soul: chronic active self-absorption.

It wasn't long before my good intentions were tested. On Good Friday afternoon, I got off the North Western commuter train at my home station of Arlington Heights, stepping into a cold, slashing rain. I was exhausted and testy, particularly when I found that Ginny was not there to pick me up. Fifteen minutes later, angry, wet and put-upon, I stomped to the phone outside the station to call the forgetful Ginny. To my annoyance, a boy of about twelve with long, greasy hair and wearing a tattered jean jacket, lounged with his back to the wall, saying not a word into the phone at his ear. I gave him my industrial-strength, "you're-a-pain-in-the-ass" glare. The little twirp was tying up the phone with some girlfriend, while I stood, wet and weary, abandoned by my allegedly loving wife. The boy became aware of my anger. His eyes widened like a frightened animal, and he dropped the phone and ran around the corner of the station. Before I could start dialing, I heard him trying to speak to someone. When I say "trying," I mean just that. Whatever he was doing, he wasn't speaking. It was just high-pitched babble. I realized that the boy was retarded and I had thoroughly frightened him. A woman, perhaps his mother, peeped around the corner at me. I pretended that I was deep in conversation on the phone. I don't remember any time in my life, before or since, when I felt more ashamed, more truly sorry.

That night I wrote in my journal: "How trivial are the inconveniences and slights of life compared to the real burdens that some people carry. How light has been the load that God has asked me to carry."

In May, I returned to Mayo for tests to see if my condition was changing. They ordered two new tests, an electromyograph, which checks nerve and muscle response, and a computerized axial tomograph, or CAT scan, which can detect abnormalities in the brain.

As Ginny delighted in saying, "the CAT scan found nothing in his head." But new x-rays of my stomach and esophagus showed that my liver disease was accelerating. Dr. Rakela told us that a condition called "varices" had developed in my esophagus or gullet, the tube that connects the throat to the stomach. In lay terms, I had developed varicose, or swollen, veins in the esophagus. Blood that normally flows through the liver, finding its path blocked by scar tissue, forces its way up other routes, including the veins in the esophagus. It's like channeling traffic on a four-lane highway into a single lane road that never was designed to handle the volume. These so-called esophageal varices occur in about 60 percent of patients suffering from cirrhosis.

As Dr. Rakela explained to us, the varices could rupture without any warning, causing life-threatening hemorrhaging in someone with poor blood clotting defenses. My chances of surviving a first bleed were poor. Just being alive a year after a serious bleed from the esophagus was a 50-50 bet.

The thought of getting killed by that Rick Sutcliffe fastball no longer seemed so funny. It certainly had far more appeal than bleeding to death.

That June, a TWA plane with 146 Americans on it was hijacked by terrorists over Athens. It happened on a Friday, a frantic time for newsmagazine editors, who are rushing to close its pages for printing over the weekend. On the plane were many people from the

Chicago area, including the pastor and twenty parishioners from St. Margaret Mary Catholic Church in Algonquin, a town about thirty-five miles northwest of Chicago. In a situation like that, the regional bureaus have the job of quickly finding out as much as possible about the hostages and how their families and friends are coping with the crisis.

When we heard about the TWA hijacking, I already was home for the day, and my deputy bureau chief, John McCormick, was driving to his home in the western suburbs. Only correspondent Pat King was in the bureau to learn from our New York editors that it was "time to scramble the jets," as editor Maynard Parker liked to call such all-points, close-to-deadline efforts. I reached McCormick at home and told him to head for Geneva, a far western suburb where several other passengers on the airplane lived. After telling Pat to stay in the bureau to relay our reports to New York, I climbed into my car and, ignoring Ginny's vigorous protests, headed for Algonquin, where parishioners of St. Margaret Mary already were gathering for a special Mass. It was the first time I had driven anywhere by myself in months.

My liver might have been sputtering, but my adrenal glands were pumping on all cylinders. For the first time in months, I was on a reporter's high. This was why I got into this crazy business. As I drove toward the tiny town of Algonquin in the Fox River Valley of Illinois, I knew that other *Newsweek* reporters all over the world were driving or flying to their own assigned destinations for reporting the hijacking story.

Unlike some journalists who like to have total control over everything they do, I thrived on the newsmagazine system. I liked the camaraderie and sense of being part of a bigger enterprise than myself. Even if I only had a small piece of a story, and often that was the case, I knew that come Monday morning millions of people all over the world would read the story. I liked being on the fringes of history. G. K. Chesterton once observed that a journalist should never regret showing up a day late for the Battle of Hastings. A good, accurate account of the day *after* the battle is a valuable thing to have.

I stayed up all that night, drinking coffee and talking to the young assistant pastor and the parishioners who gathered for a vigil at the church. In the middle of the night, they wrapped a big yellow ribbon around a honey locust tree. I wasn't the only reporter who stayed all night, but I guess I was the only one who was in as grave a danger of dying as were the passengers on that plane.

What I learned about the hostages themselves or about how their neighbors were reacting I dictated by phone to Pat King back at the bureau. She took my reporting, added what John McCormick had picked up in Geneva, wrote a combined report, and dispatched it to New York. We ended up getting a few quotes and anecdotes into the final story about the hijacking of TWA 847, and that's what we were paid to do.

The sky was just turning light gray as I started the drive home. My stomach was sour from too much coffee and too little sleep. Many times during my news career I had gone twenty-four hours or more without sleep. And I had worked on many stories where I had a larger, or the sole, reporting responsibility. But that was when I was younger and healthier. Throughout that long night, I never once thought about my aches and pains; never felt anxiety or fear, just the rush of excitement in doing what I always wanted to do since I was a kid.

For one night I escaped from the prison that chronic illness had built for me. I felt as happy as a cub reporter heading for bed after his first night on the police beat. I could still do it! Damn, but I could still do it!

4

WOODCARVING DAYS

After the hijacking story, I felt less wounded and more optimistic about my work. The doctors' estimate of my longevity was just that—an estimate. If the average person in my condition had about seven years to live when diagnosed, that meant some patients were living longer. I chose not to consider the other side of the coin—that some had to fall below the average.

Because of persistent fatigue, I could work only short days at *Newsweek*. Since I was running the bureau, I could schedule my work to match my energy levels. But I was determined to show up every day. From my father I had inherited a deep respect for the work ethic. I also inherited from both my father and mother an invincible optimism about the benevolence of the universe, a conviction that obstacles would evaporate like soap bubbles if you just didn't quit.

In late 1985, I had not told friends or anyone at *Newsweek,* not even John McCormick, that I was a "short-termer." They only knew that I had "some health problems." But Ginny made me promise not to take any more out-of-town assignments, even short hauls like the trip to Algonquin. Tucked away in my mind was the knowledge that I was under a death sentence. But in my work life I managed to squelch the thought. I was like a prisoner on death row who had his lawyers working on appeals. Someday the appeals would run out. I would worry about that when the time came.

Still, every so often I would hear death's footsteps right behind me. One time the bureau was asked in midweek to get some comments from a Chicago business executive for a national story about the threat of inflation. It was the sort of task that any journeyman reporter can do on automatic pilot. The hardest part of those assignments is getting past the business executive's personal secretary. From experience I knew that there are ways to reach top business executives if you run into resistance from the doorkeepers. One way is to call their office about seven in the morning or during the lunch hour. Most top executives are such high-energy, overachievers that they can't wait to get to work in the morning, and, unless they have an important business lunch, they often gulp down soup and a sandwich at their desks. The technique doesn't work with public officials, elected or otherwise, who begin their days at a more leisurely pace and who never miss a meal—particularly a freebie.

Sure enough, my man answered his own phone a little after seven in the morning, long before his assistants were in the office to form a skirmish line. He was quite willing to offer his opinions to *Newsweek*—working for a national publication has advantages when it comes to access. But he wanted to do it face-to-face. In thirty minutes, I was sitting in his office, a bit out of breath, jotting down in my notebook his answers to my questions—actually our business editor's questions. Had it been a longer or more complicated interview, I would have brought along a tape recorder to back up my notes. But for such a down-and-dirty interview, taping wasn't necessary.

The interview lasted a half hour, and I thought it went smoothly. The questions the business editor had supplied were pretty basic, designed to elicit answers that also were basic and not requiring much in the way of follow-up questions. Back at the bureau, I fetched a cup of coffee and sat down at my word processor to write what we call a "file." I did not need to craft a well-organized story with proper beginning, middle, and end. Nor did I need to struggle over an opening—the lead—nor come up with a satisfying ending—or kicker. In a way it was more like stenography than reporting. So I flipped open my notebook and found . . .

Gibberish. That's all I can call it. My notes were absolutely unreadable. Like most reporters, I have my own style of note taking, my own abbreviations and shortcuts. I never met a professional reporter who used conventional shorthand. But what I saw as I fanned the pages of my notebook was not just undecipherable, sloppy handwriting—it was the scribbling of a prekindergartner. I was shocked and devastated. During the interview, I thought I had accurately jotted down the man's comments. Now I began to wonder: Had I asked the questions correctly? Had I slurred my words? Did I understand his answers? Then a sudden thought made my face flush and my stomach ache. Had I behaved like some drunk in the executive's office, or some lunatic?

I sat wondering what to do. I could call our business editor and lie, saying that the executive was not available for an interview. That was the easy way out. Or I could call the man back under the guise of trying to extract a few more nuggets of wisdom and clarify some points. I decided that would be the most upright way of covering my tracks—and I might also get some hint of how I had behaved during the interview. Then I noticed the message that had been placed atop the stack of papers in the in-box on my desk. It was from the business editor: "Inflation story killed. Thanks for your efforts."

Later that same fall of 1985 I got a call from Katharine Graham's secretary, saying that Mrs. Graham was coming to Chicago to give a speech and wanted to have dinner with me the night before. It may sound strange that the board chairman of the Washington Post Co., the owner of *Newsweek,* a woman who has been described as the "most powerful woman in America," would want to have dinner with me. But it surprised me not the least. It says nothing about me, but says a lot about Katharine Graham. In my two decades at *Newsweek* it was not at all unusual for Mrs. Graham to drop in on the bureau whenever she was passing through town. It was her way of showing that she was interested in what the troops in the trenches were doing and thinking. It also gave her a chance to hear complaints and suggestions straight, without waiting for them to perk slowly up, well-filtered, through the corporate hierarchy.

The first time I ever met Mrs. Graham was shortly after I had been named Chicago bureau chief in 1971, when she dropped in unannounced as I was cleaning my new office in worn jeans and faded Notre Dame sweatshirt. By the way she treated me you would have thought I was wearing a tuxedo, had a mind that rippled like Henry Kissinger's, and was the possessor of the most fascinating gossip she had heard outside of a Georgetown cocktail party.

Normally a visit from Mrs. Graham was nothing to fear. But having dinner with her in my current state of uncertainty was more than I could handle. I had been at *Newsweek* long enough that my reputation, good or bad, already was fixed in stone. So making a good impression was not the problem. What did worry me was making conversation. Was I up to the job of answering the penetrating questions that Mrs. Graham always asked about local politics or personalities? She also always asked our opinion of stories that were in that week's issue of the magazine—which could be embarrassing if you had skimmed some of the back-of-the-book sections.

And, what if I had an attack of vertigo, or what if my mind started sputtering again? I solved my problem, as I would many a time during my illness, by leaning on my deputy bureau chief, John McCormick, who not only is a fine journalist but also a good storyteller and a great listener. I invited John to join us for dinner.

As it turned out, we also brought along Monroe Anderson, who had just joined the bureau from the *Chicago Tribune,* where he had specialized in urban and minority reporting. The other bureau correspondent, Pat King, was away on assignment. We took Mrs. Graham to a new Italian restaurant near her hotel on North Michigan Avenue. After a slow start—not unexpected when everybody is uptight about using the right fork when the boss is watching—the conversation brightened up when we stopped discussing the magazine and "important issues" and wandered into personal recollections. I don't exactly know how we got started up memory lane, but all of a sudden Mrs. Graham was telling us about growing up, and each of us added an anecdote or two about our own childhood. She seemed to be having a good time, and I realized that John, Monroe, and I were too.

The high point of that dinner came when Mrs. Graham, who had grown up as a daughter of a millionaire, recalled that, as a very young girl, it never occured to her that she lived in an elite world, unlike most other girls. "I never realized that we were rich," she said. Monroe Anderson snapped his fingers. "I know just what you mean, Mrs. Graham. When I was growing up in Gary, I didn't know we were poor."

That topped off a delightful evening. I even think Mrs. Graham enjoyed it more than just another dutiful visit with the working stiffs. I know I am ever grateful to the amiable John and the affable Monroe for getting me safely and pleasantly through what might have been treacherous seas for a sailor in my wobbly condition.

Except for three years as an officer in the peacetime navy, I have made my living by the written word. I have no other marketable skills. Compared to my tiny wife, Ginny, I have few practical skills of any kind. It was bad enough to slowly lose control over my daily life—just not being able to drive was humiliating—but I was devastated by the prospect of losing my ability to write. Later, I would have a hard time reading. But then, only writing was a problem.

Like an injured baseball player sitting on the bench gripping a bat, I tried to keep a feel for words by writing in my journal, something I had done since my navy days. One day in that winter of 1985, I realized how badly my mind had deteriorated when I tried to decifer my journal entry of the previous day only to find the scrawlings of a child. It was a repeat of the incident with the interview notes a few months before. That night I painstakingly printed in the journal: "I feel like a leaf falling too soon in the early autumn, at a time when the other leaves are still green."

Another time when I was alone at home, wandering aimlessly from room to room, I entered my den and saw the shelves of books there. The day was coming when I never again would be able to read them. I started sobbing, something I had not done since my boyhood friend, Chet Wynne, was killed in a plane crash thirty years before, just a few weeks before he was to be in our wedding. I slumped down on the floor like a little boy and shook as I tried to hold back the tears. Even alone in the house, I didn't want to embarrass myself by crying.

You must understand: feeling sorry for yourself is an occupational hazard for the seriously ill. Self-pity first clears the road, then despair has a straight path into your soul.

Another hazard that afflicts the afflicted is the temptation to glory in your illness. Later, when Ginny and I became enmeshed in the "sickness community," we ran into instances of this. Those with the fewest or the lightest ailments seemed to spend the most time talking about them. I remember one time sitting in a doctor's waiting room listening to two women spout their litanies of woes for almost an hour, neither one ever hearing what the other was saying.

Illness can become, like your job, your only measure of self-worth. Without it, you are just another face without a story. I did not immediately fall into this trap simply because I never told anybody about the seriousness of my illness. It wasn't that I was all that private a person, it just seemed to me that being ill was a terrible embarrassment, a secret that I was not comfortable about sharing with even my closest friends. Only Ginny and my doctors knew. (Our children also knew, Ginny made sure of that, but it would be some time before I realized that they knew I was dying. And they never learned it from me.)

Much as I tried to avoid it, my illness always threatened to become the only topic on my mind. It was like a maddening tune that keeps repeating itself in your head even though you can't stand hearing it. Ginny recognized the hazard long before I did. As suits her style, she decided to do something about it. After seeing an item in the local newspaper, she signed me up for woodcarving classes at the park district.

As well-intentioned as she was, my action-oriented wife had no idea what she was getting me into. Woodcarving was an avocation for which neither God nor man had prepared me. After stonewalling as long as I could, I finally agreed. Despite my grousing, I found the idea attractive. Like all klutzes, I had this fantasy about being able to work with my hands, thinking it was somehow noble, pure, and, in my case, maybe even therapeutic. If it turned out that I could no longer write, maybe I could earn a living as a woodcarver. I pictured myself as a kindly old craftsman, turning out carvings that I would sell at shopping malls and county fairs. Considering my fragile health, I wouldn't do Indian heads or ducks. In my situation it was more prudent to do religious carvings.

I was the only guy under sixty-five in the Saturday morning carving class, and the only one who never had worked with his hands. The instructor sold me a German carving knife for six dollars. "Watch it," he cautioned me. "It's sharp as a surgeon's scalpel." He gave me a block of maple, a few hints on technique, and a mimeographed sheet showing how to carve a sea lion.

Hand tremors are among the neurological symptoms of advanced liver disease. Another problem is poor blood clotting. During the very first session, I cut my thumb badly when I mistakenly pressed it against the business side of the blade.

Ginny tried to encourage me like a mother comforting her little boy after a disastrous first day at school. "Things will get better once you get used to it," she said patiently as she removed the tape the instructor had roughly applied, cleaned the cut, and neatly rebandaged my thumb. Normally patience is not one of Ginny's most cultivated virtues. In a way it pleased me to have her fuss over me; but it also made me nervous. Did her solicitous manner mean she knew something I didn't—that I was in worse shape than even I suspected?

After two woodcarving sessions, I had sliced my fingers so badly that I had no choice but to abandon my second career. I felt like I had failed Ginny, who had hoped the carving would help compensate for my loss of reading and writing abilities.

I was too ashamed to retrieve my carving tools at the third meeting of the class. Like a schoolboy, I sent the ever-faithful Ginny to get the cigar box containing my sandpaper, instruction sheet, and carving knife. I told her to forget about the sea lion, which at that point in development looked like a lopsided bowling pin.

"Tell them we're moving," I said.

5

UNEASY RIDER

ndeterred by my failure as a woodcarver, Ginny was determined to keep me from slipping further into morose apathy. With no control over this strange business of dying, I seemed always on the edge of that crevasse. After reading in our church bulletin that a group in our parish needed volunteers to work with mentally handicapped children, many with Down's syndrome, she signed me up—then told me about it.

"First woodcarving, now social work. What's next?" I protested.

After raising four children without ever getting snared into Little League, Cub Scouts, Indian Guides, or other parental excesses, I was not about to get tangled up in my dying days with a kids' organization—no matter how worthy the cause.

"I am not a joiner," I whined.

Ginny acted as if she were a passive bystander, not the instigator of my predicament. "The first meeting is Sunday morning," she said. "I told them you would be there. But that's up to you."

That is how I got involved with "my boys," Marty, Sean, Keith, David, Peter, and John. I started out thinking I was making a great personal sacrifice in spending a few hours every second Sunday so their parents could have some time to themselves. Instead, these innocent and lively teenage boys ended up teaching me more about friendship and the value of each human life than I could learn from volumes of books.

The group is called SPRED, for "Special Religious Education," and it is about the only organization, except for the United States Navy, that I ever joined in my life. I remain a faithful and enthusiastic SPRED member today—having also recruited my youngest daughter Heidi into the group.

The idea behind SPRED is to integrate mentally handicapped children and young adults into the parish community and stimulate their spiritual experiences. Each adult "helper catechist" is assigned one child as a special friend. Usually, a man is paired with a boy and a woman with a girl, but because our group never was perfectly balanced between volunteers and children, this was not a hard and fast rule.

Each Sunday meeting I sat at a table in a classroom with whatever boy was then assigned as my "special friend," and we would quietly draw pictures with crayons or paint with sponges, weave designs with yarn, play with blocks, or make animals out of clay. We were told to talk quietly so as not to disturb the couples working at other tables.

At first I felt like John Candy playing the role of a kindergarten teacher. The classroom atmosphere was so foreign to my self-image that I felt more embarrassed than elevated by my volunteer work. I was too self-conscious to simply play and talk with my assigned friend. Why did I ever let Ginny trap me into this?

Only later, as I saw how open and innocent these special children were, how gently they treated one another, and after I saw how cheerful the other adult men and women volunteers were, only then did I drop my guard and become a true member of the SPRED community. God's annoying habit of drawing straight with crooked lines no longer seemed so strange to me. My illness and approaching death did not seem all that consequential when viewed in the context of my friendship with these children.

The sessions were structured so that the children were comfortable and knew what to expect at all times. After our hour of "quiet time" play in the bright meeting room, we would move into a dimmer "celebration room." There we would sit in a semicircle around a burning white candle and vase of fresh flowers as the group leader talked, in terms the children could grasp, about simple things like friendship, forgiveness, or the beauty of nature and the changing of the seasons. The boys and girls were encouraged, not just to listen, but to talk about their own joys and pains and their experiences with friends, pets, parents, teachers, and God.

As I listened to them, I was amazed at the depth of feeling, gentleness, and humor that these children revealed. And I realized what a narrow, stereotyped view I had of the mentally handicapped. Despite their handicaps—some had severe speech problems in addition to their other limitations—they showed remarkable spiritual insights, along with simple joy in being alive.

I was struck that they all seemed to have a strong concept of what was good, but no idea—or apparent interest—in what was bad. Maybe it was because never in their young lives had they ever done anything really bad. They seemed to glow with innocence.

Despite their handicaps and the normal pangs experienced by children on the threshhold or into adolescence, these special boys and girls seemed to be less moody and far happier than the average youngster one encounters today. It took me a while before I could tell—sober-sided adult that I was—when one of them was pulling my leg.

David, a skinny fifteen-year-old nonstop talker, who already was three inches taller than my five foot, seven inches, always was putting me on, testing how much line he could reel out before I was hooked.

When time came for David to be confirmed, I innocently asked him what he had chosen as his Confirmation name.

"Hulk Hogan," he said brightly.

"You can't use a wrestler's name for Confirmation," I said adultly. "You have to pick a saint's name."

"How about Michael?" he asked, cocking his head to read my reaction.

"Very good choice," I said. "Michael, the Archangel."

"No," said David with a satisfied smile. "Michael Jordan, the Bull."

When I told Ginny the story, she immediately thought of the perfect Confirmation gift for David. Instead of giving him a crucifix or other religious article, I called the public relations department of the Chicago Bulls basketball team and got a big glossy, autographed picture of Michael Jordan flying like an archangel toward the basketball hoop. When he opened the package and saw the picture on his Confirmation day, it was the first and only time in my experience that David was speechless.

The children not only were expert teasers, they also at times could be quite mischievous. I found that out during the months I was assigned as the special friend of Peter, a thirteen-year-old the size of a playful St. Bernard. Peter had multiple handicaps, not the least being a severe speech impediment. But he also was street-smart, with an imagination as glowing as his clear blue eyes.

Because he was too hyperactive to be allowed near paints and brushes and had too short of an attention span for weaving or other crafts, he and I usually spent the hour pretending to run a restaurant. Like all the children, Peter was enamored of fast food restaurants. During our quiet time, while the other children and their adult friends were weaving, drawing, or doing other activities, Peter and I pretended to take orders and serve imaginary hamburgers and milkshakes.

I have to confess that playing with Peter did wonders to stimulate my own imagination. We made our hamburgers out of brown modeling clay, flipped them on a "grill" constructed of wooden blocks, and served them on cardboard trays to imaginary customers. Sometimes I got so mesmerized by the work in our restaurant that I completely forgot that I was over fifty years old, father of four grown children, bureau chief of a respected international newsmagazine, and—yes—someone who was dying.

Playing with Peter was hard work. Not only was he a workaholic when it came to running his restaurant, he often was so hyped up that I could not control him when it came time to close his hamburger stand and go into the celebration room.

One Sunday he was particularly hyperactive during the play time, turning out hamburgers at a pace that would have delighted any McDonald's manager. His adrenalin was still pumping in the celebration room as Judy Porst, an elementary school teacher and our "leader catechist," produced a bowl with two goldfish and started to talk about the life-giving qualities of water.

"We also share a life together," she began. But Peter wanted nothing to do with goldfish. He began banging his foot against the side of his folding chair and kept nudging me in the ribs. He wanted to get back to making clay hamburgers. He became so disruptive that the group leader, Rosemary Schumacher, gave me a raised-eyebrows appeal to escort Peter out.

I needed all my strength to wrestle Peter back to the other room. Then he decided to have some fun with me. Ignoring my attempts to interest him in a picture book on animals, he ran to the door, yelled something incoherent, and started down the corridor. The artful dodger was stronger and quicker than I, and he knew it.

I started down the hall after him, but it was like running in a nightmare. My legs turned to jelly, and my eyes wouldn't focus. I stumbled after him like a ninety-year-old man. Then all my strength whooshed out of me like air leaving a balloon. I slumped to the floor and sat exhausted, my back to the wall, like a schoolboy during a tornado drill.

A grinning Peter looked back from the end of the corridor where he was threatening to bolt through the door to the playground. Then he realized that something was wrong. He started back toward me, slowly at first, then faster as he realized I was not faking. He held out both hands, palms up, and tried to say something that sounded like, "Peas Fank Peas." Only with difficulty could I make out what he was saying: "Peace, Frank, Peace." It was a gesture and words he had seen Judy Porst use many times in the celebration room. "Peace, Peter, Peace."

This beautiful, innocent child sensed that I too was wounded, and that he was stronger and that he needed to help me. Awkwardly he pulled me up. Like two exhausted comrades with arms around each other, we wobbled back into the room. We sat at a table and looked silently at pictures of animals in a book until the others returned for our postcelebration snack of doughnut holes and Hawaiian Punch. I was too physically and emotionally drained to make any more "hamburgers."

By that time my illness was drawing me into two conflicting worlds. Sometimes I lived in this strange land of the imagination with Peter. I felt more comfortable when I became this little boy who was Peter's friend. Other times I still tried to function in the "real" world. But I felt increasingly alienated from the no-nonsense, healthy, hyper-competitive journalists who were a part of that world.

I could not clearly define this growing sense of alienation—or was it isolation? The only person I felt could understand what was happening inside me was Ginny. I found myself feeling comfortable only when I was with her—or with the SPRED children. My old world was slipping away, and nothing was coming to replace it, at least nothing that I could see on my horizon. No longer did I occupy my accustomed niche in the workaday world. No longer did I feel comfortable identifying myself by what I did for a living or for whom I did it. In one sense, that was liberating; in another sense, it was frightening. How would strangers react if I followed my instinct and answered their inevitable "what-do-you-do?" question with "I make clay hamburgers with my friend Peter."

For the first time in our married life, I also began to understand what it means to need someone's love. Before my illness, I always had simply taken it for granted that Ginny loved me and that I loved Ginny. Our love was something like the air we breathed; we didn't need to talk about it or analyze it. It just was there. But I was discovering that dying means never taking anything for granted anymore. All along I had thought I was loving, when I only was comfortable.

In early March of 1986, I was abruptly yanked back into the world of hard reality and competition. A summons went out from 444 Madison Avenue for all *Newsweek* bureau chiefs to assemble in Key West, Florida, for a three-day meeting. Our New York editors wanted to sit down with us at a neutral site to wrangle over problems and discuss the future course of the magazine. Though never a fan of sun and sand, I found the prospect of fleeing from Chicago's lingering cold for a few days appealing. That same weekend, Ginny was scheduled to drive to Indiana University for "Moms' Day" at our youngest daughter Heidi's sorority. We both could escape, if only briefly, from the cloud of uncertainty that hovered over us since our second visit to Mayo. We also needed some time away from one another. I was getting too dependent on Ginny. And she was getting too focused on me.

During that meeting in Key West, I did three things I never will do again in my life: smoke a cigar, drink a margarita, and ride a motorbike.

To reach Key West I could either take a small shuttle plane from Miami or drive the 120 miles in a rental car. Considering my vertiginous condition, neither itinerary seemed comfortable. So I arranged to rendezvous at Miami Airport with Houston Bureau Chief Dan Pedersen, who could share the ride down the coast. Like everybody else at *Newsweek,* at the time Dan did not know anything about my physical problems. As it turned out, I did all the driving. But I was at ease, knowing that if I suffered a dizzy spell, Dan could grab the wheel.

The drive also gave me a rare chance to talk with Dan, a former *Des Moines Register* reporter and one of the "Midwest Mafia" that I had recruited for *Newsweek* over the years. Of all the things I did in my twenty years at *Newsweek,* I think my most lasting and important contribution was helping hire a coterie of quality young reporters with solid experience at midwestern newspapers. In addition to Dan, there was my own deputy John McCormick, who I met while doing a story on Sylvester Stallone making the thoroughly forgettable movie, *F.I.S.T.,* in Dubuque, Iowa; Tony Fuller, a small-town Illinois boy who worked for United Press International, the *Chicago Daily News,* and later became *Newsweek*'s National Affairs editor; and Bill Schmidt, now with the *New York Times,* one of the best all-round reporters I have known in thirty years in the business. I persuaded Bill to join *Newsweek* during a three-hour lunch at the Detroit airport.

I also was proud of having trained Vest Monroe, a kid who had grown up in the gang-infested housing projects on Chicago's South Side, and who came to my bureau right out of Harvard University— of all places. Vest's climb from ghetto to Harvard to national magazine correspondent was so stunning that I was proud when he would tell people that I was one of his "mentors."

All the bureau chiefs arrived at Key West the night before the start of the meeting so we could engage in our own version of show-and-tell. We also could plot our meeting strategies before the heavy brass arrived from New York.

Bob Rivard, the director of correspondents, was our den mother. Maybe ringleader is a better description. We started the afternoon at a bar where the waitresses carried pitchers of margaritas in clusters, and the other patrons looked like extras in a South Sea island movie.

Determined not to be a party pooper, I allowed my glass to be filled and, from time to time, pretended to sip from it. Nobody noticed that I wasn't drinking. Somewhere Rivard had gotten hold of cigars the thickness of bamboo shoots and offered them around. I never smoked cigarettes, but once in a great while puffed on a cigar at a wedding reception or special occasion. I lit the cigar and soon was caught up in the camaraderie, the inside jokes, and the "war stories" that reporters like to tell about themselves and the characters they have covered.

For the umpteenth time, I told about being sent on the wild goose chase after the kidnapped newspaper heiress Patricia Hearst. (Yet another abandonment of the long-suffering Ginny.)

Our New York editors had been tipped by a source in Denver that the missing Patty Hearst had been spotted near Sheridan, Wyoming, in the company of a guy named either McCreary or McCready. My friend Bill Schmidt, then bureau chief in Miami, was sent to run down a second tip that she also had been spotted in Utah.

I spent all Friday and Saturday talking to deputies, bartenders, barbers, druggists, drifters, and town gossips without finding any trace of the elusive Hearst or McCreary (or was it McCready?). All I uncovered for forty-eight hours of sleepless effort was an "incident" report by a state trooper who several weeks earlier had stopped a gray van containing a "band of hippies." Later, realizing that one of the women in the van had looked like Hearst, he wrote the brief report.

With our Saturday night deadline fast approaching, I called New York and asked if our source could supply any more information about the mysterious McCreary or McCready character. I stayed on the line while they phoned our tipster in Denver. Yes, it turned out, there was one other small detail about him. He was half-Japanese.

I always have prided myself on being a cool professional—though I did have a reputation for exploding like a geyser at one-year intervals. After two sleepless days and nights of trying to engage a passel of "yup and nope" guys in conversation, chasing a gauzy rumor all over an unfamiliar frontier town, I blew my top. Before

45

slamming down the phone, I shouted: "Doesn't that sonofabitch in Denver think that just possibly it would have helped to know that I was after a guy with an Irish name who looks Oriental?"

I went back to a few places with my expanded profile of McCreary or McCready, but when people started looking at me funny, I got into my rented car without calling New York and hit the road myself.

The storytelling in the Key West bar went on for the best of an afternoon. I never realized that I had drunk the margarita, until someone started to fill my glass again. That was to be my last taste of alcohol and my last cigar.

Eventually we adjourned to a more upscale restaurant for a relatively sedate dinner. Later, as we sang off-key songs around the piano bar, I felt a bit out of place because everyone else was at least slightly pixilated and I was cold sober. I also was dead tired. No way could I stay up for the all-night poker game. As I settled down to sleep that early morning, I felt a glow of good fellowship; I was still part of the gang. I had hung in there for as much of the fun and games as I could possibly take.

The next day the ever-inventive Rivard decided we should greet our top editors, Rick Smith and Maynard Parker, with a bureau chiefs' motorcade from the airport. The idea was for all of us to rent motorbikes, ride out to the airport in formation, and escort the van carrying the editor-in-chief and the editor down the main street of town to the resort where we were staying. The more we embarrassed them with the horn-honking and bell-ringing hoopla, the happier we would be.

Anyone in my shape, with my history of vertigo and confusion, had no business on a bicycle, let alone a motorbike. On an isolated country road I would have been a threat only to myself. Speeding along the main drag of downtown Key West, at times only inches from other unskilled riders of varying degrees of sobriety, I was a public nuisance. Even as I wobbled along, teeth clenched, fingers frozen around the handlebar grips, I pondered what Ginny might say if she knew what I was up to. There must be something in the genes of even the most mild-mannered men that makes us less afraid of death than of being left out of the clubhouse.

Somehow our Marx Brothers' motorcade made it from the airport without any of the riders hitting a pedestrian or sliding beneath the wheels of the editors' van. My cycling days were over. Much later— in a land I then did not know existed—a transplant surgeon would tell me that they called motorized two-wheel vehicles "donor-cycles."

The Key West bureau chief's meeting was Maier's last folly.

6

HE'S ON THE ROOF

A nurse told Ginny this joke: A fellow gets drafted into the army. He calls home to his brother to see how his pet cat is doing. "The cat's dead," says the brother. "No, no," cries the distraught soldier. "Don't tell bad news that way. Do it gradually. Say 'The cat's on the roof and won't come down.' Next time I call, say 'The cat's dead.' Okay? By the way, how's mom?" (Pause) "She's on the roof."

Ginny became so weary of "How's Frank?" inquiries from our close friends that she often answered, "He's on the roof." They were glad to hear that I was doing well enough to clean the gutters.

Actually, Ginny has been on our roof more than I during our thirty-five years of marriage. Without success I have tried to keep her from dangling out second floor windows to knock down wasp nests under awnings or swaying atop our maple tree while trying to shape its upper branches. She can fix a leaky faucet, install a new sump pump in the basement, rip down paneling, build a stone wall—all the skills that our culture traditionally assigns to males.

I like to cook. Ginny has no interest in cooking. Our oldest son, Michael, says that he and his brother and sisters are the only people he knows who went to college and never complained about the food. Our married daughter, Katie, calls *me,* not her mother, for recipes.

Yet Ginny remains firmly feminine, tiny but hard of muscle.

Standing five feet tall—if she stretches—she has never strayed more than ten pounds from the 105 pounds she weighed when first we met. Her weight control doesn't come from idle aerobics or running; she is too pragmatic to waste energy without it producing something. She stays tiny and strong because she is always working, often at hard physical labor.

Her garden is as orderly as the inside of her house; she has no tolerance for weeds or unwashed dishes. A chronic neatnik, she drives me crazy by whisking up sections of the Sunday newspaper even as they drop from my hand. The biggest fights of our married life have erupted over her compulsiveness in stashing everything in its proper place—where I would never look—and tossing out anything that's not lashed down. For a writer who spends his waking hours furiously clipping articles from newspapers and magazines, intending someday to file them, life with Ginny can be challenging.

Many compulsive people are very self-absorbed. That's not one of Ginny's faults. If anything, she gets too involved in other people's problems, a trait that reflects her basic empathy for the underdog, but also her perfectionism. As she occasionally used to advise an obstreperous child, "It's my way or the highway, buster."

Perhaps because of my penchant for avoiding the uncomfortable or confrontational, I have always admired Ginny's way of giving preferential treatment to the lowly and powerless while adopting almost a pugnacious attitude toward authority figures. One of my doctors only half-jokingly gave her the nickname "The Intimidator."

I've always said that Ginny would have been terrific on the *Titanic.* Had she been in charge, no half-filled lifeboats would have been lowered in panic. No millionaires would have gotten life jackets before the last little grandma in steerage had hers. Then, after the boats were lowered and the band stopped playing, Ginny really *would* have rearranged the deck chairs.

I have known Ginny since she was "Sweet Sixteen" and the cute, short-haired little sister of my college friend, John Ryan. I was a classic example of a 1950s Catholic boy: product of an all-male high school, student at then all-male University of Notre Dame, destined soon to become an "officer and a gentleman" in the U.S. Navy. All in all, I spent the first two decades of my life in what constituted a masculine commune. When Catholic boys of my generation thought of girls, it was as "occasions of sin," as the priests unnecessarily used to caution us. I don't know of too many of my contemporaries who ever had the nerve, or the good fortune, to come close to those "occasions." Like most of my pals, I was not only totally inexperienced, but also totally unexposed to what our fathers and grandfathers then condescendingly called "the gentler sex." Looking back, I think most of us—me the foremost—were actually scared to death of women.

The first time I remember seeing Ginny was in the flickering light of a Halloween night bonfire when we both were in our late teens. I was there with her brother John and three other of my perennially dateless friends, just hanging around the edges of the bonfire, as indeed we hung around the edges of every social event, commenting on the attractiveness or lack thereof of the girls in the crowd and daring one another to try to strike up a conversation with one of them, pretty or otherwise. As participants in a dating ritual, we definitely would have been dismissed as duds by any observing social scientist.

Suddenly Ginny popped out of the darkness at her brother's elbow, along with three other girls. I remember she was wearing the "uniform" that was *de rigueur* for girls out on the town in that era—plaid skirt, pullover sweater over a white blouse with a Peter Pan collar, knee socks, and brown "penny" loafers. And that's about all I remember—except that she singled me out and, to my befuddlement, kept asking me questions, one right after another, seldom waiting for my monosyllabic answers. I wasn't sure if she was flirting or just trying to torment me. By the time I finally crafted in my mind something clever to say, she just disappeared into the darkness—and all of her friends evaporated too. I was left in an ambivalent daze, certain I would like to see her again but not sure if I was up to it any time soon.

Were it not for Ginny's innate aggressiveness, I probably never would have gotten up the nerve to ask her for a date. Two weeks before Valentine's Day, I received an unsigned three-by-five-inch index card in the mail. Taped to it was the slogan of the Hallmark Greeting Card Co.: "When you care enough to send the very best." Also stuck to the card was a dime. Since I had a very short list of female acquaintances, it did not take me too long to figure out that John Ryan's little sister was my mystery "correspondent." For the fifties, this was bordering on a brazen overture. Girls were expected to be more passive in the dating arena. I remember picking through valentines in the greeting card section of the old Walker Brothers store in Oak Park, trying to find one that was encouraging but romantically neutral. Ginny later told me that the valentine I sent—not a dime, but a quarter one—was the sort you would pick out for a maiden aunt.

While I was at Notre Dame and Ginny was at Barat, a small women's college in Lake Forest, Illinois, we had what might be described as an on-again, off-again courtship. Sometimes she called it off, sometimes I did. But there never was any finality to any of our partings—which always resulted from some trivial tiff.

One time we broke up because of an April Fool's Day joke that got out of hand. Ginny called me at school and, at the end of our conversation, casually mentioned that she had tumbled down an elevator shaft, suffering minor bruises, but mercifully no broken bones. She expected me to laugh at her April Fool's joke. Not gullible Frank. When I took her seriously, she couldn't resist keeping the joke going. I ended up sending her an expensive get well card with an emotional and, for me, romantic, note. When she fessed up by return mail that her fall down the Barat elevator shaft was a hoax, I became so furious that I didn't write or call her for months.

Actually, it wasn't all that farfetched for me to believe that Ginny had fallen down an elevator shaft. At college she always was up to some mischief. One time she and a dozen of her classmates decided to break the boredom of boarding school life by sliding three floors down the winding fire escape chute. The first one down later became a nun. The second one later became my wife.

What the sliders didn't know was that the door at the end of the chute was rigged to set off an alarm, both in the building and at the Lake Forest fire station. By the time the last dusty slider emerged from the chute, the Reverend Mother was part of the greeting committee, and the fire engines already were pulling into the driveway.

One other night when Ginny got tired of studying, she took all the oil paintings off the third floor corridor wall and put them on a nearby grand piano. She then left a note with the Reverend Mother's initials, "H. C.," on it, directing the janitor to take them, piano included, to the trunk room.

Ginny's slide down the fire chute or her other school pranks, which she delighted in telling me about in her letters, didn't cause any breakup of our romance—though it did make me wonder about what kind of an unpredictable woman I had gotten mixed up with. In a way, given my conservative nature and upbringing, I found it exhilarating to have a girlfriend with such a puckish streak.

But I did not find her unpredictableness so lovable on another occasion. That was when my roomate Frank Lolli and I hitchhiked home from Notre Dame so I could surprise Ginny with a weekend visit. Because it was easy for Notre Dame students to get a ride from South Bend to Chicago, we figured to make the trip in maybe three hours. No sooner did we have our thumbs out, than northern Indiana was struck by one of those blinding snowstorms that sweep off the end of Lake Michigan with such sudden fury. Eventually we were picked up by an optometrist, who neglected to tell us—as we neglected to ask—which direction he was ultimately heading. While we dozed in the warm comfort of his Buick, he turned south rather than west. By the time we realized we were not heading for Chicago, we were far from any well-traveled road. Lolli and I found ourselves standing in front of a closed service station on a two-lane road somewhere south of Valparaiso, wondering how any passing motorist ever would see us in the pitch blackness.

Somehow we reached Chicago about twelve hours after we had left campus. When I called Ginny's house to announce I was home and would be over as soon as I could change my clothes, her mother said she had gone to the movies with some guy named Lenny. I vowed that was the end of my romance with Ginny Ryan!

We became engaged during my senior year in college. I remember—because I asked for Ginny's hand when her father visited me at Notre Dame. A gregarious, no-nonsense Irishman, John Vincent Ryan was on campus to see his son, John, a pre-med student, and brought me banana bread baked by Ginny's mother. Asking Ginny's father for her hand in marriage would have been a formidable task under any circumstances. Doing it over a gift box of banana bread seemed about as safe as I could hope for.

He frowned through his bushy eyebrows, "Is it all right with her?"

"Oh yes. I already asked her."

"Then it's okay with me," he said, crushing my hand in his big paw.

As he left, he looked back with an impish grin. "You sure you know what you're getting into?"

I have spent the last thirty-five years delightedly trying to come up with an answer to that question.

After graduation, I went to Newport, Rhode Island, for four months of navy officer candidate school. The Korean War had just ended, but the draft was still in place. I figured that doing my military service near an ocean would be better than rusting at an army base in some forlorn patch of the interior.

While I was at OCS, Ginny—incredibly—was hired to work in the test kitchens of Quaker Oats Company in Chicago. Other than hating to cook, her credentials consisted of being a home economics major before dropping out of Barat College. (One of her classmates was Jane Burke, who became Jane Byrne, mayor of Chicago, whose first husband was a classmate of mine at Notre Dame. Bill Byrne chose to put in his military time as a marine flier, only to be killed while trying to land his plane in a fog.)

Getting married to Ginny Ryan was logistically complicated, something reminiscent of an early "I Love Lucy" show. The whole production was a preview of our married life—which can minimally be described as "interesting." Life with Ginny has been many things, but never boring.

We were scheduled for a big wedding in Chicago the Saturday after my Thursday commissioning. Since I could not come home to obtain a marriage license, Ginny had to arrange to get one by herself—which she managed to do. Don't ask me how—this was, after all, Chicago, and Ginny was, after all, Irish. But I did need to forward a report of a blood test. That was no problem because I also needed a blood test as part of my precommissioning physical.

The day after our physicals, a corpsman entered our barracks, hollered out my last name, and, when I identified myself, told me to report to the infirmary. When I got there, the chief petty officer on duty told me I had to retake my blood test. "How come?" I asked. "Because the first one says you've got syphilis," he replied. I jumped up so fast the chair fell over. "That's IMPOSSIBLE," I shrieked. "That's what they all say, sailor," he replied.

As he wrapped the rubber tubing around my arm, all I could think of was Ginny's father, John Vincent Ryan. He was going to kill me. Just as the chief prepared to jab the needle into a vein, I saw a card on the table next to my arm. Reading it upside down, I saw that the name on it was pronounced the same as mine, but was spelled differently. The guy who needed to be retested also had a different first name and was in a different section of our company barracks. The chief reluctantly agreed that I was not the right sailor. With that crisis settled, I naïvely believed that the hard part of getting married was behind me.

The day of my commissioning I was ordered to report to the Newport navy base temporarily until I could be reassigned in a few weeks to permanent duty. We had been told to expect at least a seventy-two-hour pass as a reward for surviving the rigors of training camp. But, when I reported to the officer of the day, he assigned me to stand-by duty over the weekend, which meant I could travel no more than fifty miles from the base. He was unimpressed with my marriage plans back in Chicago—as he was unimpressed with my shiny new ensign bars. So, my first act as an officer in the United States Navy was to go AWOL to get married. I was much more intimidated by John Vincent Ryan than by the Secretary of the Navy.

We were married on Saturday, flew the next morning with two suitcases to Providence, Rhode Island, took a bus to Newport, and began married life in Mrs. Crilly's boarding house on Catherine Street, only a short walk from the cliffs where the elegant mansions of the wealthy overlooked the Atlantic Ocean.

We didn't own a car, a television set, a stereo system, a microwave, or any of the impedimenta that young couples today think are the bare essentials for starting out life together. Like many of our friends in the same predicament, we learned to make do with what we had. Many a time we rounded up pop bottles for refunds to go to the movies. When we started out, all we had was $1,350 in the bank and high hopes.

The love we planted in each other's heart was just starting to sprout. We didn't know then, but would come to understand later that what you sow in the spring of your life, if tended and watered, will yield a golden harvest in the autumn of your life, when you need it most. We had no way of knowing back then how meaningful the promise to be loyal "in sickness and in health" would become for us one day.

I ended up spending three years on an attack transport ship out of San Diego, never managing to get transferred to a coveted public information job, which would have been useful experience for a future journalist. I outlasted three captains and eventually became the senior officer in terms of service on the ship. Everybody knew how to get off the bucket but me. While I was careening around the South China Sea or the Western Pacific at a top speed of 16 knots, landing sea-sick marines on unpronounceable atolls, Ginny was learning what it was like to be married to an absentee husband. The navy did not provide good training for my eventual career; but it was perfect training for her.

Surprisingly, my ship was in port for the birth of our first child, Michael, at the small hospital on the Coronado Island Navy Air Station. But the next day we sailed for three weeks of exercises off San Clemente and Catalina Islands. Tom Harte, a high school friend who also was stationed in San Diego, brought Ginny and baby Michael home from the hospital, the first of many friends and neighbors who would end up being my surrogate in family emergencies. By the time I dropped anchor again, Ginny had the shingles and had taken up coffee drinking and smoking for the first time.

It was while living in Southern California that I gave Ginny the nickname I've used for her ever since. I started calling her "Monk" because she wore her hair in a short style that looked like a Franciscan friar.

After my discharge, my first job in the news business was sports editor—actually the one-man sports department—of a daily newspaper in Elgin, a town about twenty-five miles west of Chicago. By now, our second child was on the way. And my base pay was $1.25 an hour. The only possible way for even a single person to survive on such a Scroogian stipend was to be willing to perform almost round-the-clock overtime duties. Breaking into the news business then, as it is today, was difficult for even the most aggressive and well-connected young person. I was deliriously happy when I landed the job—which consisted mainly of covering high school sports and writing a column three times a week. (Without a byline. The publisher figured if any of his trolls developed a personal following he might have to pay us a living wage.)

It was great training. Because the paper was so small and the management so cheap, I got to do everything, including taking pictures with an old speed graphic camera and covering fires, auto crashes, library board meetings, political cornboils, and other shenanigans of small town life.

But on every Friday and Saturday during the high school football and basketball seasons, I worked forty-eight hours straight. I would attend the most important games and arrange for the team managers of other schools in our circulation area to call in their results and box scores. Since I was off covering one or two games, quite often I was not back at the paper to take the incoming scores from my "stringers." If they couldn't reach me in the newsroom, they called our apartment where the uncomplaining Ginny took down the box scores, not for one instant understanding what the numbers meant. Being a telephone person, and having only a bawling baby for company, she often kept the boys on the line to chat after they unloaded their scores from Hinckley–Big Rock, Hampshire, Hebron, and other sports centrals in the area.

My first Christmas at the paper, the managing editor came around with our yearly bonus: the choice of either a cigar or a pack of cigarettes. If, like me, you didn't smoke, you were out of luck. They also offered me a dime-an-hour raise, which I found so insulting that I quit. I probably couldn't have kept up the pace into my twenty-seventh year anyway. Maybe Ginny could. She enjoyed talking to those kids every Friday and Saturday night.

My next job was in Rockford, the second largest city in Illinois, where I became police reporter for the morning paper, chasing death and disaster all over town from four in the afternoon until midnight. It was a brutal job that was physically and spiritually exhausting. I witnessed enough death, brutality, pain, and tears to supply a lifetime of bad dreams.

After eighteen months, I asked to be taken off the police beat. From seeing and writing about so much death and violence, I had become paranoid, convinced that it was only a matter of time before something terrible happened to someone I knew and loved. I didn't realize it then, but that was when I began building a wall around my emotions, a way of buffering myself from other people's pain. It became a wall of indifference that stood uncracked for many years until one day I rounded a corner and bumped into Death myself, the very guy I had been trailing for so much of my working life.

After the police beat, I was assigned to cover politics, a cheerier job though almost as physically exhausting. Not only did I report on nonstop local, state, and national political campaigns, but also the sessions of the Illinois legislature in Springfield. In my absence, Ginny had total responsibility for raising our children and running our household. In my smugness, it never dawned on me that her job might be as difficult and tiring as mine.

As my career advanced, from Elgin to Rockford to the *Chicago Daily News* to *Newsweek,* Ginny was left to handle by herself all the crises and calamities of family life—from rushing kids to hospital emergency rooms for stitches to unclogging the kitchen sink.

When I taxied to the airport to fly to Austin for the Texas Tower shooting, I left Ginny to somehow retrieve our car which I had abandoned in downtown Chicago. When *Newsweek* sent me winging to Sheridan, Wyoming, in pursuit of a rumor that the elusive Patty Hearst had been spotted there, she was left to host a Saturday night dinner party by herself. When our daughter Katie had a tumor removed from her leg, Ginny sat in the hospital waiting room alone—I was off in Springfield covering the governor's annual budget address. When she was in labor with Danny, I was at her bedside, but not exactly holding her hand. I was busy writing a deadline story on a yellow legal pad. (That was before fathers were encouraged to get involved in the birth of their children.) When Ginny herself had foot surgery, I dropped her off at the out-patient clinic and rushed to the airport to meet an arriving editor from New York.

While I galavanted around the country, convinced that I was making tremendous personal sacrifices for my wife and four kids, she took care of all the logistics of our life. More important, she assumed the "bad guy" role in disciplining the children. During the week, she was the one who had to tell them "No" and make them do their chores and homework, and go to bed on time. On the weekends, I would come home bearing trinkets from my travels, full of stories of my adventures, eager to take the kids to the zoo or a ballgame, fully expecting to be pampered by my spouse who had luxuriated at home while I was out eating the dust of the road in a fiercely competitive job.

In retrospect, I am amazed that never once during this era of our life did Ginny suggest that I might be a complacent jackass. Her friends know Ginny as someone who doesn't suffer fools patiently. She made me the loving exception to this rule.

Part Two

DEATH

7

THE OTHER
SIDE OF
SILENCE

ewsweek's Chicago bureau chief has the best view from his office of anyone at the magazine, including the top editors in New York. My office looked south from the seventy-ninth floor of the Amoco Building over Grant Park and Soldier Field to the smokestacks of Gary and the Indiana Dunes at the foot of Lake Michigan. When we first moved into the marble-clad skyscraper, I would spend my lunch hours with binoculars trying to pinpoint favorite restaurants in Chinatown and the Italian neighborhood near the University of Illinois at Chicago campus, or watch the lake freighters pulling into Calumet Harbor or the planes taking off from old Midway Airport.

Before I became jaded with the magnificent view, one of my trademark pranks was "turning on" the Buckingham Fountain for visiting editors from New York. During the spring and summer, the famous fountain in Grant Park went on promptly at ten each morning. If possible, I would arrange for the visiting New Yorkers to be sitting in my office a few minutes before then. I would casually ask if they would like to see the fountain work. Whatever their reply, I would pick up the phone and pretend to call someone at the park district named "Floyd." After small-talking about weather and family—while watching the seconds tick toward ten o'clock—I would say: "Floyd, I've got some people here from New York who've never seen Buckingham Fountain working. Could you turn it on for them? Thanks, Floyd. My best to Millie." No sooner would I put the phone down than the fountain would burst into a rainbow of water spraying fifty feet into the air. My guests always were properly impressed, convinced more than ever that you could do anything in Chicago if only you knew whom to call.

On my return from the bureau chiefs' meeting in Key West, a lethargy as gray as the March days settled over me. Unable to churn up any enthusiasm for the assignments on the weekly story list, I sat at my desk like a hypnotized child, staring down at the tiny toy cars and buses on Michigan Avenue or the Lilliputians flowing in and out of the Art Institute. Since it wasn't yet spring, I couldn't even amuse myself by turning on Buckingham Fountain for visitors.

Fortunately, we were in a slow news time, very little mayhem was occuring in the ten midwestern states we were responsible for overseeing. Without breaking news, the bureau correspondents worked on stories with future deadlines. I assigned myself to answer the week's routine queries from New York, most of which could be done over the telephone.

On the Tuesday afternoon before Easter in 1986, I finished my last phone interview for a business story on the growing practice of homeowners' refinancing their mortgages. Weary and woozy, I decided to go home, get a good night's rest, and write the piece in the morning. By the time I got off the commuter train in Arlington Heights, I was nauseated and exhausted. No matter what Ginny thought, this time I really did have a touch of the flu. She agreed that a lot of it was going around the neighborhood.

I was up all night with a wrenching stomach ache that would not subside despite frequent vomiting. I was in such distress that I did not notice in the dim glow from the bathroom night-light that I was vomiting dark fluid. As incredible as it sounds, never during that long night did I consider that I might be suffering from anything more serious than the mischief caused by the flu bug that was "going around." Actually, I was bleeding to death.

The varices that Mayo's doctors had detected the previous spring had ruptured in my esophagus. Only later did I learn how much in jeopardy my life was on that early March morning. The mortality rate from a hemorrhage of the esophagus is high, and my chances of being alive a year after a bleed, even with good medical care, were only 50 percent.

At dawn, I was so sick and weak that I finally woke Ginny. Even then I was in denial, figuring that somehow I could bluster my way through this episode. Despite stomach pain and light-headedness, I kept worrying about that unfinished story on home refinancing. I wondered if John McCormick could stitch the story together using my notes at the office and comments phoned from my sickbed.

Ginny took one look at me and said, "You're going to the hospital." I started to protest, but, instead of words, a gusher of blood shot out of my mouth, exploding all over the green carpet in our bedroom. The entire room turned sideways, the floor came rushing up at me, and I remember Ginny screaming.

Two figures in navy blue carried me on a gurney through a blinding white blizzard to the waiting fire department ambulance. By this time, I was surprisingly at ease, like a potentate being carried in his sedan chair through the marketplace. My stomach cramps were gone, and I felt quite calm, indeed almost euphoric. I remember thinking it strange that the snowstorm continued to whirl around me even in the ambulance. One of the paramedics talked on the radio to the emergency room of Northwest Community Hospital, the other took my blood pressure and asked me questions. I answered in what I thought was a neighborly way. For some reason, the last thing I wanted to do was get the paramedics excited; as long as they didn't act panicky, I was okay. Soon they had a clear IV solution draining into my arm and were wrestling my legs into pressure leggings.

I wondered why they didn't turn on their siren and start rushing toward the hospital. I asked one of the young men how long he had been a paramedic and if he liked his work. You would think I was the Duke of Windsor talking to his gardners. Where was Ginny anyway? I suggested to them that, since I was feeling better and not spitting up more blood, they should just carry me back into the house and ask Ginny to call the doctor. The truth was that I had very little blood left to spit up.

Finally, the siren began to wail and we slipped slowly away from my house. I felt alert, like a traveler ready for adventure as his train pulls from the station. I wondered what the day would bring. At first the driver did not seem to be going very fast; I thought he might be lost in our neighborhood of winding streets. I asked his partner, hunkered down by my stretcher, if they knew about the construction detour on Cleveland Avenue. He assured me that they knew the fastest way to the hospital. I thought: these really are nice lads. Nothing can go wrong as long as they are taking care of me. Maybe I can get to the bureau by tomorrow and still make the deadline on that story.

The world seemed wrapped in a glaring white fog, and I began to shiver violently. Above everything else, I wanted everyone to remain calm. As the paramedics pulled me from the ambulance, snapped down the gurney's legs, and rolled me into the emergency room, I remember thinking: If I'm dying, why am I so calm?

I recall little from then on, except protesting when a nurse snipped off my T-shirt and a doctor pushed a cold tube up my nose. My strength was draining from my body like sap from a tree—and I couldn't stop it. The last thing I remember was asking for Ginny. I wanted her to call the bureau and tell John McCormick that I wouldn't be in today.

What I know of the next six hours comes from Ginny and others who were there, and from reading my hospital records months later. I survived that first bleed only because I was fortunate enough to be near a major hospital that had doctors and nurses who were experienced in dealing with what constituted a true medical emergency. Bleeding esophageal varices cannot be stopped easily, particularly by people without the training or tools to handle it.

The ER doctor first administered a drug called vasopressin that sometimes helps control hemorrhaging. Blood was ordered from the bank in anticipation of a transfusion. At first, they thought I was suffering from a bleeding ulcer, a diagnosis that alarmed and frustrated Ginny, who arrived at the hospital by car with all of my Mayo records in her arms. But the doctors—none of whom had ever seen me before—did not seem all that interested in what Mayo's experts had to say or what Ginny told them about my condition. She went to the phone, called Mayo Clinic, and soon had Dr. Jorge Rakela on the line. He told her that, from the description she gave, I was in a "grave situation and might not survive." He offered to discuss my case with any of the attending physicians if that could be useful.

To this day, Ginny still feels that the doctors fighting to save me that morning in ER should have taken the time to consult my Mayo records and talk, however briefly, with Dr. Rakela on the phone. I certainly was in no condition to assist in my treatment or discuss my medical history. Ginny was my proxy and should have been listened to. I wasn't really aware of anything during most of the time they worked on me in the emergency room.

As would be the case during subsequent crises in our medical adventure, it was Ginny—not me—who had to face the raw fear of the moment, deal with the frustrations that laypeople feel when first confronted with medical jargon and the wall that many medical practitioners erect rather than make the effort to explain what is happening.

They also lost an opportunity to possibly learn something about this fifty-ish, white male with little blood pressure and even less blood who was lying mute on the table before them. When I was rolled into the ER, there was no one there who knew more about me or my condition than Ginny. But she was to learn from that first bleeding crisis that we—meaning mostly, she—would have to fight to get information about what was happening and to keep some measure of control over my treatment. I am alive today because those men and women yanked me back to life that morning in the emergency room of Northwest Community Hospital. For that I am forever grateful. But I believe just as deeply that I am alive today because in the months ahead Ginny fought like a cornered wildcat to see that nothing was done to me without a proper explanation.

As we later got tangled up in the unfamiliar and, at times, terrifying jungle of modern medicine, we were amazed to discover how many patients with serious illnesses—with their very lives on the line—are too timid to ask their doctors even the basic question, Why? So many ailing people do not understand that they have, not only the right, but the obligation to participate in the decisions made about their treatment. The doctors, nurses, and technicians are there for the patient's benefit, not the other way around.

To attempt to stop my bleeding, the doctors inserted a Sengstaken-Blakemore tube through my nose and down my esophagus. A balloon in the tube was then inflated so that it pressed tightly against the ruptured veins in the esophagus to stop the bleeding. A

Preston traction helmet was then slipped onto my head to hold the tubing rigidly in place. It is like a tight-fitting football helmet. As I slowly floated back toward consciousness, the pain from the helmet biting into my forehead was the most excrutiating I have ever felt, before or since. For months afterwards, I had a five-inch scab where the helmet bit into my forehead. The faint scar is still there today, a white gash in the summer when I get a bit tanned. I plan to tell my grandchildren it was from a bullet grazing my head when I was a cowboy.

I once interviewed Dr. Elisabeth Kubler-Ross about dying—and I have since read books by noted thanatologist Dr. Raymond A. Moody Jr. about near-death experiences. As a reporter I have tried to recollect my experience of being on the threshhold of death as accurately as possible. Never in those frantic hours in the emergency room and later in the intensive care unit did I experience the range of phenomena that so many people in that predicament have reported to researchers—the out-of-body experience, the meeting of dead relatives, or the sensation of passing through a dark tunnel toward a creature of light.

But I did share two of the feelings that frequently are reported by those who claim to have undergone near-death experiences. First, despite the pain of the helmet on my forehead, I remained at peace and devoid of anxiety about what was happening. And, for some time, I floated in a world that was beyond time, beyond expression.

Sometime before, I had read a book by the late Frank Sheed in which he used the phrase, "the other side of silence," to describe the state of clarity and insight we might find in a different dimension after life. Reporters are not known for their introspection, but more for their observation. So I wander through strange country when I report that during those crucial hours of my first dying I floated somewhere on "the other side of silence."

I later described it in my journal as "a land where I knew things intuitively, but cannot explain them to anyone, even to Ginny. The experience truly was ineffable. Maybe to some it might be a frightening place. But, I recall it as a land where God touched me deeply, directly, and lastingly."

Some friends who have an interest in the phenomena have asked me if I had a near-death experience that first time in the emergency room. I tell them that I did not, at least not in the way people who were revived after being clinically "dead" have described it to researchers like Kubler-Ross and Moody. But, in a real sense, I had a near-death experience, not for a brief time, but for the many months I sat on death's doorstep, waiting to be called inside. Because I lived so close to death for such a long time, I got to know something about it. Once you are introduced to death, you may continue to respect it, but you never again can be awed by it.

If someone pointed a gun at me, my stomach would go cold, and I would dive for the floor as fast as anybody in the room. That would be my instinctive reaction to a perceived threat of bodily harm. But, from my own experience and from talking with others who have survived close encounters with death, I view death as no more frightening, maybe a lot less frightening, than life. As my journalistic hero, the late Red Smith, once said in a eulogy for a friend: "Dying is no big deal. The least of us will manage it. Living is the trick."

It must have been about six hours before I began to "regain" my body, began to feel across my forehead the sharp bite of the helmet holding in place the pressure balloon down my throat. Through the slowly lifting fog I began to understand that I was adrift in treacherous waters. Gone was the holiday mood in the ambulance, the euphoria apparently caused by the shock of my brain being deprived of blood.

I remember people whispering in my ear, Ginny among them, but I have no recollection of what they said. One of the voices had a bright Irish lilt—a young woman's voice that kept calling me "Angel." I learned later that it was Margaret Kennedy Moser, a neighbor who belonged to the Care Ministry of our church, St. James. She had been in the intensive care unit comforting an elderly parishioner when she saw Ginny and learned of my predicament. During those hours, though I don't remember it, a priest gave me the last rites of the Catholic church—the first of three times I would receive this final sacrament within twelve months.

As I struggled to understand what the voices were saying, I began to think of myself as a small child again—it was a phenomenon that was to recur as my condition deteriorated in the months ahead. I was back in a classroom in St. Edmund's grammar school in Oak Park, and a young nun with an almost-familiar face was telling all of us that, whenever faced with pain or sorrow, we should "offer it up" for someone who was suffering even more.

After that I kept visualizing a baby named Candice, the first-born of a close friend of my daughter Katie. The infant had been born a few days before with a deformed heart. When Ginny had told me about her, I felt sad, but then pretty much dismissed it from my mind. But now, as I struggled to make sense of my own predicament, I kept thinking of this baby. I decided to bargain with God: since it now looked like I was about to die, take me now and save that baby. Make it an even trade. I know that sounds terribly unsophisticated to the worldly, and I confess it does to me too. In my helplessness, I reverted to thinking of God as I had as a child, as a kindly old Bookkeeper in the Sky, someone you could make deals with.

Weeks later Ginny told me that I kept asking about baby Candice after the tube was taken from my throat. But she had died in her mother's arms that first night I was in intensive care.

Easter night they removed the helmet and slipped some slivers of ice and a few chunks of lemon gelatin into my mouth. Our oldest son Michael sat by my bed reading me the *Chicago Tribune,* including a story about the great wealth amassed by the deposed dictator Ferdinand Marcos of the Phillipines. I remember thinking how all the treasures of the world seemed valueless compared to the soothing ice and soft, wiggly gelatin the nurses had given me.

When my night nurse in ICU tried to elevate my head, the bed would not crank up. She called a repairman who slipped under the bed like it was an old Chevy. Soon I was bouncing up and down in rythmn with his wrench banging on metal. The nurse soon chased him off and apologized to me for the rough treatment.

For the first time since arriving at the hospital I found words to complete a thought: "I hope he isn't the guy who fixes your heart-lung machine." She laughed at my feeble joke.

That's when I decided that I wasn't ready to die—not if I could still make a pretty girl laugh.

8

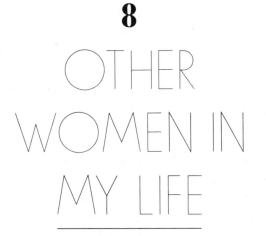

OTHER WOMEN IN MY LIFE

Warning: Hospitals can be dangerous to your health.

I spent six days in the intensive care unit before being shifted to a general care floor of the hospital. Before reading my records, the nurses there thought I had been in a car accident because of the ugly scarlet scab across my forehead. When Ginny told them it was from a Preston helmet, they had no idea what she was talking about. Only later did a doctor explain to us that nurses outside the emergency room and ICU rarely saw a patient who had worn one. "There's a saying," he said. "When the helmet goes on, the game is over." When the helmet was removed from most patients, they were transferred, not to a hospital room, but to the morgue.

We were just starting to uncoil from the fear and tension of my first brush with death when another crisis struck from an unexpected direction. On my tenth day in the hospital, a raging fever erupted in me like tissue paper touched by a match. Before the day was over my temperature "spiked" at 104 degrees and neither Tylenol nor applications of cold compresses could bring it down.

They called in Dr. John McGillen, an internist with a specialty in infectious diseases, who diagnosed my problem as probable bacterial endocarditis, an infection in my heart. Bacteria called staphylococcus aureus had invaded my system via the catheters, tubes, and IV lines that had been used to save my life. In the medicine trade, it is called a "nosocomial" infection, one that you pick up inside the hospital.

The bacteria were attacking the most vulnerable parts in my body, the valves of my heart that had been damaged by two bouts with rheumatic fever when I was a teenager. Rheumatic fever normally strikes children in their early teens, causing a variety of symptoms. In my case, I had been kept in my bed with arthriticlike pain in the joints and fatigue for two six-month periods when I was in seventh grade and a freshman in high school. Like so many other children of that era who had contracted the disease, I was left with a slightly enlarged heart with leaky valves, a condition that never was detected by doctors who examined me when I joined the navy.

Had the Mayo records that Ginny brought to the hospital been consulted, maybe this latest crisis could have been averted. Among them was a recommendation from Dr. Titus Evans, the cardiologist I had seen at Mayo, that I be given antibiotics before any invasive procedure—even before having my teeth cleaned.

I remember being puzzled because Dr. McGillen began examining my fingers, as if trying to divine the source of my fever through them. Actually, he was trying to determine if I did indeed have endocarditis, which sometimes reveals its presence by dark lines under the fingernails. He immediately ordered intravenous doses of penicillin to defend my heart valves from the bacteria attack and told us that, to be on the safe side, I would need to stay on IV antibiotics for six or seven weeks.

"You mean I have to stay in the hospital that long?" I moaned.

"It can be done at home, if Ginny is willing to be the nurse."

"What if we do nothing?" I asked. "Will it clear up by itself?"

"If we do nothing, and if you do have it, you will die."

As the antibiotics began their counterattack, my fever dropped. To restore my leg muscles, weakened from too much time in bed, Ginny forced me to get up and walk. I must have looked like a wobbly garbage picker tangled up with a discarded Christmas tree as I wheeled the IV pole with its dangling plastic pouches of penicillin up and down the hospital corridor. But slowly Ginny began to rekindle in me, if not a glow, at least a spark of life.

For one thing, the ever-practical Ginny realized that we were in for a long war, not a short battle. There is a big difference between being acutely ill and chronically ill, both in how it affects the one who is sick and how it impacts on family, friends, and, in many cases, fellow workers at your job.

Among the first letters we received from friends while I was still in critical shape in the hospital came from *Newsweek*'s correspondent in South Africa, Rick Manning, and his wife Diane. Rick had worked with me in the Chicago bureau and on a special six-month assignment for *Newsweek*'s Golden Anniversary, so we were friends as well as colleagues.

In this joint letter from the Mannings, Diane gave Ginny some practical advice that was to be of great service during my illness. She told her to immediately "beg, borrow, or steal" an answering machine for our telephone (something I had stubbornly resisted, mainly because I got so annoyed at the inanely cute messages some people seemed compelled to put on them). Indeed, upon coming home exhausted from the hospital, Ginny was swamped every night by calls from our relatives and friends wanting to know how I was doing or simply showing their concern for us. She found herself repeating over and over the same basic condition report on me at a time when she should be catching up on lost sleep. Since both Ginny and I come from large families and have lived most of our lives in the Chicago area, we have a larger circle of relatives and friends interested in our welfare than do couples who come from smaller clans and who have moved more frequently in this highly mobile society.

Another bit of advice from Diane Manning was that Ginny establish telephone chains to disseminate news on my condition and forestall most of those incoming phone calls. Ginny did this immediately, making her sister, Martha Maddock, the switchboard operator for her side of the family, and my brother Joe's wife, Colleen, the health-caster for my relatives. Our oldest daughter, Katie, was assigned to keep our closest friends informed on my condition. This left Ginny with only three phone calls at the end of each long, exhausting day. She still was free to call anyone she particularly needed to talk with, but on her terms and at her convenience. This telephone chain was kept intact throughout the months of my dying and surprising resurrection, saving Ginny hours of wear and tear on both body and soul.

Two weeks after the paramedics had delivered me, in shock and near death, to the emergency room, my weight had dropped from 165 to 140 pounds. My complacency about my condition also had dropped. No longer could I bluff myself; Death, the grim spector whose deeds I had spent so much of my career documenting, had turned its attention my way. The game was nearly over, time was running out, and there was nothing I could do to stop the clock.

Positive thinking, cockeyed optimism, walking on the sunny side of the street—all the clichés in my armory of psychic defenses—none of them could, in the end, fend off the hepatitis virus that was destroying my liver or the bacteria that was lodged in my heart. Positive thinking and good humor certainly play a role in fighting illness and maintaining health, but neither the Marx Brothers nor the Mayo Brothers can restore a wasted heart muscle or rejuvenate a liver ravaged by hepatitis. Laughter can be a healing balm. It can charge up the old immune system like a cheering crowd at a football game. But sometimes laughter and happy talk can only help heal your soul, not your body.

It was during the long nights of my first hospital admission that I made up my mind to die with as much dignity as I could wrap around me. My greatest concern was not death itself but the fear that I might, at the end, whimper or whine on my way out the door. I was determined to provide a good example for my family and friends. For one thing, I wanted to show my faith in God's ultimate kindness, a faith that I always had easily professed—perhaps all too easily. Only later would I realize that my early stoicism in the face of death was rooted more in pride than in a deep religious conviction. Part macho man and part little boy, I was determined to die with cool dignity, like Gary Cooper did in the movies.

Ginny and I could not possibly know then that the endocarditis attack that so threatened my life during that first hospitalization would prove to be a fortuitous event in our medical adventure. In truth, had I not fallen victim to that hospital-bred bacterial infection, I would not have come under the care of the mild-mannered John McGillen and his partners. And, as it turned out, I never would have even considered undergoing the liver transplant that dramatically postponed my death.

But all of that awaited us over the horizon that spring of 1986. At that time, Ginny's and my problem was not avoiding my death, but learning how to cope with it. We needed to find a new definition for the word *hope.* The old definition—the conviction that the road would be smoother and the day brighter up ahead—no longer fit our situation. Knowing that the road would get steeper and the clouds darker, we needed to create for ourselves, or find along our way, fresh reasons for greeting each day. Hope is like water. None of us can survive long without it.

It was during that seventeen-day stay in the hospital that "other women" entered my life for the first time. It marked the start of the dissolution of "Front Page Frank," who never in his life had developed any real friendship with a woman. Ginny was my friend, but that didn't count. She was my wife. Except for a few women reporters I had worked with and respected for their professional abilities, I never had talked seriously to any woman about much of anything of substance.

I grew up in a world where the boys kept the girls out of our tree house. This attitude was reenforced as a student at then all-male Notre Dame, later as a navy officer, and as a reporter in Chicago's tough-guy, "Front Page" tradition. I was born and raised in a church that over the centuries had become so male dominated that it regarded women as lowly handmaidens who could fix the flowers and iron the linens for the altar but better not covet any higher liturgical ambitions.

In my early years with *Newsweek,* it also was a male bastion with only a few token women reporters in the entire bureau system, and only one female writer and no editors in the New York home office. When I joined *Newsweek* in 1970, most women working for the magazine were in either secretarial positions or the all-female research department. When the magazine did a cover story on the women's movement in 1970, it had to hire a woman free-lancer to write it.

I remember giving a speech to journalism students at Northwestern University soon after becoming bureau chief. Our publicity department in New York sent a film that depicted a typical day in

Newsweek's editorial offices. As I watched the film for the first time with the students, I realized that not a single woman editor, writer, or reporter was in it. The only time a woman appeared in the thirty-minute film was when a secretary shuffled into the editor's office like Edith Bunker with papers for him to sign.

When the film ended and the lights went on, I knew I was a speaker already in deep trouble. I began my talk this way: "How many of you saw anything disturbing in that film?" All the women's hands shot up. All the men looked puzzled. I still think it strange that I—a man who graduated from college in the "dark ages" of the 1950s—was more sensitive to what that film subtly revealed than were the young men of the 1970s, who supposedly were maturing in a more enlightened era. The first memo I sent to New York as Chicago bureau chief was a recommendation that they scrap that film.

I do not want to leave the impression that I was an early recruit in the fight for women's rights. My concern was more selfish than that. I had no desire to be the follow-up speaker to a film that was sure to alienate half my audience. Considering my background, it is a wonder that I was not more of a male chauvinist than I was. I can thank Ginny for that; she wouldn't have put up with me.

During that first hospital stay, I moved into a more female world than I ever had experienced. I entered the world of the "caregiver," and that world is populated mostly by women. When I speak of "caregiver" I do not mean, for the most part, the physician—though many of them can be called that. The physician is the one who treats the disease. The caregiver is the one who treats the patient. It can be a nurse, social worker, friend, or family member—anyone who assumes the thankless job of caring for the bodily and spiritual needs of the chronically ill. I found out that most of the people comforting the afflicted and visiting the lonely in hospitals, nursing homes, and, often, in private homes are women. For someone like me, who had spent his adult life playing a self-centered game in which points are awarded for aggressiveness and ambition, not for compassion, this was indeed a strange, new world.

I was to learn later that many of these women care-givers were truly "sandwiched" between conflicting obligations, having to care for elderly parents or ailing spouses, while still carrying the burden of raising their own children.

The first time this hit me between the eyes was while I was still in the intensive care unit at Northwest Community Hospital. There was an elderly man in a nearby "stall" who, I learned from overhearing the nurses talk, had been "dumped" there by a nursing home. It seemed no one wanted the old man, who was not critically ill enough to remain in the hospital, but who was incontinent and unable to feed himself. One whole day, I watched the nurses trying to feed the man, only to have him vomit up whatever they managed to get him to swallow. He also keep soiling the sheets. Every time he made a mess, one or more nurses would come and gently rebuke him. Then they would clean him up and change all his bed linen, knowing that in a short while they would have to do it again.

I lay watching, amazed. Considering my recent escape from death, I was admittedly in an emotional state. But I felt tears warming my eyes as I saw how gently and with what dignity those nurses treated that old gentleman. After their shift, they would go home like anyone else after work, maybe to screaming kids or a surly spouse or a collection of unpaid bills or maybe to their own loneliness. They were unaware of the pure goodness that radiated from themselves as they just did the job they were so inadequately paid to do.

By no means do I want to give the impression that women have an exclusive franchise on compassion. A few of my best nurses were men—and, as it turned out, some of my best doctors were women. (The percentage of women graduating from medical school has climbed to 40 percent—a blessing down the road for the chronically ill.)

However, some of the most caring people Ginny and I encountered during our journey were men. But these men were confident enough of their masculinity that they found room in their hearts to nurture the virtues we traditionally consider feminine: empathy, sensitivity, compassion, and, not least among them, the ability to listen—really listen to what someone is saying.

The caregivers are those chosen few among us who, like King

Solomon, are wise enough to ask God for only one gift: "an understanding heart."

Some time after my ordeal was over, when I was recuperating from my liver transplant, an energetic young woman reporter who had trained under me in the Chicago bureau, said to me in tones of admiration: "All you went through must have made you much tougher." I didn't want to trample on her aggressiveness, but I had to reply: "Just the opposite. It made me much softer."

A common trait of the best caregivers Ginny and I encountered was their cheerfulness. We never met a doleful caregiver. Certainly the two tiny women who came into my life after my first hemorrhage are the least lugubrious of mortals. Margaret Kennedy Moser, a pretty young mother of two teenagers who came to this country as a sixteen-year-old Irish lass, first whispered something into my ear while I was drifting in a fog in ICU. She was the one who called me "Angel," the one with the brogue that sounded as cheery and warm as a cup of tea. Then there was the lay Catholic chaplain at the hospital, Terry Schott, one of those women who smile more with their eyes than their mouths, a small package of energy who, after her four sons were raised, studied to become a lay hospital chaplain.

As I recuperated in hospital and later at home, Margaret Moser added me to her daily route, which included a long roster of ailing and elderly St. James parishioners in hospitals, nursing homes, or their own homes. She not only stopped at each home for a chat and some praying, but often pitched in to help tidy up, run errands, drive them to the doctor, or even bathe some of the old people when no one else was there to help.

Being a lay minister, Margaret was authorized to bring communion to the confined. She brought me communion in ICU shortly after the helmet and stomach tube were removed and I could take only ice and gelatin. From a small round pyx hung around her neck, she took a white wafer, broke off a tiny sliver, offered it to me, and said, "This is the Body of Christ, Angel." (Margaret would end up "hearing" my last confession, but that's a story I will tell you later.)

Terry Schott also stopped at least once each day when I was hospitalized, often just to tell me what was happening in the outside world, but mostly to bolster my spirits. At first, I felt rather awkward with my women visitors. They made me more aware of my helpless condition, the feeling that I was no longer in control of my life. One thing that never changed for me during all my days in hospital beds: I never completely lost my embarrassment about receiving guests while lying in a disordered bed, hair uncombed, face unshaven, arms bruised purple from IV punctures, and dressed in a flimsy gown that tied at the neck and was open up the back.

But I began to look forward to my daily visits with Margaret and Terry, relaxing in their company and not feeling like a schoolboy at his first dance when they held my hand as we talked. Neither of them ever was solemn. Even the prayers they suggested we say together had a bubbly and cheerful tone.

The day before my release from the hospital, I asked Terry Schott about executing a living will, a document that would declare my wishes that I not be kept artificially "alive" by machines once I was in an irreversibly terminal state. It was something I had considered doing ever since Mayo's experts gave me a death sentence. The last thing I wanted was to lose all dignity and control in the final chapter of my life or leave my family with the expense and pain of a prolonged departure. Control—that was a big word for me. I feared losing it more than I did my life.

We went to Terry Schott's office near the chapel on the third floor, where she gave me a form for a living will that had been drafted by the American Protestant Health Association. It was labeled, "A Personal Statement of Faith," and I remember how it began: "I believe that every person is created by God as an individual of value and dignity." It instructed my family and doctors that, to the extent possible, I wanted to participate in decisions regarding my care, and specifically directed physicians and attendants not to use artificial or mechanical means to prolong my life when there no longer was reasonable expectation that I could recover. It expressly ruled out any "direct intervention" to shorten my life. I do not believe in active euthanasia and wanted that clearly spelled out in any last instructions.

I didn't sign the living will until after I went home—when Ginny decided to sign one for herself. Our neighbors from around the corner, Roger and Barbara Dress, came over one evening to witness our living wills. One lesson we pass along from our journey: in this era when medicine has the awesome ability to keep a person "alive" indefinitely, every adult should execute a living will—if you love your family and value your dignity. Just as you need a legal will directing the disposition of your wordly goods, so do you need a living will directing the final treatment of your body.

As I talked with Terry Schott about the living will and about my grim medical prognosis, to my amazement, I burst into tears. I began pouring out all my anxiety and sadness over what I knew awaited Ginny and me. More than anything, I felt devastated at the prospect of abandoning Ginny just when our four children were raised and the mortgage was almost paid off—just when we could start fulfilling many of our dreams.

Much as I tried, I could not suppress the tears that welled in my eyes and then rolled down my cheeks. It was the first time I had cried in front of another person, let alone a woman, since I was a little boy. As I sat, shaking and trying to control my tears, Terry told me not to be afraid to express frustration, anger, and fear—and certainly not to be ashamed to cry. Had I been wearing my reporter's hat, I might have used the word "blubbering" to describe my condition.

Growing up I had been taught to hide my feelings; as a reporter I had built an added outer wall of detachment to guard against becoming too involved in other people's pain and loneliness. As I kept babbling and apologizing for my tears, Terry talked very little, but gave me her total attention.

When she did speak, it was about simple things, like hope and patience and love, and how suffering can make us less self-absorbed and more sensitive to other peoples' hurts. But she also encouraged me to keep on crying—strange advice to give a man who had been indoctrinated since childhood to do just the opposite.

"Don't be afraid to show your feelings, give yourself permission to show that you're human, just like the rest of us," she said. "Remember, Frank, God gave us tears to wash our pain away."

For me that half hour in Terry Schott's office was like the start of spring, a time when the ice first began to thaw in my heart. I couldn't wait to talk to Ginny and share with her what I was feeling and what I had faintly begun to hear—a trickle of hope beneath what had been a cold, forbiding winterscape.

Back in the dark time, when I had the painful helmet on my head and the tube down my throat, I had whispered to God the words I had learned as a child, "Thy Will Be Done." But it was an empty prayer coming from someone like me, who was so determined to keep control over all aspects of my life—most especially my dying.

After listening to Terry, I began to understand the consequences of saying that simple prayer, acknowledging that God's ways are not our ways; accepting pain and suffering, not for themselves, but for what we can do and what we can become because of them; learning to reach out to help one another, tolerate one another, love one another.

There would be other mountains for Ginny and me to climb up ahead, and many more lonely hours when tears would flow. In a way nothing had changed; I still was going to die. But in another sense, everything had changed.

Buried somewhere in the calming words of Terry Schott was a revelation—I just knew—a message that would somehow carry us through, no matter what happened.

Before I was dismissed from the hospital, a nurse implanted a heparin lock in a vein in the back of my right hand and instructed Ginny how to attach the intravenous antibiotic drip line to it. Every four hours for the next month and a half, round-the-clock, she was directed to feed me a dose of a drug called oxacillin, a form of penicillin which Dr. McGillen said was "strong enough to knock out half the power in St. Louis."

Once a week a delivery man from a drug company brought plastic pouches of the drug which we stored in the freezer. When Ginny forgot to get a pouch out in time for it to thaw, she would warm it by holding it under an arm pit while she ran the vacuum cleaner. She never was one to waste motion. Once a week, a visiting nurse came to shift the heparin lock to another vein in my hands or arms.

Nothing went smoothly. Within two weeks I developed a violent reaction to penicillin, forcing Dr. McGillen to shift me to a drug called vancomycin. Then my overabused veins started to collapse. It became ever more difficult and more painful for the visiting nurse to find a suitable vein for the heparin lock. Ginny had to pack my arms with hot towels for half an hour before the nurse's arrival to make the veins expand.

Ginny and I will never forget the afternoon of April 30, 1986.

It was to be the darkest day of our journey. That was the day I gave up.

The liquid antibiotic, which was supposed to run into my arm in forty-five minutes, would not flow. The vein had simply closed down after too many hours of intravenous feeding. After ninety minutes of raising and lowering the IV pole and adjusting the angle of my arm, we could not get the antibiotic to flow. In desperation, I lay down on the bed and tried turning my body to see if that might somehow cause the fluid to move. Nothing would work.

Then I heard my voice like it belonged to someone else: "I wish I would just die."

Ginny got down on her knees, put her arms around my neck, and we cried uncontrollably. Just then someone opened the front door downstairs and a hearty woman's voice hollered, "Anybody home?" It was Margaret Moser on her daily rounds. She came up to our bedroom, got down on her knees, somehow wrapped her arms around both of us, and then began cooing, "There, there, Angels. It's all right to cry." By now you would think I knew this.

I don't know how long we were locked in this triple embrace. After a bit I realized how crazy we must look, my head dangling over the foot of the bed, one arm pointing skyward toward a plastic pouch of clear fluid swaying atop a metal pole—with two women hanging around my neck. My tears turned to shaking laughter. Margaret and Ginny started laughing too.

The antibiotics still wouldn't drip, but Ginny was laughing on the phone when she reached the visiting nurse to ask her to come shift my heparin lock.

9

SPILOTRO'S
LAST
HIT

There is an old axiom among Chicago news reporters that goes like this: "If your mother says she loves you, check it out." A number of editors have been credited with first proclaiming this prime rule of hard-nosed journalism. No matter who deserves credit, it has become basic dogma for those of us who are paid busybodies. And that's what a reporter is: a professional busybody.

At the risk of sounding like a fuddy-duddy, I offer the opinion that reporters who learned their trade in the "good old days" had a healthier skepticism about their sources of information than do their counterparts today, many of whom think reporting is showing up for a press conference and grabbing the first handout sheet. Not only were we indoctrinated by demanding editors and our elders in the newsroom to double-check everything before putting it into a story, we also were taught to question the motives of anyone supplying us with information—even our own mothers. We were expected to keep our biases and bile out of our work.

Of course, only wishy-washy nebbishes have no personal opinions. That was not expected of us. No one whose body is above room temperature should pretend to be perfectly objective or free of prejudice. I would hold suspect any journalist or writer who claimed to have achieved that holy state. The goal held up for us was fairness, no matter what our personal views or limitations. It was a matter of pride to get it first, but it was more important to get it right—or as close to right as you could under the pressures of a deadline. Not to make a serious effort to get "the other side" of a controversial story, even if it meant added work, was a hanging offense in the better newsrooms of the country.

"If you want to be an advocate, become a missionary or a PR guy for the circus," was the advice of my first city editor, the fastidious Oliver Cremer of the *Rockford Morning Star.*

I learned the basics of my trade from Ollie Cremer, a hulking editor of the strict observance, who taught us never to presume anything and to always make that one extra phone call—even if it meant more work or, as often happened, the collapse of the entire supporting framework of your story.

The first time I short-cutted Ollie Cremer's standing orders on double-checking, I got burned. It nearly brought my reporting career to a screeching halt even before I finished my apprenticeship. That was when I was on the police beat. The time I killed a man.

This is how it happened. One afternoon an elderly man was stricken in his home on North Church Street in Rockford—let's call him Oscar Gustafson. The police ambulance took him to one of the three hospitals in town, St. Anthony. Answering police calls in the newspaper's radio car, I recorded the man's name, age, and address in my notebook for future reference and went about my duties, chasing after stories with larger potential for violence and mayhem.

Late that night, shortly before the presses were scheduled to roll for the morning edition, I telephoned from police headquarters to the emergency rooms of each hospital to inquire, as I so indelicately put it, if there were any "late deaths" to report. When I checked with the little nun who always had night duty at St. Anthony, she replied: "No, dearie. But we have one hanging by the golden thread." Looking at my watch, I saw that I had fifteen minutes to deadline, so I told her I would make a final check later.

When I called back just before midnight, she told me: "We just lost Mr. Gustafson." She began to read his basic ID from the admittance sheet, but I cut her off. "I've got him in my notebook. Good night, sister." I redialed the phone, asked for the rewrite desk, and dictated the following obit: "Oscar Gustafson, 72, of North

Church Street, died late Wednesday in St. Anthony Hospital, where he had been taken earlier in the day by police ambulance. Funeral arrangements are incomplete."

I went home to a good night's sleep and awoke the next morning feeling terrific. So did Oscar Gustafson. I had killed the wrong guy. It never occured to Frank Maier, cub reporter, that there might possibly be another man named Gustafson hospitalized in a town that had almost as many Swedes as Stockholm.

When I came to work that day Ollie Cremer summoned me to his desk, which unlike other work spaces in the newsroom was neat as the starched cuffs that flashed from his coat sleeves. (Lou Grant might have done his televersioned chores in shirtsleeves, but Oliver Cremer, who didn't have to pretend to be a city editor, always wore his suit coat.) In describing Mr. Gustafson's unexpected resurrection, Ollie kept his voice matter-of-fact and low-volumed. I would have felt less threatened if he barked and screamed, but that wasn't his style. He just quietly lacquered me, head to toe, with sarcasm. After suggesting that I might have a future selling vacuum cleaners door-to-door, he squinted up at me with his head cocked almost onto his shoulder and said, "Got it?"

I got it—and I still "got it" as I attempt to tell the story of what happened to Ginny and me and how we changed during our medical adventure. The lessons I learned from Ollie Cremer remain planted deep in my hide, flashing yellow lights that caution me not to presume anything, to be ever aware that more is left out of a tale than is put in to it.

All of us are selective in our remembrances. We are selective also in what we choose to tell and what we choose not to tell. From experience, I can assure you that the patient's viewpoint often differs substantially from that of the medical professionals. And a spouse's or family member's perspective during a prolonged illness might differ from that of either the patient or the doctors.

Storytelling requires creating order out of chaos, shaping a mosaic from bits and pieces that, standing alone, make no sense, form no pattern. Seldom do we understand the meaning of what is happening to us, or the changes occuring in us, until after the final curtain has fallen and we can reflect on the entire play and all of its players.

In the spring of 1986, Ginny and I felt a veil of isolation falling around us because of my terminal illness. To be chronically ill is to be chronically alone. Most Americans are impatient and intolerant with the seriously ill or the dying. Everything in our culture glorifies the trim, the fit, and the beautiful. Age and illness are a national embarrassment. Maybe the sick and the dying remind people of what they do not want to contemplate, how fragile life really is.

Whatever the reasons, Ginny and I at first were bewildered by our growing isolation. For my part, suddenly withdrawn from a life packed with action, travel, lively people, and excitement, I became a semi-invalid, not even trusted to drive a car or take a walk by myself through the neighborhood. Ginny, whose days always bubbled with human contact and vigorous action, was equally confined, her world reduced to being my chauffeur, nurse, and cheerleader.

Shortly after my first serious hemorrhage, most of our friends and family members rallied around us. But some of our acquaintances and many of my contacts in the news business began drifting out of our lives. Undoubtedly it was because I was no longer useful to them professionally and Ginny no longer entertaining.

But I am convinced that many simply felt uncomfortable around the chronically ill or dying, like those people who find excuses to avoid wakes and funerals because they worry about "what to say." Knowing they could not solve our problems, they found it easier, less stressful, to avoid us altogether. Were it not for those friends and family members who stuck by us and newcomers who entered our lives only because of my illness, we would have been devastated by people's indifference.

We became weary of people who told us, "I know exactly how you feel." If there is one phrase that should be excised from the active vocabulary of all would-be comforters of the afflicted it is that one. Ginny finally responded to one woman who clucked-clucked the I-know-how-you-feel platitude: "No. You don't know how I feel, or how Frank feels, any more than I know how it feels to lose a child or to be all alone in a nursing home."

Rather than the dispensers of platitudes and advice, the seriously ill cherish those who simply hold their hand or sit with them in comforting silence. Never tell someone in pain that you know exactly how that person feels.

We also grew weary of people telling us that we were "in their prayers," an expression that sadly can become the ecclesiastical equivalent of "Have a nice day."

I do not want to belittle what theologians classify as "prayers of petition." They certainly have a place in our lives. If you think of God as a father or a mother, you know that you can ask for help. But one of the lasting lessons I slowly absorbed during my months of dying was a new concept of what prayer was. This did not come in a sudden flash of illumination, but emerged over time. For me, prayer came to mean listening for God's whisper, not presenting Him with a nagging list of petitions. I came to think of prayer more as God trying to reach us than as us trying to reach Him.

Quite independently of me, Ginny came to the same conclusion. One time I overheard her telling a neighbor: "I'm at the point where if I hear one more person say, 'I'm praying for you,' I think I'll scream. God isn't sitting in heaven with a tablet, counting 'Our Fathers' or 'Hail Marys' to decide whether to solve our problems."

Later, when I asked Ginny what she meant, she shrugged. "I'm no theologian, but I think our only prayer ought to be 'Thy will be done.'" With a laugh, she added, "And it better be the same as our will, right?"

I was equally confident that God knew our needs without someone constantly having to remind Him of them. The people we valued most were not those who offered easily given, easily forgotten prayers, but those who showed up to cut the lawn, do the ironing, or put up the screens, or who came, like Margaret Moser, just to visit—with or without tuna casseroles.

More than anything, Ginny needed someone who would volunteer to watch over me while she took some time to go to the beauty shop, walk through a shopping mall, or just sit in the park. Everybody remembers the sick person, but few remember the caregiver, who often is the person shouldering the most stress and fatigue.

Those who gave us the most practical help in everyday life were the people who most made us feel God's presence, reminding us that His providence does extend even to the birds of the air and the lilies of the field.

85

People who never have been sick usually fail to realize how kind it is to simply be quiet around the very ill—just to sit quietly and to listen. Active people have not learned to appreciate silence the way the sick have. I was astonished during my hospital days when visitors would descend upon some of my poor roommates like hordes of squawking geese, determined to stamp out silence as if it were an embarrassment.

When people first offered to help us, I had a difficult time accepting it. It added to my fears of losing control over my life. In fact, my pride became a point of conflict and, sometimes, harsh words between Ginny and me. It takes humility to admit that you need help, that you can't control everything in your life, and I fought against doing that. Whenever I overheard Ginny on the phone accepting someone's offer of help, I would yell, "Tell them, thanks. But we can do it ourselves."

Until I was sick, I never realized how stubborn and stiff-necked I could be. Ginny finally convinced me that, with a few exceptions, the people who offered to help were sincere and deserved to be given the chance to be generous.

"Look at it this way. You are doing them a kindness by letting them help us," she said. "Besides, we really do need help."

Besides, I had no choice. Pride was a luxury I no longer could afford. Many friends and strangers offered and delivered help when we really needed it. One couple even deposited $1,000 in our checking account without telling us, just because they thought we might need it for something. But there were other people who casually offered to do things for us, and then never did them. And that was disappointing because we never wanted to remind them of their promises to help.

Even though my medical prognosis was grimmer than ever, the rupturing of the varices in my esophagus at least changed me from a passive to an active patient. In an odd way, that made me more optimistic—at least some treatment was required now that a medical emergency had occured. In addition to the home IV doses of antibiotics to fight the infection threatening my heart, I underwent regular treatments at the hospital for the bulging veins in my gullet.

At one time or another, four specialists in gastroenterology performed the procedures called endoscopic sclerotherapy: Doctors

Jerrold Schwartz, Igor Jurcik, David Sales, and Loren White. The first endoscopies were in the emergency room or ICU during my emergency bleeding. But, after my discharge, we went to the outpatient wing of the hospital for treatments.

First I would be given antibiotics to protect my heart valves from any more bacterial invaders during the procedure. Then a nurse would spray my throat with a bitter local anesthetic to dry the mouth and minimize gagging. The doctor would have me count backwards from a hundred as a mixture of Valium and Demerol was injected into my IV line. By ninety-four I usually was gone.

After I was asleep, the doctor slipped a flexible scope deep into my gullet to look for any bleeding or bulging veins. If he spotted any varices, he would "zap" them with sodium tetradecyl sulfate to clot them and help prevent further ruptures.

Ginny and I lost count, but we estimate I had a dozen endoscopic treatments during my illness. To be truthful, as my disease began to take a harsher toll on my liver and the itching, fatigue, nausea, and swelling of my belly increased, I began looking forward to the endoscopic treatments. They were the only time when I could drift into a peaceful, dreamless sleep, if only for an hour or so.

At first there was some stoic streak in me—perhaps inherited from my father—that made me ashamed of wanting to be knocked into oblivion. I felt like a drug addict wanting to escape from a little discomfort. I didn't even confess this sense of guilt to Ginny—and by then I was withholding very little from her.

Eventually I learned to accept this desire for temporary relief as not shameful; I began to treat myself with more kindness and tolerance. Looking back on those troubled days, I realize now that, in being gentler to myself, I also began to think and act more tolerantly and kindly toward others. There is a deep truth in the maxim that you cannot love others unless you first love yourself.

Wasn't it amazing what I was learning from being sick?

As my liver, my detoxing station, continued to deteriorate in the next months, it had to struggle harder after each endoscopic treatment to clear the anesthetic from my system. Eventually, it started taking two hours or more to rouse me after a treatment, even with Ginny and the nurses shaking me and trying to talk me back to consciousness—a recovery room fandango called a "stir-up."

It must have been comic, them poking and joking me toward consciousness, and me trying to get a few more minutes of snooze time, like a teenager escaping his chores on a Saturday morning. But they dared not allow me to continue sleeping for fear my poor overworked liver would just give up the fight and I would drift off forever.

On June 1, my birthday, Ginny drove me to the *Newsweek* bureau for an hour's visit, my first real outing since my hemorrhage. Even though I had little stamina, I wanted desperately to get back to work—even on a part-time basis. Ginny and Dr. John McGillen agreed that I could go to work whenever I felt strong enough— provided I was accompanied on the commute by her or one of our children. As it turned out, my second son, Daniel, who then worked as a press aide in Washington for U.S. Senator Alan Dixon, was assigned that summer to work in the senator's Chicago office. No one told me, but I suspect that this special arrangement was made all because of my illness. In any event, on those days that I felt I could do some work, I commuted on the train with Danny—or occasionally Ginny would ride into the city with me. I always had a baby-sitter.

Most days I could only stay a few hours, and I never did much more than a few routine phone interviews or the editing of a younger correspondent's copy. But I felt productive again.

Then in late June a prominent Chicago mobster and his brother were found bludgeoned to death in a shallow grave in northern Indiana. I immediately saw my chance to prove to myself and to my editors in New York that I could still hit the fastball. Over the years I had done my share of mob stories, so it seemed only proper that I assign myself to do this one. The sudden passing of Tony "The Ant" Spilotro, the Chicago Outfit's man in Las Vegas, and his brother, whose only crime apparently was hanging around with bad company, provided me with an uncomplicated, easily reported story for my reentry to the working world.

Unlike television reporters who needed pictures, print reporters did not have to rush out to the Indiana cornfield where the bodies of the severely beaten Spilotro brothers had been dug up. My task was to round up the usual sources and extract anything they could or would tell me about why Tony Spilotro had been "whacked," as the mobsters so colorfully and euphemistically describe such untimely deaths.

I spent a stimulating morning on the telephone to FBI agents, prosecutors, Chicago and suburban police, and assorted professional mob watchers—of which Chicago has more than Los Angeles and New York have gossip columnists. I spent the noon hour reading old clippings on Spilotro's criminal career and then two hours writing what I hoped would be a compact, colorful Chicago mob story that could be enjoyed by *Newsweek*'s readers around the country.

I finished the piece in late afternoon, became weak, wobbly, and nauseous on the train ride home, and, before sunset, was staring up at the ceiling of Northwest Community Hospital's emergency room as doctors again frantically worked to stop new bleeding from my esophagus.

One part of me felt elated that I had done some useful work again. Another part told me how stupid and pigheaded I was in trying to go back to work too soon.

While vomiting dark purple blood into a metal basin held by a nurse, I was struck by an ironic and frightening thought: "I'm going to be Spilotro's last hit."

10

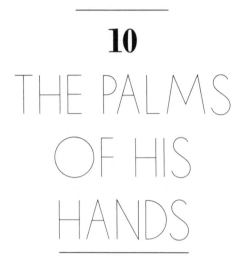

THE PALMS OF HIS HANDS

I ended up spending 125 days and nights in hospital beds because of four major hemorrhages, my liver transplant, two minor surgeries, and a painful case of shingles. As a result, I became an authority on hospitals in the gritty, haphazard way a street person gets to know a neighborhood. As a reporter, I enjoyed every minute that I can recall—even those times when I was tormented by pain or discomfort. As a patient, I also saw that hospitals—particularly at night—can be lonely and terrifying places.

For someone like me, who likes to think of himself as a detached professional observer, hospitals are like circuses with something happening in three different rings at once, a lot of it without the knowledge of the people in charge. I soon learned all the "codes" used over the public address system to declare emergencies without causing panic among inmates or visitors: Code Gray for tornado, Code Red for fire, Code Yellow for any disaster that might bring many casualties to the hospital, Code Blue to summon the resuscitation team.

It took me several admittances to Northwest Community Hospital before I figured out that when "Mr. Strong" was paged three times, it was a call for designated male heavyweights to come subdue an obstreperous patient or visitor—sort of a call for the bouncers. I never could decode the call that went out many times a day for veteran movie star "Cesar Romero," until a nurse told me it wasn't a code name, but the actual name of a respected surgeon on the staff.

During my hospital days, I learned from one patient how to hot-wire a car. He was an enormous man built like a football defensive lineman, who was a "skip-tracer" in the risky business of reclaiming cars from deadbeats. He didn't put his neck on the line to reclaim Pintos or Novas, but specialized in expensive models like BMWs and Mercedes. He told me wonderful tales of being shot at by lawmen who didn't know he was a "repo" man and being chased by angry owners with tire irons.

Another patient, a grossly overweight truck driver who was agonizing through a liquid diet, showed me how to sneak down to the coffee shop to buy milkshakes. "Just act like you're a damn intern," he growled. When I protested that the hospital didn't have interns and, if it did, they wouldn't be walking around in bathrobe and slippers, he shrugged, "See. They'll never know."

One roommate, an old man with a urinary tract infection, was a retired bus driver who once drove streetcars. He told me how conductors on the streetcars used to "knock down nickels," sort of an unauthorized profit-sharing plan.

Another roommate, a kindly old man who was a part-time preacher, suffered from severe diabetes and was in the hospital to get regulated. He telephoned his wife every night, not to talk to her, but to his pet cat. He would coo and purr to that cat for up to an hour each night. To my dismay, he snored like a 747 revving its engines at O'Hare Airport, so I spent most nights reading old *New Yorkers* and *Reader's Digests* in the solarium at the end of the corridor along with other insomniacs.

I had many characters for roomies, some kindly and some outrageous. Only one was mean-spirited: a vile-tempered, middle-aged man with sunken cheeks and soul to match. He always was ringing for the nurses. If they did not respond quickly enough, he would bang his bed pan against the wall. During the day he fumed, moaned, and cursed. In the middle of the night, he enjoyed switching on the television at high volume just to annoy me. We would engage in a spirited duel. I would use my hand set to turn the TV off; he would switch it back on. He got even one night by turning the set on full blast after I was sound asleep. Heart pounding and mind scrambled, I sat bolt upright, staring at a rerun of the "The Gong Show" on the far wall. When I came to my senses, all I could do was laugh at him, while he pretended to be asleep. In a way, he took my mind off my troubles. And I suppose in his own perverse fashion, he was having a good time. I never did find out what was wrong with him.

Another time, I had a roommate with an enormous family, all of whom felt obligated to visit him daily. The poor man was never left alone. Not only did his wife come, but also their children, their spouses, and his grandchildren. They always brought exotic-smelling fast food carryouts, not for the patient—he slept through all of their visits—but for themselves. With him asleep, or pretending to be, all they did was eat and watch one soap opera and game show after another. I always pulled my bed curtain, but that could not muffle the television or block the aroma of the fast foods. My discreet protests to the nurses brought expressions of sympathy, but no relief. They had more pressing things to do than act as room monitors.

On the day he was discharged, one of his teenage daughters was so hypnotized by a soap opera that she lay on his bed, watching until it ended twenty minutes after he had left in his wheelchair. Neither the man nor any of his army of visitors ever spoke a word to me and, except for logistical messages like, "Gimme some ketchup," never said a word to each other.

During those hospital confinements throughout 1986, I also caught a glimpse of what awaits the medical profession over the horizon as the nation's population ages. Many days I was the youngest patient on the floor at Northwest Community Hospital, a general medical center that serves the growing northwest suburbs of Chicago. I was fifty-three at the time but always seemed to be the "kid."

One roommate, John Anderson, a retired man in his early sixties, and I took it upon ourselves to be the jolly boys of the floor. Like two adolescents, we felt it our duty to cheer up the nurses and the cleaning women because the place was jammed with terribly old and feeble men and women.

We used to badger our regular cleaning woman, Kathy Zaletanski, to smuggle us a contraband pizza for a party we told her we were planning after visiting hours. "You boys can't have pizza," she would say. "Then bring a six pack," John would answer. We would tease her unmercifully as she cleaned our room, accusing her of being a chicken for never sneaking us the pizza and beer. She always took a long time sprucing up our room, leaving with a promise to bring the pizza that night—provided she could bring a few of her girlfriends to the party. "The more the merrier," John would tell her.

As the clown princes of the floor, John and I also kept a stash of candy for the nurses—even though we couldn't enjoy it ourselves. One nurse, who was a stickler for order, always got upset when she came on duty to find anything in our room out of place. One morning, as she was grousing about a missing thermometer, John produced a box of Gummy Bears and offered her one. After giving him one of those tuck-the-chin-in, over-the-eyeglasses, schoolmarm glares, she took one of the chewy things and left. "You watch," said John. "By the next time, I will win her over." And he did. We became suppliers of her daily Gummy Bear fix, and she became as pleasant as Florence Nightingale.

After my third bleed in August of that year, I watched from my bed in ICU as the nurses struggled to control an old gentleman named Roy, who kept pulling out his IV lines. Roy had fallen and cut his head and bruised his ribs the day after his wife, Helen, had suffered a heart attack. While Roy was in ICU, Helen was several floors above in CCU, the cardiac care unit. He kept calling for her and trying to get out of bed.

A few days later, I encountered Roy again after we both had been moved to a regular floor. I'll never forget the scene, which was both comic and sad. Hearing a commotion in the hallway, I wobbled to the door and saw to my amazement three nurses wrestling with Roy, who was naked as a scarecrow and swearing like a longshoreman. He had shed his hospital gown and was hollering about getting dressed so he could go see Helen. The nurses were alternately laughing at their predicament and sternly rebuking Roy for trying to whack them with his flaying arms.

The tallest nurse got behind him, pinned his arms to his side and said: "Roy. You've got to get your clothes back on. You're not a stripper, and this isn't the Sugar Shack." The image of Roy performing at the Sugar Shack, a notorious male strip joint just over

93

the Wisconsin border, was so outrageously funny that I staggered back to my bed, shaking with laughter. Only later, after the noise in the corridor had subsided and the rush from my laughter had faded, did I begin to feel another emotion—a melancholy sadness as I thought about poor Roy, poor old confused Roy, fighting with all the might he still could muster, ignoring the pain he must have felt in his own brittle body, determined to get to the bedside of his ailing wife of so many years, his Helen. Did ever Don Quixote fight more recklessly, more selflessly for his Dulcinea?

Many nights I listened to old men and women crying out in loneliness and pain. The saddest and longest night I ever spent in a hospital bed was Saturday, June 28, 1986, when I was recovering after my second bleeding from my esophagus. I was alone in a room on the fourth floor of Northwest Community Hospital, too discouraged and tired to try to read the many books that friends had sent. Reading was becoming increasingly difficult. The meaning of the words kept drifting away from me. I would fan the pages of the books, enjoying their nostalgic fragrance, and then arrange them neatly on my bedside table like a boy stacking his favorite toys. But I could not read them.

Down the hall that night, an old woman, who might have been suffering from Alzheimer's disease, kept up a rhythmic shout, "Doctor. Doctor." Later she shifted to, "Nurse. Nurse." Finally, she began calling more urgently, "Daddy. Daddy." It wasn't that the nurses were ignoring her. There was just nothing they could do for her. I couldn't flee to the peace of the solarium because I was shackled to an IV drip line myself. All I could do that long terrifying night was listen to the lonely chanting of that old woman.

Finally I fell asleep, only to waken deep in the night to her continued weak pleading down the hall. Now she was talking directly to God, asking for relief from her miseries. Tears of frustration and anger welled up in my eyes, and I said out loud, "Goddammit. Why don't you help her?" Why would a good God not do what any decent human being would do: give her peace?

I wrote in my journal: "There are worse things than dying too young. One of them is dying too old."

I began to wonder about the attentiveness of the God I had grown up with and had prayed so casually to all these years, the One with the reputation for never missing the plight of a single falling sparrow. The gusher of faith and hope that Terry Schott had tapped in my soul in this same hospital only a few months before now seemed to have dried up. I allowed myself a daring thought: having an indifferent God, an absent God, was worse than having no God at all.

Since God no longer was listening, I started praying to my long-dead Grandma Mitchell, my mother's mother who had lived with us when I was a boy. I figured she could act as my heavenly ombudswoman. Maybe I was hedging my bets ecumenically since Grandpa and Grandma Mitchell were Presbyterians. When I was little, my parents let me accompany them to their church services after I first attended Mass at the Catholic church. I fell into ecumenism before it became popular. I remember being impressed with the hearty way Protestants sang during their services and how forceful the preachers were compared to most Catholic priests.

I was very close to my grandparents, who came from Missouri to live with us during the Depression. My mother said they favored me because I looked like her brother Earle, who had drowned in 1907 at the University of Missouri after friends on the cross-country team threw him into a river during a freshman hazing ritual. Grandpa and Grandma never got over his death.

My Grandpa Mitchell took me to my first Cubs game and used to throw me baseballs in Kelly's lot next to our house. Even when pitching, Grandpa wore a starched white collar, tie, and vest.

In shifting my prayers from God and making Grandma Mitchell my heavenly intercessor, maybe I was passing through my own version of what spiritual writers have called "the dark night of the soul." All I know is that it was a time when despair seemed to wrap around me like a dirty fog. Coming when it did, at a time when I knew my life was winding down and I had important decisions to make and positions to take, it was frightening. Much as I tried, I could not convey this emptiness to Ginny. It was a hollow feeling that was beyond expression.

Actually, those dark hours were the prelude to the dawning in my spirit of a brighter hope than I ever experienced before. But that was later. For the moment, all I could do was hang on and keep talking to my Grandma Mitchell about the good old days. That was what my prayers consisted of: talking to Grandma about picking crab apples for the jelly she made each fall; listening to her stories of being a young school teacher and about the general store Grandpa owned back in Mound City, Missouri; about my mother going to Chicago to study music and winning a contest to sing with the Chicago Symphony. And we talked about her son Earle, who wanted to be a lawyer and serve on the Supreme Court one day, but who died when he was only seventeen.

I thought about those evenings when I went up to my grandparents' bedroom after dinner and sat cross-legged on their bed listening to Grandma reading to Grandpa from the Bible. Protestants were much more attentive to the Bible than Catholics, who only in recent years have come to read and study it. As a boy, I was far ahead of my schoolmates in knowing the stories of both the New and the Old Testaments, all because of those nights I spent listening to Grandma reading to Grandpa in their rocking chairs.

Later, when I was recuperating at home, Margaret Moser came visiting two mornings a week, bringing communion for Ginny and me. No matter what the weather was like, it always seemed that the sun was shining when Margaret showed up at our door. Sometimes she wore a bright print skirt and cardigan sweater that made her look like a young Irish housewife. But other times she wore faded jeans that made her look like the twin of her teenage daughter. One thing about Margaret—she always was either laughing or looking like she was about to laugh.

In our growing isolation, Margaret became our window to the outside. She brought us all sorts of news about what was happening in the "real" world, from small doings like someone in the neighborhood remodeling a kitchen to sad happenings like one of her "customers" taking a turn for the worse or dying.

Like Ginny, Margaret is a born talker. (Like Ginny she also hates to cook, though I'm not sure if there is a message in that.) But unlike many chatty people, Margaret also is a great listener—I should say, a "skilled" listener. After giving it some thought, both Ginny and I came to understand that listening—deeply listening—was Margaret's greatest gift to the elderly and the ailing whom she so cheerfully ministered to. Although she had a long list of calls to make each day, she never looked the least bit concerned about time, never giving the slightest hint in word or gesture that she might have anything else to do but sit and visit with us.

And the most blessed thing about dear Margaret was that she never offered advice, never felt compelled to tell us what we should do or how we should feel. Sadly, this was not true of many acquaintances, who thought that we needed their advice when all we needed was their presence.

At some point during her visit, Margaret would take my hand and Ginny's and recite with us "The Lord's Prayer." Then she would open her well-worn Bible and read us a short passage, invariably a joyful or poetic selection.

I realized that our house, which was jammed with books and magazines, did not have a Bible except for a digested, picture-book version for children. The next time Ginny took me for an outing, we stopped at a book store and I bought one containing both the Old and the New Testaments. That very night I began flitting through its pages, hoping to come across some words of hope, something I might clutch to keep from slipping further into the dark hole.

As a reporter, I was used to people saying to me, "No comment." But being rebuffed by God was a new experience for me. That's what seemed to happen. It was like the other end of the phone line going dead just as you are trying to make an emergency call.

For me, faith in God had always been an easy faith, His existence as self-evident as each morning's sunrise or the tinkling laughter of children. I knew Him by experience, which is the best way to know anything. Until you actually have had a toothache, you may know its definition but you really don't know what *toothache* means. Until you have fallen in love, you don't know what love means. Sophisticates might call it a reflection of my spiritual shallowness, but I always had this easy relationship with God. I never quite understood why some people got into wrestling matches with Him. He and I "talked" all the time, even before I was sick, even when I was enmeshed in the gritty business of gathering and reporting death and violence.

In fact, when one pietistic, albeit well-meaning, lady once asked me if I had made my peace with God, I couldn't resist telling her—rather smugly, I admit—that no peace treaty was needed because God and I never had been at war.

But now the God I thought I knew so well had abandoned me. I was talking into an empty void. Everything I saw or heard only reinforced this sense of emptiness. When I saw a large crowd of refugees on the television news, I would slump further into my depression. How could God be mindful of each of the millions of people suffering throughout the world? And why would even an omniscient God focus much attention on the trivial problems of Frank and Ginny Maier when the world was filled with sick and starving children, tortured prisoners, lonely old folks. The Lord who kept His eye on the sparrow and delighted in each lily of the field made for beautiful poetry, but what did poetry have to do with one person's real life and one person's real death?

One night when I could not sleep because of my itching skin and swollen belly, I went down to my den and tried to find words of consolation or meaning in my newly purchased Bible. I fanned through the pages, starting a passage here and another one there, but never finding anything that cut to my heart. Part of the problem, I felt, was that I simply could no longer concentrate. How could I expect to find inspiration in words when I could barely understand them.

Then my eye fell upon a verse from the Old Testament prophet, Isaiah, that looked familiar. They were words that I remembered from somewhere, but never had taken to heart before.

"Can a mother forget her infant, be without tenderness for the child of her womb? Even if she should forget, I will never forget you. See, upon the palms of my hands I have carved your name." (Isaiah, chapter 49, verses 15–16.)

I was stunned by the words. The writer in me marveled at their simple imagery, the carved hands and the idea of God as mother not as father. But the dying man in me felt the words as if they had been carved into my own hands. That God should love each of us—me included—individually, unconditionally, without footnotes or subclauses, even to the extent of carving our names into the flesh of his hands, astonished me.

Those three sentences from Isaiah were to become the mantra for my dying. On nights when I could not sleep I repeated them over and over.

On one of those nights I remembered where I had first heard those words of Isaiah—from Grandma Mitchell, reading so softly to Grandpa and me so long ago.

11

MONTHS
—NOT
YEARS

ife goes on. Katie is getting married and we need a new car."
That entry in my journal in early September lacks the emotion of some of my other scribblings in the eventful year
1986. But it shows how we were trying to maintain a sem-
blance of order and balance despite my illness and dwindling
capacities. What we needed more than anything was to experience an ordinary day. Just an ordinary day.

The morning that we went car shopping, Ginny sighed, "Whenever we do this I feel like I'm married to Bob Newhart." Normally
a crack like that would have triggered my male glands to secrete
pints of defensive juices; I was acutely aware of my mediocre combat
record against car dealers. But I felt so chipper that morning that
I only chuckled—in my suave Bob Newhart way. This time I had
a secret edge entering the jousting arena. A dying man can be
reckless in a showdown with even the slickest car salesman. With
nothing to lose, I was eager for battle.

Funny. Sick as I was, I still wanted to impress Ginny. There was
this insecure guy living in my attic who still needed to prove to his
wife of three decades that he knew more about cars than she did
and that he could blow any salesman out of the water.

The only thing I blew was my cover as an authority on automobiles and an expert negotiator. At our very first stop, I formed an

instant, irrational attachment to a hulking Oldsmobile station wagon, insisting that we take a test drive. By the time we returned from the spin around the neighborhood, I was sold. I did not even throw a feint at another vehicle or suggest that we visit the dealer down the street.

The salesman looked disappointed at netting me without even token foreplay, but he steered me toward his cubbyhole office for the celebrated contract signing. That's when Ginny disrupted our negotiations. "I don't think so," she said firmly. Her reasoning, of course, should have been obvious to me. "Have you lost your mind?" she asked. "We've never had a station wagon with four kids, and now that they're all gone, you want to buy one?"

In the end, Ginny picked out a modest two-door hatchback (I insisted it be fire-engine red). I kept up the pretense that I was in charge, but the salesman knew better and thereafter directed all questions and answers to Ginny.

When he asked if we wanted to pay cash or finance the car, I said, "Cash." Ginny said, "We'll finance it." When he asked if we wanted to take out credit insurance on the loan, I said, "Absolutely not." Ginny said, "Yes."

Now I had her. I could regain a measure of respect in this bargaining ritual. "Credit insurance is the biggest rip-off there is," I lectured her. "We don't need it. No way. Absolutely not."

Ginny would not bend an inch. We financed the car for the longest term possible and took the credit insurance.

It never dawned on me until several days later why my tough-minded wife was so adamant about the financing arrangements. She was facing reality while I was still doing my best to ignore it. She calculated that I never would live to make too many payments on that car. The credit insurance would pay off the balance of the loan.

When I admonished her for being so pessimistic about my future, she laughed like a schoolgirl and said, "Don't worry. I've never won anything in my life." With an impish glance to see my reaction, she added in an undertone, "Maybe we should have bought a Mercedes."

At first, the impending wedding of our oldest daughter, Katie, seemed the perfect opportunity for Ginny to direct her considerable energies to a project other than keeping me alive. Ever a stickler for details and decorum, Ginny should have been at her best helping plan her daughter's wedding. Katie and I saw it as wonderful therapy for her. After so many dreary and anxious months of being my full-time nurse and cheerleader, for a change she could think about flowers and music and buying a mother-of-the-bride dress.

A wedding can be a stressful, though semicomic, experience for any family. When a lingering cloud like serious illness hovers overhead, that normal stress is compounded. Much as she wanted to, Ginny could not handle my growing incapacities and at the same time help Katie with wedding arrangements. I was slipping into a slow, steady physical decline. My belly was swollen from ascites, a buildup of fluid in the abdominal cavity; my hands trembled, a flapping condition called "asterixis;" my skin turned yellow-green from jaundice and itched unmercifully. Some days my strength was so depleted that Ginny had to bathe me in the tub and dry me with a towel like I was a little boy.

Rather than brightening her days, the approaching wedding drove her close to physical and emotional collapse. As it turned out, Katie and her husband-to-be, Rick VanEgeren, did most of the planning and arrangements on their own.

One night a few weeks before the wedding, Ginny suddenly said, "I wish I could climb to the top of a mountain and scream." In all of our years together, she had never talked like that. She was the least melodramatic person I knew. Neither a screamer nor a crier, she also never talked about screaming or crying. Her outlet always was action. Kids got her down? Wash the car. Miffed at Frank? Vacuum the house. Feeling sick or down in the dumps? Go to the park and swing on the swings and swoop down the slide like a schoolgirl. That was Ginny.

To say that Ginny gave up a career to care for me would be an understatement. She never had a single job going at one time, even in the days when she was raising our children single-handedly while I was on the road recording what I considered to be the instant history of the world. She always was juggling several entrepreneurial balls in the air while managing to maintain an orderly, spic-and-span household.

One summer she decided to go public with her gardening skills and formed the "Green Thumb Gardening Service," the total work force consisting of Ginny and our then teenage boys, Michael and Danny. That led to her appointment to the Arlington Heights Beautification Council, of which she became the two-term president.

Other times she billed herself as a self-employed "space consultant," showing the disorganized how to stow anything anywhere. The local newspaper even ran a feature with pictures of her work. Her slogan: "A place for everything and everything in its place." I was pleased to have her tied up on this enterprise because it kept her so busy that she didn't have time to throw out more of my precious magazines and other memorabilia.

One winter she packed plastic milk containers with bird seed and had the kids peddle them to motorists to carry in their trunks. They served two purposes: provided drivers with traction to pull out of slippery ruts and fed the birds at the same time.

When not involved in one of her own ventures, she managed a gift shop, worked as a "sales associate" in a department store (until she quit because her purchases far outpaced her earnings), and helped out at a bicycle and ski shop owned by our friends, Dick and Mary Ellen Spirek. One night a blizzard swept into town, stranding Ginny at the shop. Airports were closed and all the streets were drifted over. She phoned to say she was coming home despite my protests. To make the journey, she bought a set of cross-country skis—she was going to buy them anyway—had Mary Ellen put on bindings, and then skied home to join the family for the pot roast I had prepared.

With my sickness, the irrepressible Ginny was forced into restraints that she never had experienced in her life. She accepted voluntarily what she never would have allowed anyone to impose on her—never complaining, never sighing, never hinting at her sacrifices. If she cried, she did so privately, never in front of me.

To me she was like a beautiful bird trapped in a cage, still trying to sing and flash her wings for my enjoyment despite her own predicament. When I told her how guilty I felt about being sick and tying her down with my care, she flipped my maudlin words right back at me: "Guilt is a wasted emotion. We have more serious problems than that."

Indeed we did. Uncertainty was our worst enemy, not being able to make any long-range plans. Even short-range plans were tentatively made and often abandoned—like my trying to go to the bureau for a few hours of work or our going to a movie. There was no question I was dying, but no one would be more specific about my timetable than that first estimate by Mayo's doctors that I might have seven to eight years. In light of my three hemorrhages and decaying body, that was certainly an obsolete estimate.

The uncertainty bothered Ginny more than me. Although some days were better than others, I usually felt so exhausted and depleted that I lost all concept of the future; just making it through a day was enough for me. Besides, illness had not changed my basic nature, which was to avoid hard questions whenever unsettling answers were expected.

But Ginny needed concrete answers. One afternoon while I was sleeping, she wrote down ten questions to ask my main doctor, John McGillen. When she told her sister, Martha Maddock, about her list of questions and her intention of taking them to the doctor, Martha looked alarmed: "You aren't going to do it before the wedding." It was a statement, not a question, and Ginny, seeing concern in Martha's face, understood what it reflected. "No. I have an appointment with him on the Friday after the wedding."

Everyone tells me the wedding was beautiful and went off without a hitch. I remember bits and pieces of the day, particularly our neighbor Barbara Dress from around the corner coming to put pancake makeup on me to cover my jaundiced complexion and the raccoon hollows around my eyes.

That next Friday Ginny told me she was going to the beauty shop. Instead she drove to see Dr. McGillen, who had set aside time after his last patient of the morning. She took the folded sheet of questions from her billfold and read the first one: "How long does Frank have?"

She expected him to hedge, retreating behind the euphemisms of his trade or wrapping his answer in layers of conditional clauses. That's why she had the other nine questions, to pin him down.

The soft-spoken John McGillen, who once studied for the priesthood, answered with expected kindness but unexpected directness. "Ginny, he could bleed to death at any second of any day."

Ginny burst into tears. After that answer, there was no reason to ask the other questions on her list. Much, much later, when she told me about her private meeting with my doctor, she said something that endeared her even more to me: "I felt so sorry for John, having to tell me that. He didn't need for me to break down crying, to have to go through that."

Serious illness, like any other crisis, has the potential for uniting a couple as never before—or driving a wedge into their marriage that shatters it beyond repair. We were to see examples of both during the months we spent among the seriously ill and dying.

So many anxieties converge on a family that at times the illness becomes secondary. Paying your regular bills and wondering how you ever will pay off the accumulating medical expenses becomes a nagging worry, even for those fortunate few who have good health insurance.

Beyond the financial stress, a couple with young children or teenagers faces the added challenge of not letting the illness dominate the household to the point that it deprives the children of the nurturing and attention they need. Fortunately, unlike many stricken couples we met, our children were older. Far from being a burden, they ended up rallying around their mother and helping us cope with my dying.

Ginny's own mother had been a widow for a quarter of a century, so she was all too aware of how lonely life can be for a man or a woman who loses a spouse before the usual time. We were fortunate in having a network of family and friends nearby, a dividend from having spent most of our married life in the same part of the country. But even the closest relatives and friends cannot substitute for the one special person you have freely chosen to love and to forgive from the very bottom of your heart.

Because our children were older, we never had to face the decision of whether—or when—to tell them that their father was dying. The only one still in our nest was Heidi, and she was away most of the year at college in Indiana. Michael, our oldest, was a television cameraman in Chicago; Katie worked as an office manager for a robotics company; Danny was working as a senatorial aide in Washington.

As my condition deteriorated, Ginny made sure that the children knew what was happening. For my part, I tried to keep up a blustery exterior, partly because I did not want my illness to dominate the childrens' lives and partly because I did not want them to see me weak and helpless.

Ginny did something that I never detected at the time. There were many occasions when we got together as a family. But she also deliberately set up situations where each of the children could spend time alone with me. It was a sensitive idea that I never would have thought of had our roles been reversed. It gave each child and me a chance to share special memories and talk about each child's special interests.

I never specifically brought up the subject of my dying with the children, though one Sunday when all of them were to be home for dinner I came close. At Mass that morning I asked God if it was time to formally tell the children that I was dying. If so, I prayed that I would say it gracefully, in a way that would provide them with a good example of faith and dignity. On the way home from church, I decided that the best time would be when I said grace before the meal.

Maybe it was divine intervention that saved me from delivering my maudlin speech, but the announcement of my death was canceled when Michael, who had caught a serious cold shooting an outdoor assignment, became so ill with a fever that he spent the afternoon on the living room sofa, needing more care and coddling than I did. I decided it was not the right time for a dramatic self-eulogization.

Later, when I told Ginny of my aborted plan to go public with my dying, she gave me one of those patented wifely looks and said: "Do you really think we have raised four dummies for children? They know. And they've known for a long time."

For me there were other problems that I was reluctant to admit to myself. Being chronically ill was a blow to my self-esteem, to my sense of being the titular head of the family, to my need to feel in control of my own life and of some value at home and at work. One of the worst things about being chronically ill is that you no longer feel competent to do anything. And without this sense of competence, you lose all your dignity and self-respect.

As my illness progressed, I resented Ginny's calm competency. To be honest, I must admit that I always felt threatened by her ability to handle tools and understand how some things worked or why some things didn't. Whenever we had a workman in the house, I would hide behind my books to preserve my dignity. She always knew if they were botching a job—and often she would lend them a hand to get it done right—and quicker.

In addition to my long-standing sense of inferiority when it came to such manly arts, my sickness created other anxieties. I was ashamed that I could not work regularly, drive a car, or even carry out the trash. It is humbling to have to ask your wife to open a jar of pickles because you have no strength in your wrists, or to watch helplessly as she climbs a ladder to clean the gutters.

At least in my healthier days I could fool myself—if not Ginny—into thinking I was capable of handling minimum chores around the house. No longer could I keep up that charade. Dying is not anything like the drama it is made out to be in films and pop culture. It hurts in so many small ways.

We have a lot of trees in our yard, many of them planted over the years by Ginny and the boys. Every fall Ginny ferociously attacks the gold and russet leaves with the fury of a peasant fighting off an invasion of locusts. She never stops her relentless raking and bagging until she has captured the last scrap of maple or cottonwood hiding under the smallest shrub.

On a Friday in early November, Ginny kept interrupting her traditional battle with the leaves to come stare at me dozing on the living room sofa. She never said anything, just looked at me like a mother peeping at a sleeping baby. Indeed, that was exactly what she was doing every fifteen minutes. Her motherly instincts told her that something strange was happening to me. That night and all day Saturday she kept asking me if anything was wrong. "Other than dying, I don't think so," I joked.

That Sunday morning we went to Mass and then brunch with neighbors at a little restaurant called Eros. I have no recollection of being there—and that was precisely the problem. Ginny told me later that my conversation consisted of non sequiturs and absolute nonsense. She said I could not even find the arm holes when I tried to fumble my way into my windbreaker. My hand flapping was more pronounced than ever.

By that night, as my attention kept straying off the conversational path, she decided that I had suffered a minor stroke—but she withheld her diagnosis from me. On Monday, I was scheduled to make a rare visit to the bureau to interview a woman from a local newspaper who wanted to know about job opportunities at *Newsweek*.

"You are not going down to the bureau," Ginny told me at bedtime. "We're going first thing to see John McGillen."

I protested, saying that I could do the job interview, then take an early train home and see the doctor. She would buy none of it.

"This is not 'Let's Make a Deal.' Frank, if you try to do that interview you will embarrass yourself and *Newsweek*."

First thing Monday morning we were at John McGillen's office. He barely looked at me before saying, "I know the problem." He took something from his pocket and held it up for my inspection. "What is this, Frank?" I considered the object for some time and then made a tentative stab: "A pencil?" He smiled. "Almost. It's a pen." When he made me extend my arms and bend my wrists up, my hands shook as if I had palsy.

He fumbled in my medical folder and pulled out a report from the gastroenterologist who had done my last endoscopic treatment. It noted that I was more than a little confused coming out of the anesthetic and warned that I might be falling into a condition called "hepatic encephalopathy" and should be watched carefully.

We had never heard of the disorder, much less had Ginny been warned by any of our doctors to watch for it. It meant that I was descending into the final stages of liver failure. The intermittant reading, writing, and memory problems that I had suffered earlier were only vague signs of the approaching storm that was descending on me as my liver struggled to clean toxins from my body.

The confusion and physical impairments were caused by a buildup of ammonia in my system. That is what was causing my slurred speech, writing difficulty—the experts call this "constructional apraxia"—and my drowsiness. If untreated it could drag me into a deep coma.

To flush the ammonia from my system, Dr. McGillen put me on a low protein diet and a liquid medication called Chronulac, which actually is a strong laxative that can cause the side effects of severe diarrhea and cramps. "How can I go to work taking that stuff?" I protested. Ginny and the doctor looked at me like I was crazy—which, I guess I almost was.

Chronulac—its generic name is lactulose—is not a tasty medication. Ginny teased me into taking the prescribed two tablespoons three times a day by dubbing me "Captain Chronulac," an endearing term that my youngest daughter Heidi soon picked up on: "Here he comes! Yellow-skinned, belly-bloated, slower-than-a-tortoise, able to leap out of hospital beds in a single bound—not a bird, not a plane, it's Captain Chronulac!"

Despite the best efforts of Ginny and our children to laugh me through this latest symptom of end-stage liver disease, hepatic encephalopathy turned out to be the worst part of dying for me. Until you lose your control over words, you never realize how you depend on them. Without words you cannot connect with reality. For someone like me who could not make a living except with words, it was devastating to drift in and out of a state that resembled early senility.

If I did not know what was happening, that would have been bad enough for my family and friends. At least I would be oblivious of my condition. But with hepatic encephalopathy, I usually realized, even as it was happening, that I was not functioning on all cylinders. It was like being trapped in a nightmare and being unable to force myself awake.

After catching me giving a $30 tip to a waitress for a $17 luncheon check and discovering imaginary deposits I had made in our joint checking account, Ginny took away my money, credit cards, and checkbook. I walked around without a penny in my pocket—just like the president of the United States.

To my humiliation, one night I caught myself urinating into the corner of our bathroom instead of the nearby toilet. I was aware enough to clean up the mess by myself and was so ashamed that I never told Ginny—until right now. Another night when trying to wash my hands I could not figure out how to turn on the faucets and mix the water to the right temperature. I stood at the sink in frightening confusion thinking, "Why am I here? How do I do this?" I could not understand how to turn the cold or hot faucet to produce a stream of water. I might have stood there for minutes—

maybe hours—I really don't know. Nor do I recall if I ever managed to turn on the water.

The youngest of John McGillen's partners, Dr. Vern Kerchberger, gently warned Ginny that the day might be coming when she would have to think about putting me into a nursing home. She kept this entirely to herself, not mentioning it even to those closest to her. Thankfully, she told me nothing about this warning. I would have been devastated had I known that it was even a possibility.

About this same time, Dr. Kerchberger became the first person to suggest that I might consider trying for a liver transplant as a last resort. His brother, an anesthesiologist, had worked with the newly formed liver transplant team at the Mayo Clinic and reported their early promising results. Dr. Kerchberger suggested that Ginny sound me out about going there for evaluation. There was no certainty that I would be accepted as a transplant candidate, he said. But I had no options left.

When she casually mentioned it over dinner, I erupted in anger. I began pacing through the house, snarling that she was upsetting me by such nonsense. The idea of a transplant seemed totally bizarre to me. Why didn't she and Dr. Kerchberger suggest that I try out for the astronaut program? Far-out talk of a transplant only served to give me false hope. I was reconciled to dying. The last thing I needed was to have my last days complicated by fantasies.

I remember shouting at her: "I know I'm dying. I've accepted it and now you're saying maybe I don't have to die. All you're doing is confusing me! Stop it!"

Ginny listened without a word to my rantings, and I suspect she—like me—thought that was the last of that crazy idea. Later that night I wrote in my journal: "I am absolutely opposed to the idea of a transplant and would never consider it."

Some days my confusion from the hepatic encephalopathy would lift like fog burning off in the morning, and I would rush to write in my journal and read anything I could. But I had to read in bits and pieces; I could not concentrate enough to get through a long piece of writing. Under those conditions, words became particularly precious for me. I would examine them carefully and tenderly, like a child playing with stones in a river bed.

For me, reading a paragraph was like wading through hip-deep snow. Somehow, slowly, I managed to make it through parts of the *Imitation of Christ* by Thomas à Kempis, after the Bible the most widely read book in history, and *The Cost of Discipleship* by Lutheran theologian Dietrich Bonhoeffer, who was only thirty-nine when executed by the Nazis, and through all of *Man's Search for Meaning,* by Holocaust survivor and psychiatrist Viktor Frankl and several small volumes on spirituality by Dutch-born priest Henri J. M. Nouwen. I also kept scanning the Bible, hoping to find other insightful words like the ones from Isaiah that had come to mean so much to me.

Despite all that was happening to me, even though I had accepted the general principle that I was dying, I still did not have the courage, as Ginny did, to ask Dr. McGillen for a more specific estimated time of departure. After sharing so much during our married life, Ginny and I had switched onto different tracks without even knowing when it happened. She wanted to talk about my death and its consequences. If she tried to bring the subject up, I either made a joke or simply walked away.

Frustrated by my attitude, Ginny went to see Father Patrick Render, a young priest we knew from the time he was principal of the high school where our boys had graduated. Now a provincial of his order, he was experienced in counseling parents about their puzzling offspring and, on occasion, the parents about their own crises.

After Ginny told him of Dr. McGillen's grim estimate on my life expectancy and my stubborness in addressing our joint fears, Father Render told Ginny about a young married couple he knew who had just gone through a similar death experience. The man, only in his twenties, was dying of cancer. Nothing could change that. He told Ginny how this young couple shared everything in the final months of his dying: every hurt, every melancholy dream of what might have been, and every small joy that lightened their day.

"After he died, she was left with sadness, but with no regrets about what was left unspoken. They shared everything right to the end," Father Render said.

The story touched Ginny, who compared my attitude to "wall building." Once again, the expert builder had erected a barrier to protect his own emotions. But it was a barrier that also cut her off.

"Frank always handled obstacles by pretending they didn't exist," she told the priest. "In dying he's following the same pattern."

He told her that I was on a different time schedule than she was, but that somehow she must try to nudge me into sharing everything with her and with our children. "If you don't reach that point, there will be regrets later." She came away from her two-hour visit with Father Render convinced that somehow she needed to get me to "climb over the wall," to acknowledge that I was dying so that we could talk.

Thereafter Ginny watched for every opportunity to break down that wall. But I resisted whenever she moved the conversation in that direction.

Two weeks before Christmas 1986, we drove to the crossroads village of Long Grove near the Wisconsin-Illinois border where we wandered through the shops that smelled of evergreens and tinkled with holiday carols. We bought cinammon-apple donuts, hand-dipped chocolate cherries, and pine-scented candles. Then we had steaming corn chowder and hard French rolls at a restaurant over-looking a frozen pond. The smells, the tastes, the clinking bells, and winking lights created a swirl of memories that both delighted and saddened me.

We sat over coffee and the remnants of deep-dish apple cobbler, silently wrapped in each other's presence, until afternoon shadows slanted across the pond and only a few patrons were left in the restaurant. I felt a rush of emotion—not quite joy and not quite pain. I put my hand on Ginny's and said, "I wish we could do this again next Christmas." She looked at me with glistening eyes and answered, "The important thing is that we're doing it this Christmas."

The next day we went to see Dr. McGillen. I had decided it was time for me to face my dying. The scene remains etched in my memory as if it happened moments ago. He sat on a low coaster stool, the bulging folder containing my records open on his lap. Ginny stood in the corner, my shirt and sweater folded over her arms. I sat on the end of the examining table, feet dangling awk-wardly, hands gripping the table as if I would lose my balance.

Even then I would not ask a direct question. All I would allow myself was, "How am I doing, John?"

Forewarned by a phone call from Ginny that I would be asking THE question, John McGillen was prepared to be direct in his reply.

"Frank, you should start thinking of your life in terms of months, not years."

There was an embarrassing silence. He coughed nervously and I coughed back. Ginny looked at me with a sad smile that seemed to say, "So now you know, love."

My face flushed, but I was determined not to show any emotion. "How is it likely to happen?"

"Most likely you will start bleeding somewhere, and we won't be able to stop it."

Abruptly he rose and said he wanted to confer with one of his partners. It was an excuse to leave us alone.

"You already talked to him," I said to Ginny, who nodded. That was all we said until he knocked on the door a few minutes later and came back in.

"He agrees," John McGillen said as if he had talked it over with one of his three partners.

To normalize things, he went through the motions of listening to my heart and lungs, taking my blood pressure, tapping me here and there, and asking a few general questions. I asked how his writing was coming (I knew he wrote in his spare time, and we often talked about writing and about doctors who had become successful authors.) Like Ginny before me, I found myself wanting to take the pressure off John McGillen, who undoubtedly had been the messenger of bad tidings more times than his gentle nature deserved. Ginny and I knew that, as an infectious disease specialist, John was one of the doctors in the area who treated patients with AIDS.

Besides, right then I needed to find a center of calm in myself. I felt that my best hope for maintaining my dignity and not breaking down was to act as if he had just given me the day's weather report. I needed to pretend it was something that might cause me a minor inconvenience but was ultimately of little consequence.

We drove from the doctor's office to a place called Arnold's Diner where we sipped chocolate milkshakes at the old-fashioned soda fountain and talked about our plans for Christmas.

Strangely, like a nervous traveler, I felt much calmer now that I had a rough idea when my train was going to pull out of the station.

113

12

UP IN THE
CHOIR
LOFT

That was Tom's great secret—the scheme to re-
turn home with his brother pirates and attend
their own funeral.

> —*The Adventures of Tom Sawyer*
> by Mark Twain

ntil Dr. McGillen provided the more specific estimate on my departure, I had been content to view my death as an abstraction, a riddle that I tried to solve by reading and writing in my journal (when I *could* read or write). For Ginny it was a reality that required planning and preparation. She always was big on logistics.

In early January of 1987, she suggested that I plan my funeral. At first, I was stunned by the suggestion—as perhaps you might be. Someone not in our situation might consider it a cold and impersonal proposal. I can understand that. But Ginny knew me better than anyone. She knew that I needed to feel more in charge of my dying—there were so few things left that I could control.

The idea of planning my funeral also appealed to that little boy in me, the one who was increasingly taking over. It reminded me of that wonderful scene in *The Adventures of Tom Sawyer,* when Tom and his pals, Joe Harper and Huck Finn, sneak up into the choir loft to listen to the minister's maudlin eulogy at their own funeral.

First I checked with Father Patrick Render to see if he thought it was a morbid idea. He agreed with Ginny that it would be good for me to take an active role in planning my funeral, even suggesting it would be a kindness that might ease the burden on my family. On this last point, I think he was only trying to make me feel I was doing it for them, rather than for me.

I sat down in my den one midnight with a yellow legal pad and planned down to the last detail all the arrangements for my funeral and the party afterwards. Here is what I wrote:

"My wishes upon my death:

"This is how I want things handled. But everything here is subject to Ginny's wishes, which take priority.

"I want the following persons contacted as soon as possible—I am presuming that my children, close relatives, and friends already know:

"John McCormick, to inform my editors at *Newsweek* in New York and friends in the news business; also ask him to write my obituary.

"Paul Fullmer, secretary of Notre Dame Class of 1955, to inform those classmates who know me best and the university alumni office.

"My aunt Maryalice Rasmussen in Milwaukee, the family switch-board operator, to inform all my relatives on my father's side of the family. My oldest sister, Bunny McCafferty, will do this on my mother's side.

"My lawyer, Eugene Schlickman, has a copy of my will.

"A list of insurance policies are in my desk, along with inventory of contents of our safety deposit box. If instant cash is needed, contact Navy Mutual Aid Association, Washington, D.C., which will wire $2,000 of death benefit immediately. Policies themselves are in the bank safety deposit box.

"I want a one evening wake at the funeral home Ginny prefers. Although I previously talked to Ginny about having a closed coffin, I have since learned that it is better for survivors if the coffin (moderately priced) is open. I want to wear my good navy blue blazer

115

and gold and blue rep tie. I know it is a Catholic tradition to place rosary beads in the hands of the deceased, but I prefer a small wooden cross.

"In the obit, request no flowers; donations to either the St. James Special Religious Education program or the American Liver Foundation.

"I want the funeral service to be cheerful, and I want everyone who comes to either the wake or Mass to be treated as if they were guests of honor. If anyone shows up who surprises you, don't be.

"Remember the wisdom of Garrison Keillor to 'cry at weddings and tell jokes at funerals.'

"I would like the funeral Mass to be said by either Father Peter Bowman, the pastor of St. James, or Father Patrick Render, whoever is available. As servers I want altar girls rather than altar boys—just because.

"Select pall bearers from among the following (if none are willing or able, hire some guys from central casting who look like they would have a good time at a funeral): Tom McCabe, Frank Lolli, Jim O'Shea, Jack Pittas, Jack Flynn, Dick Burke, Mike Ward, Jack Reardon, John McCormick, Vest Monroe, Ed Gilbreth, Jim Griffin, Bill King, John Ryan, Ernie Banks (no harm in asking).

"Ask Margaret Moser and Terry Schott to do the scriptural readings. One of the readings must be from Isaiah, chapter 49, verses 15 and 16.

"If people want to tell stories, let them. But I definitely want my brother Joe to talk because he will get everybody laughing.

"For music I want organ and trumpet (the young man from DePaul who played at Katie's wedding might take the job). Some suggested songs: 'The Navy Hymn,' 'On Eagles Wings,' 'Morning Is Breaking,' 'Notre Dame Our Mother,' 'Amazing Grace,' Gounod's 'Ave Maria' and maybe some Bach. For the recessional, I want sons Michael and Danny to arrange for a loud rendition of the Boston Pops playing 'Stars and Stripes Forever.' (Father Bowman will approve, I'm certain.)

"Afterwards there should be a party at our house for anyone who wants to come. Daughters Katie and Heidi will make sure there is a bountiful buffet and ample liquid refreshment. The only beer served will be Leinenkugel's from Chippewa Falls, Wis. I met Bill

Leinenkugel while working on a beer cover story for *Newsweek;* during my illness he called regularly to see how I was doing.

"I want our children to pay special attention to their two grand-mothers. We must not forget how the death of a child can hurt—and I am a child to them.

"If anyone should come to the funeral from *Newsweek* in New York, please treat them as family and invite them to the party afterwards."

About two in the morning I finished my funeral plans and tucked the yellow sheets into the pages of my journal. I felt as mischievous and happy as Tom Sawyer up in the choir loft with his pals at their own funeral.

About this same time I went through my files and destroyed most of the practice writing I did over the years, including several pounds of puerile fiction that I wrote in college and the navy. I did not want Ginny or my children to find them and think it was my wish to try to have them published.

I also searched through my old journals for any item I had written that could conceivably hurt someone. Given the choice, I would rather be kind than totally honest. As it turned out, I blacked out just one long angry passage I wrote during my early illness. I did not want my grandchildren finding it someday and thinking their grandpa was a cranky old man. Had it been powerfully written rage, I would not have struck it out. But the world—and my grandchil-dren—can do quite well without a mediocre example of fury.

When you are seriously ill, you can become so self-absorbed that you forget that your family and friends also are hurting because of you. Not long after I was told that I had only months to live, Ginny began sobbing at the kitchen table where we were having a light meal of soup and cornbread. She staggered into the living room holding her stomach and curled into a fetal position on the sofa.

She cried like an abandoned child, gasping and choking for breath between sobs. I tried to put my arms around her, but she shuddered me away and buried her face deeply into the cushions. I had seldom seen Ginny cry; never had I seen her cry like this. I thought about calling one of the children—or maybe Dr. McGillen. But all I did was sit down on the floor next to her and slowly rub her back and neck. "It's okay," I said over and over. "It's okay."

117

After five minutes of sobbing, she stopped as abruptly as she had started, sat up, and asked me for some tissue. I helped her upstairs to bed, but she did not want to undress. Without objection, she accepted one of the sleeping pills that the doctors had prescribed for her the night of my first emergency. But sleep never came.

All night she cried, vomited, and slept fitfully while I tried ineptly to comfort her. Never in our married life had I seen her in such agony. It was frightening because it was so unlike her to give in to pain. She always had a high tolerance for pain—even refusing Novocain from the dentist because she didn't like the numbness afterwards.

It was to be the only time during our ordeal that she broke down—at least in front of me. I could understand why young Dr. Kerchberger jokingly called her "The Intimidator."

In the morning she was pale and uncustomarily quiet. I wanted to tell her how much I admired her loyalty and strength, but it came out awkwardly. "I'd rather have you in my foxhole than anybody in the world," I said.

She smiled coyly and answered, "That's the best offer you've made in months, soldier."

In late January we flew to Sanibel Island, Florida, for what I knew would be my last vacation. The only reason Dr. McGillen allowed it, even for a week, was that we were going with Ginny's brother, John, and his wife, Patti. Since John was a doctor, he could keep an eye on me for signs of distress and handle any emergency. At first I fought the idea, but then—realizing how badly Ginny needed relief from her grinding caretaker duties—I decided to be as lively and pleasant a traveling companion as my energy would permit.

We actually spent little time together, except at dinner each night. Ginny went for long tranquil walks along the beach, gathering shells and running like a little girl with clapping hands through the swarms of irate seagulls that were trying to rest on the white sand. Sometimes she took off on a rented bicycle and was missing for hours. For my part, all I could do was lie in a hammock and try, with little success, to read some of the paperbacks I had optimistically bought at the airport.

Ginny must have mailed thirty postcards to friends. As is her custom, she sent one showing an ancient cemetery to our friend,

118

Jack Pittas. She always sent a postcard of a cemetery to him, but not out of sick humor over my predicament. That strange custom started when, at a dinner party, he called everyone's attention to Ginny's "dark Irish" habit of bringing up the subject of death, wakes, or obituaries. He nicknamed her "Mother D," insisting that she could not go more than five minutes without discussing some aspect of the Grim Reaper. And, like a self-fulfilling prophesy, it seemed that poor Ginny never could be around Jack Pittas without blundering into his trap, usually by mentioning that she had learned of so-and-so's demise on the obituary page—or, as Pittas called it, the "Irish Scratch Sheet."

It was John Ryan who finally nudged me out of my hammock, leading us on sidetrips to the home, museum, and arboretum where Thomas Edison spent much of his latter years in nearby Fort Myers and then to the 5,000-acre bird sanctuary named for "Ding" Darling, the late political cartoonist and naturalist. These sidetrips benefited me more than Ginny, who I think was more interested in being left to herself about then.

But I was reinvigorated by visiting the Edison homestead, marveling at the output of this uneducated genius who had obtained more than 1,000 patents for inventions that changed the face of the world, including the first workable electric lightbulb, the phonograph, even the process for Portland cement.

In the Edison arboretum, I learned that bamboo is a grass, not a tree, and that it can grow as much as forty-three inches in a day. We walked around the third largest banyon tree in the world, some four hundred feet in circumference, with huge roots and tendrils that grow down from the extended branches in search of water. The whole tree resembles a forest of individual trunks that started as tendrils.

Ginny's brother also proved to be an accomplished bird-watcher, pointing out all sorts of rare species as we drove through the bird sanctuary. I marveled at the antics of the anhinga, a bird that dives underwater and darts like a fish after his prey. We watched one persistent anhinga pursue a fish for minutes, break for air, then return to the chase. He finally speared a small fish and surfaced to enjoy his lunch, only to have a pelican swoop down and steal it right off his beak.

During the day we spent at Edison's estate and the bird sanctuary, I completely forgot about being sick or dying. I was almost in a trance, immune to pain and anxiety, wrapped in awe at seeing things I had never seen before, learning things I had never known before. I had loved going to school, and maybe that is why I loved being a general assignment reporter—a busybody and scribe-of-all-trades who actually got paid for the delectable task of asking questions and poking into everything.

That night I told Ginny how happy the day had been for me. And I told her that I had finally figured out where and what heaven is. "Heaven isn't a place; it's wherever God is. And I think He's going to be filled with surprises for me. I can't wait." I actually said that: "I can't wait."

Back home, my mind remained relatively unscrambled because of the daily doses of Chronulac syrup. But, as happens with liver disease, when one problem is controlled, something else always seems to go wrong. Fluid began to accumulate in my belly, a condition known as "ascites." For some liver patients ascites is more agonizing than the itching skin or hepatic encephalopathy. In my case, my waist went from thirty-four to forty-two inches, and I gained forty pounds in two weeks. It was like acquiring an instant beer belly, and I had neither the back nor stomach muscles to support it. Unable to wear regular trousers, I had to wear sweat pants with an expansion waistband. Sleep was impossible because the fluid pressing on my lungs made it hard to breathe. During the day I could barely walk because of the back pain. For the first time I could sympathize with my pregnant daughter Katie, who complained of constant back aches as her baby grew.

Dr. McGillen and one of my gastroenterologists, Jerrold Schwartz, were not enthusiastic about tapping the fluid from my belly. They agreed it was a drastic procedure that could cause other complications without providing a permanent solution. Instead, they put me on heavy doses of two strong diuretics. That helped to drain off some of the fluid in my belly. But a week later I suddenly started to slur my speech and could not write legibly in my journal. The diuretics had upset the delicate balance of electrolytes in my body and needed to be drastically reduced. It was another trade-off: rather a swollen belly than a scrambled brain.

On the morning of March 16, 1987, I suffered my fourth and final hemorrhage from the esophagus. I was dozing in an easy chair in our living room. Ginny was kneeling on the floor in a warm shaft of sunlight reading the newspaper. Our daughter Heidi, home on spring break from college, was sleeping upstairs. She had been all set to go to Florida with friends, but changed her mind at the last minute. "Florida will always be there," she told Ginny when she arrived home unexpectedly the night before.

Without any warning, a shudder rippled through my entire body. I could not speak or move my arms. Then a black curtain shut off all light. Ginny told me later that I never made a sound, that my head jerked back suddenly and clots of blood shot from my mouth. She thought that I had suffered a cerebral accident and that this was the end of me.

I woke to Heidi cradling my head and wiping blood from my face with a cold, wet towel. "It's okay, Dad, it's okay. Mom is calling the paramedics."

By this time I knew the drill and kept my mouth shut while the paramedics carried me to the ambulance for the fourth time within a year. As the ambulance pulled away, I arched my head up so I could see my house through the rear window. I figured that was the last time I would see it.

It was Dr. Schwartz who got the call this time to stop the bleeding with an emergency endoscopy. At least they did not need to put the painful Preston helmet on me this time. The most painful part of this last emergency room visit to Northwest Community Hospital was the blood transfusion. My veins were so abused that it was difficult to plant the lines for the transfusion. The head nurse on duty in ICU, Ken Peterson, had to be called to make the hookup. I knew Ken well from my previous visits. How could I forget someone who managed to persuade a little old lady patient to surrender her television set long enough for me to watch a basketball game?

The next day was St. Patrick's Day—the nearest thing to a national holiday in Chicago. I was in bed 19 of ICU, confused about what had happened, exhausted from the painful blood transfusion, and parched because of the "nothing-by-mouth" order on my chart. In the afternoon, Heidi sat by my bed—the nurses in ICU were lenient with my visitors because I was such a good customer—and Ginny was in the waiting room watching the St. Patrick's Day parade on television. I remember Heidi running her fingers through my hair and softly singing to me the very songs I had sung at bedtime to all my children: "A Frog A-Courting," which I had learned from my Grandma Mitchell; "When the Bell in the Lighthouse Rings" (they always liked it when I did the deep "ding . . . dong"); and "When Irish Eyes Are Smiling."

"Heidi," I whispered. "Wouldn't you like to get something to drink?

"No, Dad."

"Heidi, I think you should get yourself a nice 7-UP, with ice."

"I'm not thirsty, Dad."

"Heidi, I'm SURE you would like it."

"Dad, you know you're not supposed to have anything to drink yet."

"What they don't know . . ."

Heidi slipped away and a short time later returned to give me the tiniest sip of 7-UP from a paper cup. She let me have one sliver of ice. It was wonderful.

"The other kids will wonder why I left you all my money," I told her as I drifted off to sleep.

About mid-afternoon the man in the next bed in ICU suffered a cardiac arrest. When the resuscitation team responded to the Code Blue alarm, the nurses told Heidi to leave me and join her mother in the waiting room. I was sleeping and was not even aware of the commotion a few feet away.

As it turned out, the man—who was about ten years younger than I—could not be revived. Ginny was helping comfort his wife and children in the waiting room when a second Code Blue sounded in ICU. This time it was for me. Monitors attached like tentacles to my body detected my heart slowing down from its normal seventy beats per minute—a condition called "bradycardia." At 4:44 in the afternoon on that St. Patrick's Day, my heart stopped for what my records describe as "a long episode." (Months later when I inspected the records, the "444" jumped out at me because it is *Newsweek*'s address on Madison Avenue in New York.)

The crisis resulted from an imbalance of electrolytes in my body caused by the blood loss and the malfunctioning liver. Most important, the level of potassium had become so high in my body fluids that my heart began slowing down and eventually just stopped.

Dr. John McGillen and one of my four regular gastroenterologists, Dr. Loren White, were both in the hospital and rushed to help the resuscitation team. Terry Schott, who was about to leave for the day, also responded. She watched the resuscitation efforts and kept Ginny and Heidi informed of what was happening.

Ginny remembers trying to comfort Heidi by saying: "Don't worry. God wouldn't let Dad die on St. Patrick's Day." Heidi was in no state to remind her that SHE might be Irish, but I was German and God was neither.

The rescue team used drugs, including insulin, glucose, and sodium bicarbonate, and physical stimulation to get my heart beating again. There was no cardiologist in the hospital at the time, but Dr. McGillen managed to reach Dr. Manjeet Sethi, who was twenty-five miles away at a hospital in Evanston. She drove across the entire metropolitan area to help out, though she never had seen me before. To make sure my heart would not start slowing again, she threaded a temporary pacemaker down the subclavian vein near my collarbone into the right side of my heart to keep it beating in proper rythmn.

At one point, I tried to talk to my rescuers but could not form the words. Without success, I tried to tell them that I felt I was choking under the oxygen mask. Sometimes I was unconscious, at other times I was aware that people were doing things to me. Six or seven fog-enshrouded figures hovered on all sides, including Ken Peterson and a pretty nurse with red hair wearing a kelly green sweater. I thought she was appropriately dressed for the holiday. It bothered me that Ginny and Heidi had to go through this experience. And I wondered if this time I really was about to die. Then I drifted off, leaving them the job of keeping me alive or letting me go. I don't remember seeing Dr. Sethi at all that night.

By coincidence, the pastor of our church, Father Peter Bowman, showed up right after I "coded." While at a St. Patrick's Day party in our neighborhood, he had heard that I was back in ICU. Instead of ministering to me, he ended up giving a final anointing to the man who had just died in the next bed. The man's wife had told Ginny that her husband was Catholic and, though not a regular church-goer, would have wanted the final sacrament of his church. As for me, Ginny told Father Bowman that, since I had already received the last anointing three times in the last year, there was no sense doing it again.

"In his condition, he hasn't had the energy or the opportunity to do anything bad anyway," she told him.

After I was stabilized, Ginny spoke with Dr. McGillen. She reminded him that I had signed a living will expressing the wish not to be kept alive by extraordinary medical treatment, and that I believed in the Biblical injunction that "there is a time to live and a time to die." She asked John McGillen if we had reached the point where a "Do Not Resuscitate" notation should be put on my chart.

"No," he said. "We haven't reached that point. But if his kidneys should fail, that might be it."

Three days later it was one of Dr. McGillen's three partners, Dr. Vern Kerchberger, who came to see me on morning rounds. I could tell something was up because Ginny had come to the hospital earlier than usual and was standing quietly at the foot of my bed while the doctor hop-scotched his stethoscope around my chest and back.

Kerchberger, who was raised in Sioux Falls, South Dakota, was the youngest of the eight local doctors who were involved at one time or another in my care. He barely looked old enough to date our oldest daughter, and Ginny liked to tease him about his youthful appearance and mod haircut. He was married to Mary Kane, a gastroenterologist and daughter of a prominent local surgeon. Ginny, who by now could write a newsletter on the doings of the hospital and its staff, always was fascinated by the ease with which so many younger physicians could maintain a marriage, children, and two medical practices.

When he had finished examining me, Dr. Kerchberger pocketed his stethoscope, swung a lanky leg up on the metal frame of my bed, and leaned on the side rails like a cowboy. Ginny edged closer to the foot of the bed. Now I knew for sure something was up.

"I have something to say, and I want you to listen very closely," he said.

He told me that my doctors had done about all they could do for me. The next time the paramedics brought me to the hospital, it would likely be my final trip. Either I would be bleeding and they wouldn't be able to stop it, or something else would happen—like another heart stoppage. One way or another my time had just about run out.

"You have only one hope—and it's a slim hope."

I held up my hand to stop him right there. "Ginny already brought up the transplant. I don't even want to talk about it."

At that point, Dr. Kerberger could have shrugged and gone about his morning rounds. He had done his duty to inform me of every option and that was all that was expected of him. Instead he said, "Be quiet, Frank, and let me have my say."

He repeated what he had told Ginny before—that his brother had been a fellow in anesthesiology at Mayo and had worked with the liver transplant team that had been organized only two years earlier. While liver transplants were still rare, Mayo and a handful of other major medical centers recently were experiencing promising results with this high-risk procedure on the frontiers of medical science.

"There's no guarantee that you would be accepted because of your age and condition, but you ought to try."

I adopted a macho-religious argument: I did not want my last act on earth to be selfish. I was fully prepared to die and did not want to deprive some younger man or woman, maybe a parent with young children, of a scarce liver.

He told me that my argument showed I had no idea how the selection process is done. I would not be competing directly with anyone for a liver, that transplant matches are made on the basis of blood type, size, and other medical criteria. "Besides," he added, "Most donors are younger people killed in accidents—the recipients are mostly your age."

We volleyed back and forth while Ginny stood there silently. I realized that I was shutting her out of a decision she had every right to share, and I wished she would speak up.

"You're too young to just give up," he said. "You're about to be a grandfather for the first time. Your kids are all raised, and now you can enjoy the fruits of your labors. You still have a lot to do. You can do something not many people can do."

"What?"

"If they do accept you and if you do survive, you can write about the whole experience. Transplantation is a whole new field of medicine. You can do something most doctors can't do. Write about it."

I did not want to be convinced. Death no longer was my enemy. In some ways, it looked more like a friend that was about to free me and my family from a grueling ordeal. I was not sure that I wanted to come back to life—certainly not to what life had been for me and Ginny in the last few months.

Just then young Kerchberger threw his curve ball.

"Frank, if I left the hospital this morning and got killed out there on the expressway, I'd be happy if someone like you were kept alive with my liver."

I was stunned by what he had said. I looked up at this young doctor who was taking such a personal interest in Ginny's and my pain, and my eyes filled with tears.

"I'd do the same for you, Doc."

He jumped back and threw his arms up in mock horror. "I'd just as soon not have your liver, Frank."

That broke the tension. After we laughed a bit, he left us.

For some time we said nothing. I was still waiting for Ginny to voice her opinion, to give some indication of her feelings. But she was determined not to influence my decision. It was my dying. I would have to decide on my own how to go about it.

Despite Dr. Kerchberger's appeal, which had touched me deeply, I remained unconvinced that I should try for a transplant. Yet, deep inside, I knew that I owed too much to Ginny to quit now. I looked at her, and she looked at me. Then I made up my mind.

"We're off to see the Wizard."

13

MY LAST CONFESSION

nce the decision was made to try for the transplant, events began to move swiftly—almost too swiftly for me. Dr. Kerchberger called Dr. Jorge Rakela, the liver expert who had treated me earlier at Mayo Clinic, to ask if I might be considered for a liver transplant. The answer was simple and direct: I was to come to Mayo as soon as possible, check into Rochester Methodist Hospital where the sixty-member liver transplant unit was based, and begin physical and psychological testing to see if I would be accepted as a candidate. There were no guarantees that I would be chosen.

Ginny and I also learned that the cost for this most complicated single-organ transplant could reach $250,000—provided everything went smoothly. The estimate did not include the cost of antirejection medications that transplant patients must take daily for the rest of their lives. These could run anywhere from $7,000 to $12,000 a year depending on a patient's individual metabolism and physical condition. And it did not include the cost of the regular blood and physical checkups, which could run several thousand dollars a year.

Even in my semiconfused condition, I was taken back by these figures. Obviously, the only people who could afford a liver transplant in the United States were the extremely wealthy, those who were able to generate enough public sympathy for effective massive fund-raising, or those fortunate few who happened to have excellent health insurance. Unlike kidney transplants, for which public funds were available, liver transplants were then considered experimental by most private insurers and by the federal government.

The last thing I wanted was to undergo this exotic and dangerous surgery only to die and leave Ginny with an overwhelming debt. I was determined not to allow arrangements to proceed without finding out whether *Newsweek*'s health insurance would cover a liver transplant. If it did not, then that would be the end of such talk. I would be obscenely selfish to cling to life if it meant leaving my loved ones deeply in debt.

The logistics of reaching James Murphy, *Newsweek*'s benefits officer in New York, were overwhelming for me. By this time I was in a regular hospital room with a telephone beside my bed. But, because the hepatic encephalopathy intermittently scrambled my thinking, I could not remember my telephone credit card or *Newsweek*'s phone number in Manhattan, both numbers I had used several times daily for years. My roommate at the time, the kindly John Anderson, tried to help, urging me to relax and just try whatever numbers popped into my head. That didn't work. If only Ginny were there, but she was home making arrangements for closing up our house for our indefinite sojourn at Mayo Clinic.

To this day I don't remember how I managed to reach Jim Murphy in New York to ask about the insurance coverage. But, within a short time, he called back to tell me that the company's insurance would cover most of the cost of a liver transplant. That was all I needed to know. When John McCormick, my deputy bureau chief, telephoned to see how I was doing, I insisted that he relay a message to my editors, telling them of my plan to seek a transplant and tendering my resignation as bureau chief.

Ginny walked into my hospital room as I was dictating this message to John. What she heard stunned her. In my confusion, I was dictating a letter of resignation from *Newsweek,* not my resignation as bureau chief. If I resigned from *Newsweek* I would sacrifice my health insurance coverage. She left and called John from a pay phone, explaining my confusion and countermanding my message.

As it turned out, between Ginny, John McCormick, and bureau correspondent Pat King, a proper message was drafted, explaining to my editors that I had reached what doctor's call the "end-stage" of my disease, and that I was going to Mayo to be evaluated for a transplant. I also recommended that John take over as Chicago bureau chief.

As Pat King reassured John and Ginny, "That's what Frank would have said if he were sane."

For me the next week was less a time of hope than a time for saying good-bye. Deep in my heart I did not expect the experts at Mayo Clinic to accept me as a candidate for a liver transplant—not with my history of heart valve disease, my age, and my rapidly deteriorating physical condition. I was going through the motions for Ginny's sake. I owed her that much.

For the evaluation, I had the option of going to about forty hospitals or medical centers that at the time had done at least a few liver transplants. But only a dozen, including Mayo, did most of the 1,200 that were then being done each year. In addition to performing a sufficient number of liver transplants and having an experienced transplant team and support system, Mayo presented several other advantages for us: It was relatively close to home—only about a five-hour drive; Ginny and I were familiar with the clinic's logistics and favorably impressed by the doctors we had encountered there; I also felt Rochester would be cheaper for meals and lodging, and would be much safer than a larger city for Ginny, who would be wandering around town at all hours of the night.

Lastly, Dr. Kerchberger had told me that the Mayo transplant team reported lower average blood use during the long surgery than most transplant centers. This point was not lost on me because I was all too aware of how many units of blood I had already received in transfusions during the previous year. As a reporter, I knew the dangers of getting the AIDS virus through blood transfusions. Since March 1985, all blood and plasma donors were supposed to be tested for AIDS antibodies, but I knew that this requirement was not foolproof and that researchers still were concerned about the purity of blood donated at commercial plasma centers. Adding to my concern was the recent death of a friend of mine from AIDS he had contracted from tainted blood given him during open heart surgery.

In my condition, I probably was being overly cautious in worrying about getting AIDS from blood transfusions. One day when I mentioned my concern to Dr. Kerchberger, he smiled: "Frank, the last thing you have to worry about is getting AIDS." But, truth is, I did worry about it. And it was one more factor in my decision to seek a transplant in a small town in Minnesota rather than in Chicago or another large city such as Pittsburgh, which is the liver transplant center of the entire world. My odds of being alive in a few more months were not bright to begin with. Why make them worse by risking a contaminated blood transfusion?

Ginny once calculated that, from start to finish of my ordeal, I received 165 units of blood products—either whole blood, platelets (which promote clotting), plasma (the main fluid in blood), or packed red cells (the oxygen carriers). No matter what reassurances we were given by my doctors, I felt the risk was high that I might receive some infected blood that had slipped through the screening process. In fact, a report in the *Journal of the American Medical Association* three years after my transplant confirmed that intravenous drug abusers were continuing to sell blood and plasma at commercial blood centers despite the regulations.

My doctors did not want me to risk the trip to Rochester until they had me stablized after my latest brush with death. They decided to keep me hospitalized in Arlington Heights for at least a week. They also ruled out the five-hour car drive or a commercial airline flight, fearing I might have another hemorrhage on the journey. That left us with a transportation problem until my editors in New York stepped in to charter a private plane to carry Ginny and me to Mayo.

The week that I was being prepped for my trip to Mayo, I felt much like a prisoner on death row, methodically detaching myself from people and familiar surroundings as my time wound down. Old friends and family came to say good-bye. My college roommate, Frank Lolli, brought me a Mickey Mouse watch, which I still wear daily to the delight of small children and the bafflement of adults. College classmates and many people I knew in the news business telephoned to cheer me up, a number of them joking that a younger liver might do wonders for my libido. By then I could not even spell "libido" much less care whether it was functioning or not.

One evening my daughter Katie came to the hospital with a sonograph that her obstetrician had made to judge the size and development of the grandchild I never expected to see. The picture looked to me like a fuzzy weather map until Katie pointed out the contours of the infant's head and a leg that resembled a cloud formation. Nurses brought a stethoscope so I could try to hear any sound inside her belly. Katie stood there patiently as a nurse maneuvered the listening device all over her abdomen, but the baby was resting comfortably and would not even gurgle or kick for me. It was an emotional interlude for me since I had happy memories of my own grandparents and always had looked forward to being a grandfather. One of the saddest parts of dying for me was knowing that I would miss the joy of being a grandpa. I knew I would have been a great grandpa. Seeing the ultrasound picture was as close as I was going to come to seeing one of my grandchildren.

After Katie left that night, I scribbled in my journal: "If only I could live long enough to take a grandchild to see the Cubs in Wrigley Field! That's what my own Grandpa Mitchell did for me."

Besides showing me the sonographic "snapshot" of my grandchild, Katie also brought welcome news. Her friend Nancy Reed, the mother of baby Candice, who had died a year earlier during my first visit to the intensive care unit, had just delivered healthy twins, a boy and a girl. At a time when I was balancing between hope and resignation, I interpreted the news of the twins' birth as a sign of the deep freshness that surrounds our lives—if only we are responsive enough to detect it. Perhaps I was imposing more meaning upon events than they were meant to carry, but the closer I came to my own death, the more alert I became to the signs of life in others.

As usual, Ginny spent long hours at the hospital, arriving each morning with a steaming styrofoam cup of coffee and a newspaper, which I no longer could find strength or interest to read. Although she was beginning to look haggard and weary around the eyes, she always dressed like we were going to some snazzy place for brunch. Thinking back on it, I realize that not once did she ever show up at my hospital room looking the least bit sloppy or disarrayed, a simple kindness that always lifted my spirits. After spending so many days in hospital beds, I can attest that caregivers should try to be as neat and bright in dress as they are cheerful in words and facial expression. It's such a simple way to help lighten a patient's gray outlook.

One night Paul and Sandra Fullmer, two of our oldest friends, came to see me for what we thought might be the last time. Then they insisted on taking Ginny out to dinner. They could sense beneath her veneer of perkiness that she was beginning to wear down.

Late that night I woke to find Ginny scrunched up in a chair beside my bed, sound asleep. I was not surprised to see her. She was a bold gate-crasher, often slipping back into the hospital after visiting hours to say a late goodnight to me. As I lay there looking at her sleeping face, I suddenly was astounded that someone like Ginny would choose to love someone like me.

In a way, it is comforting to be able to take someone's love for granted—something I had done with Ginny for more than three decades. But real love isn't just for the good times; eventually it means having to share in someone else's pain and sadness. That's when you no longer take love for granted, but for what it is: a gift freely given.

When Ginny noticed that I was awake and staring at her, she climbed up on the hospital bed and lay down beside me. My room-mate, John, had been discharged that day so we were alone.

"Just like in *A Farewell to Arms*," she said.

"Not quite," I answered. "My spirit is willing, but my flesh is weak."

We held each other for a long time, like two cozy, but frightened, children during a thunderstorm.

That night, I experienced the same awe that had overwhelmed me a few nights before when, in the middle of the night, I awoke with a jolting thought: how absolutely mysterious and wonderful it is that anything exists at all!

If it did nothing else, my approaching death was making me much more mystical in my musings. I do not think this was related to the recurring episodes of hepatic encephalopathy; the insights were too vivid and numinous to be products of a mind-fogging ammonia buildup in the brain. And they could not be caused by any mind-altering medications, because I wasn't given any. Even mild pain killers are prescribed sparingly, if at all, to patients with impaired liver function. A ravaged liver just cannot perform the job of filtering drugs efficiently from the body.

All during the week that I was being prepared for my trip to the Mayo Clinic, sparkling insights kept exploding in my head, epiphanies so fresh, so simple, and so self-evident that I wondered why I had never thought of them before. It reminded me of those rare times in my life when I had been jolted out of the everyday world into a state that I can describe only as both enlightening and somehow holy.

I can recall a few times in my life prior to my illness when I felt particularly insightful and in tune with the universe. But only once before my illness did I ever have what I call a numinous flash of the sort I was increasingly experiencing as I neared my death. That was in the autumn of 1972 when *Newsweek* sent me on a week's auto trip through South Dakota to see what the home state folks thought of Senator George McGovern, then the Democratic nominee for president.

On a golden September afternoon, I stopped my rented car at the side of a country road, got out, spread the map of South Dakota out on the hood, and began searching for the elusive dot that represented the village of Pumpkin Center. Knowing the whims of my New York editors, I figured that some interviews with the voters in a place called Pumpkin Center would top off my story.

As I squinted at the map, suddenly the lone cloud in the sky wrapped itself around the sun, and the world turned from warm gold to cool gray. Shivering, I looked up from the map and realized that I was standing on the open prairie with not a tree, a house, a cow, or another human being anywhere between me and the horizon. Then I experienced for the only time in my life complete, absolute silence—not the chirp of a bird, not the swish of wind through tree or grass, not the rumble of a truck, or the howl of a train. Nothing but pure, primordial silence. As a city boy I never had "heard" total silence before—and it was both thrilling and frightening. Above all else it was holy, hinting of something just beyond my understanding, but something I longed for, was made for.

I stood stunned by silence on that empty highway, in that empty land, and understood—or came closer to understanding—what

Augustine must have meant when he wrote so many centuries ago: "Our hearts are made for Thee, Oh God, and they will not rest until they rest in Thee."

It was during the intensely emotional week prior to leaving for Mayo that I made my "last confession." To my amazement, I made it—not to a male priest—but to a lay person, a woman in fact. Margaret Moser heard my final confession.

Being ill as long as I had been—and having been advised in nonqualified terms that I was soon to die—I had received what Catholics now call the "Sacrament of Reconciliation" several times in the traditional manner, from a priest. But even then my confessions had been perfunctory and unsatisfying. As a practical matter, my illness certainly left me with little inclination or energy for bold, active sinning.

Near to death as I was, I still could not totally shed the habit I shared with so many life-long Catholics of thinking of sin as a technicality, as a violation of some rule or regulation, rather than a deeper, systemic selfishness that shattered my relationships with God and my fellow men and women.

What set me up for my impulsive last confession to Margaret was another of those sudden insights during a sleepless hospital night waiting for dawn to break. I was thinking of the friends and acquaintances who had stuck by Ginny and me throughout our troubles, particularly those people who had not previously been close to us. Among them was a former college classmate, a Chicago lawyer with a dry wit named James Griffin, someone I had seen only infrequently in the three decades since our graduation. Yet, when he learned of my illness, he called regularly just to see how I was doing and to get Ginny or me laughing.

A few years before, Jim Griffin had suffered a serious and agonizing back ailment that had hospitalized him for months in a body cast and had left him unable to play the piano, for which he had great talent. When I had heard of his troubles, I had felt sorry for him, but had gone on with my life. It never occurred to me to send a card or telephone, much less visit him. A reporter doesn't get involved, remember? I had too many important stories to write.

It was because he had gone through his own ordeal that Jim Griffin had acquired his empathy for someone else who was caught up in chronic suffering. Reflecting on that, for the first time I acknowledged to myself what always had lurked just below the "Mr. Nice Guy" image I so liked to project: I realized for the first time that my sins were not so much what I had done, but what I had failed to do.

I saw myself as a smugly satisfied boob who had insulated himself from other people's pain by hiding behind a reporter's "don't-get-involved" mask. I'm sure it has been written in different ways by far wiser heads than mine, but I experienced an insight that I hope never to forget: that the opposite of love isn't hate. It's indifference.

With that fresh understanding, I was prepared to talk the next morning when the ever-cheery Margaret Moser popped into my room on her daily rounds. What started out as a "chat" with Margaret evolved into my last confession as she simply opened her heart and listened to me tell about something that had been bothering me, without my really being conscious of it, for several years.

One of my closest and most reliable sources when I was doing a lot of political reporting was a lovely older woman who was active in Democratic politics. Over the years, she not only was a font of information for me in my work but also someone I grew to like and respect for her absolute integrity and unwavering good humor. One day I heard that she was dying of cancer in another city where she lived. I was deeply saddened by the news, and reacted in my expected fashion. As that sappy, self-indulgent popular song puts it: "I did it my way." I did nothing. Absolutely nothing. Every so often I thought about her and soothed my conscience by vowing someday to take a day off and drive to see her. I never even phoned her. I don't recall even sending a card. Then one day someone told me that she had died. And I felt sad. But I didn't even go to her funeral. I was too busy, the crucial chronicler of the day's news, with important duties to perform that far outweighed the simple piety of saying good-bye to a former friend.

Margaret heard me out and, thankfully, did not try to plaster any platitudes on my wounded conscience. The last thing I needed was for my confessor to downplay the seriousness of my offense or dilute my remorse. Her words of absolution were nonjudgmental but completely satisfying.

"I understand," was all she said, and all I needed to hear.

14

ON THE YELLOW BRICK ROAD

Monday, March 30, 1987. Today Ginny and I begin our great adventure. It is the last and most dangerous part of our journey, a journey that we did not volunteer to take. It was thrust upon us. All great stories are about journeys—from "Exodus" to The Wizard of Oz. *We do not always find what we expect at the end of a journey. Often we discover that the prize we were seeking is a treasure we've had all along.*

ong before sunup, I wrote that in my journal, before other patients were stirring or the day shift nurses had reported for duty. The corridors of Northwest Community Hospital were still dim and silent when a nurse came to make my morning blood pressure, pulse, and temperature checks, the so-called vital signs.

"You're up before the birds," she said cheerfully. Indeed, I already had shed the hated hospital gown, shaved, and washed as effectively as possible at the sink in my room and put on the tan corduroy trousers and plaid sports shirt that Ginny had brought the night before. After tugging loafers onto my swollen feet with great effort, I sat on the side of the bed, listening expectantly for the hum of voices at the nursing station down the hall and the first paging of a doctor on the public address system.

Since my hemorrhage the day before St. Patrick's Day, I had lived within the narrow strictures of the hospital routine. Now I felt like an excited schoolboy waiting for the bell to ring on the first day of summer vacation.

A private King Air jet plane chartered by *Newsweek* was scheduled to pick Ginny and me up in four hours at a private airfield only fifteen minutes drive from the hospital. The flight to Rochester, Minnesota, would take less than an hour. By noon I would be checked into a new hospital to begin our final adventure, the evaluation process that could lead to a new life-saving liver or, more likely I suspected, the start of the final countdown on my life.

Though the sun was just rising, I fretted because Ginny was not yet at the hospital with our bags. I was convinced that some snafu would upset our plans; maybe one of my doctors would fail to show up to discharge me or the nurses would not have my medical records ready in time for me to meet the plane. A hospital patient lives in a narrow world where insignificant details take on disorienting importance. After spending so many days in a rigid routine where every decision was made for me, I was both excited and paranoid about the prospect of venturing into the real world again, even for a short trip.

Neither John McGillen nor Vern Kerchberger, my regular doctors, were in town to discharge me and send me packing to Mayo Clinic. Another of their partners, Dr. Joseph Franger, was deputized to do the job. That did not bother me at all since his subspeciality was gastroenterology and, besides, he had graduated a few years behind me from my old high school, Fenwick, back in Oak Park. I was comforted by anything or anyone familiar.

As anxious as I was about the details of my leaving the hospital, I knew that if Dr. Franger were called away in an emergency, then Dr. Miles Lynch, the senior doctor in the practice, was familiar with my case and could easily handle my checkout. He was the one who had removed the heart pacemaker that had been planted in me during my St. Patrick's Day emergency. He also was a favorite of Ginny's because he reminded her of her late father, a classical West Side Irishman who knew all of the same families, folklore, and characters as she did.

One thing that a hospitalized patient values is continuity of care, the feeling that the doctors and nurses bouncing into your room really have a handle on your individual problems. That was a concern Ginny and I did not have with the medical workshop of Lynch, Franger, McGillen, and Kerchberger.

I often thought that maybe it was because all the doctors in the practice knew me as "Ginny Maier's husband" that they always seemed on top of my case. Patients today become terribly anxious seeing a changing succession of doctors and nurses revolving through the day like substitutes in a football game. Because so many physicians today work in group practices, a hospitalized patient often is confronted by a confusing array of new medical faces, depending on who is on duty or assigned to rounds that day.

This round-robin of care is even more pronounced with the nursing staff, which changes three times every twenty-four hour period. It can become particularly distressing for a patient who gets the impression that the only thing the caregiver knows about him is what he or she hastily reads on the chart just before bounding through the door.

The worst time for patients is over a weekend or long holiday. That's when part-time nurses often are on the job, the so-called weekend warriors. They may be qualified and caring professionals, but the truth is they do not have the same experience and knowledge of the routines as do the regular nurses. I had one weekender try to give me the wrong medication and another leave a pair of pliers in my bed. Try sleeping on a pair of pliers—it takes your mind off your other troubles! One weekend, Ginny diverted a nurse delivering me a high-protein dinner tray at a time when I was supposed to be on a low-protein diet because of my state of hepatic confusion.

One maxim that any regular hospital patient learns is never to have the heparin lock for your IV line changed after regular hours or on a weekend. That's when you get the least experienced implant-ers, who can turn what is always an uncomfortable procedure into an agonizing ordeal. For that matter, it is best not to have any blood work done in off hours. In my case, my veins were too worn and abused to have anyone tapping them who still was undergoing on-the-job training. I needed someone with a lot of experience and a very light touch.

Despite my anxiety, my discharge went smoothly. Dr. Joe Franger had all my records in order, gave me a swift examination and a handshake. A friend, Arlene Rauch, had volunteered to drive us to the airport. She brought me a small carry-on bag filled with candy, pens, notepaper, and four paperback mysteries. Like a schoolboy afraid of losing his homework, I insisted on carrying the thick manilla envelope containing my medical records, rejecting Ginny's sensible suggestion that I put them in one of our traveling bags.

Since we were an hour early for the plane, I asked Arlene to swing by our house en route to the airport. For some reason, I wanted to sit in the cool kitchen, which always smelled like cinnamon and apples even though Ginny never baked. I always wondered if she sprayed some essence of apples and cinnamon when I wasn't looking. I can't explain why I had to sit in the house we had lived in for more than two decades; perhaps I feared I never would see it again, or maybe I needed to recharge my spirits in a familiar environment after being in a sterile institutional setting for so long. Whatever the reason, I felt much happier and refreshed as we pulled away and headed for the airport.

Without any notion of how long we would be at the Mayo Clinic, Ginny arranged to shut up our house like rich folk going on a junket to Europe. She stopped the newspaper deliveries and lined up a neighbor boy to cut the lawn when needed. Our married daughter Katie, who lived about a mile away, volunteered to pick up our mail and check the house every few days on her way home from work. It also was decided that Katie would become the main local "switchboard operator," relaying my condition reports from Ginny to the rest of the family and our close friends.

I felt like a pioneer abandoning home and most of my belongings to explore unknown territory where few had ventured before. I was the first patient from Northwest Community Hospital, a large medical center in a growing metropolitan area of Chicago, to seek a liver transplant. At that time, fewer than 1,000 liver transplants were being attempted yearly in the entire country. Just five years earlier, only sixty-two livers had been transplanted. Even many medical professionals had virtually no knowledge of the emerging technology of organ transplantation.

Up to that time, none of the eight doctors who had helped keep me alive during the last year had yet treated a liver transplant patient. They could not tell us what procedures or timetable to expect at Mayo. And they could offer no estimate on how long I might have to wait for a transplanted liver, provided I were accepted as a candidate. We did not even have a concept of our logistical needs at Rochester—such basic questions as where Ginny would stay while I was being evaluated at the hospital, how much cash to take or even if we should take summer clothing with us.

Before our jet had reached cruising altitude over southern Wisconsin, Ginny had poured us coffee from a thermos and, ever the explorer, decided to go up front to get acquainted with the pilot, a young man named Dennis Foley. To my dismay, she climbed into the empty copilot's seat and began asking him all sorts of questions about how the plane's controls worked and why he became a pilot.

"Don't touch anything," I hollered at her from the back of the plane, where I was contemplating the snowdusted fields below and thinking gloomy thoughts.

"Don't worry, Frank, were having an nice conversation," she yelled back.

"Don't let your feet touch the pedals," I shouted. By now my stomach was churning like a cement mixer.

"Frank . . ." she said in an annoyed tone.

"It's okay," Dennis yelled back to me.

Next thing I heard was Ginny lecturing poor Dennis about not wearing sunglasses.

"What would your mother say if she knew you were flying in this glare without sunglasses?"

"Ginnn—ey!" I shouted. "Let the poor man fly the airplane!"

Soon, Dennis was telling Ginny his life story, ignoring—or so it seemed to the anxious passenger in back—the babble of radio messages from air controllers in Minneapolis and Rochester. I was convinced that the messages all were aimed at our plane, if only

Dennis could hear them. I had visions of the jet crashing into a Minnesota stubble field because Dennis, blind without his sunglasses, was unable to hear landing instructions above Ginny's chatter.

Ginny has this easy nack for talking to strangers. Maybe it is because she really listens that people so easily open up to her. Her innate talent for striking up conversations always fascinated and, at times, annoyed me. I remember how upset I would get when she would answer an unsolicited phone call and stay on the line talking to some aluminum siding or penny stock salesman, ignoring my frantic shouts, "Tell them we don't want any!"

Our children used to say without exaggeration that their mother could talk for a half hour to a wrong number. (Once Ginny fainted by the swimming pool while on vacation with her sister-in-law, Patti Ryan, who paid her the ultimate compliment: "Ginny, you'd be proud to know that you kept talking all the way down.")

On our flight to Mayo Clinic we reverted to preillness habits—me grouchy and uptight, she gregarious and curious. One thing I learned about dying: it may give you sharper insights and peace of spirit, but it doesn't automatically change all the bad habits of a lifetime. If you are basically a Nervous Nelly—as I am—you remain a Nervous Nelly, only more so.

In early afternoon our taxi pulled up to the emergency room of Rochester Methodist Hospital, one of two hospitals operated by the Mayo Clinic. At first, the duty nurse could not locate my clinic records, which were supposed to be awaiting my arrival. She did not seem at all interested in my own packet of medical records which I tried to foist on her. Despite Ginny's efforts to calm me, I began stewing like an outraged theater-goer when his expected tickets are not waiting at the box office. All the resignation and peace that had enfolded me the previous week simply evaporated, leaving me an exhausted wreck with an upset stomach. What was I doing here anyway? All I wanted right then was to turn around and fly home as fast as possible.

Finally my Mayo file was located and I found myself whirling along a long corridor in a wheelchair, overnight bag on my lap, and my precious packet of medical records still clutched to my breast. The young woman "escort" pushing the wheelchair carried the newly located Mayo records, which I was beginning to understand were the only ones that counted.

Ginny had disappeared, and I was completely confused, not knowing if I were in the basement of the hospital or an upper floor. "Where you from?" the uniformed escort asked. I was to discover that this is the inevitable opening line of every escort I ever encountered at Mayo—sort of the medical equivalent of the yuppy bar's "What's your sign?" (At first I always answered, "Chicago," but later, after hearing the inquiry once too often and needing some harmless amusement, I would make up exotic hometowns—Skagway, Alaska, or whatever popped to mind.)

Soon I was in a sixth floor room, grudgingly putting on the required open-backed gown that always made me feel so vulnerable and powerless. Part of Rochester Methodist is designed like most hospitals, with nursing stations centrally located on long corridors. But other sections, including where I was assigned, were of radial design with the nursing station in the center ringed by patient rooms. These silo-shaped units are comforting to the patient, who always is in sight and sound of the nursing station, and comforting to the nurses, who do not have to put as much mileage on their feet as they do working on a conventional hospital floor.

I was starving but the nurses would not order me any food until a doctor examined me. Before I could even stretch out on the bed, another of the uniformed escorts appeared at the door like a smiling genie. Soon I was again speeding down a corridor in a wheelchair, this time wrapped tightly in a light blanket. Other wheelchairs pushed by other escorts passed us like traffic on an busy expressway. The hospital was a beehive of activity.

"Where you from?" asked the dark-haired young man.

"Where we going?" I asked in return.

"X-ray. Always start with x-ray."

There was no waiting. The chest x-rays were done in less than five minutes. Still another escort, this time an older man, pushed me back to the sixth floor at a much slower pace. He forgot to ask where I was from. Maybe he had been at it too long. By now I was seriously hungry, having had nothing but orange juice at dawn's early light back in Northwest Community Hospital. The nurses were sympathetic, but firm. Nothing by mouth until a doctor saw me. Where was

Ginny anyway? I felt like a little boy abandoned by his mother without his lunch box on the first day of school.

By mid-afternoon I became resigned to my fate and stretched out on the bed to watch an old Perry Mason rerun on television. The hunger pangs actually had subsided, leaving me drowsy and almost contented.

I was awakened by a man's cough. I looked up to see a dark-haired young man with trim moustache and studious-looking horn-rimmed glasses. He wore a light blue lab coat, unlike the usual Mayo physician's business suit. "Hi, I'm Mark Perrella," he said, shaking my hand and pulling a chair up to the bed.

"I was just looking through your records . . .," he began hesitantly.

I reached over to the bedside table and produced my own records for his inspection.

"Not those," he said. "These," he said, tapping my Mayo file. "There's something I don't understand."

By now I was used to doctors telling me all sorts of things, some good and some bad, but never had they told me they didn't understand something.

"What is it?" I asked.

"If your trouble is with your pancreas, why are you here for a liver transplant?"

That was indeed a very good question. I had no idea what my pancreas—wherever it was and whatever it did—had to do with my failing liver. Had the doctors back home missed something? Or had Mayo's experts told Ginny and me about a problem with my pancreas when they had first told me the bad news about my liver, and we just didn't hear it?

Dr. Perrella, who I later learned was a resident doing his gastrointestinal service, looked at me for some explanation. I could think of nothing—except to again shove my records from home at him. Without other options, he finally looked down at my packet of records. Then he did a double-take.

"You aren't from South Dakota?" he asked in disbelief. Everybody at Mayo seemed interested in where I was from.

"No."

"Is your name Franklin Maier?"

"No."

Welcome to Mayo Clinic, the world's most prestigious and efficient medical center—where ultimately the whole house of cards rests on the competence of human beings.

Somewhere in the records room in the bowels of the Mayo complex a clerk had pulled the wrong file, carelessly identifying it by name rather than the assigned Mayo number, which, like your social security number, never changes. Young Dr. Perrella had been given the file of a patient with a name similar to mine, but with an entirely different disease.

While my correct file was located, the nurses relented and gave me something to eat: a dab of cottage cheese, a piece of low-protein dry toast, and a ripe pear. I thought it tasted terrific.

I couldn't wait to tell the missing Ginny about the records mix-up. That really would give her something to talk about.

15

GINNY'S FELLA

While I began my battery of physical tests and interviews in the hospital, Ginny set up housekeeping in an economy motel a few blocks south of the main clinic building in downtown Rochester. Within days she received two job offers, one from the motel manager after she volunteered to wash the long-neglected windows, the other from clinic grounds keepers, who were impressed with her stopping to pull weeds on the way to visit me. As a dedicated neatnik and addicted gardener, Ginny no more could pass a paper-strewn or unweeded patch of earth than Mother Teresa could ignore a starving beggar.

But Ginny was too busy learning the geography of Rochester, probing the innards of the Mayo Clinic complex, and getting a quick education in transplant medicine to think about a job. First thing she did was buy a pair of walking shoes so she could explore the hilly city of some 63,000 mostly benevolent souls; a fine town for walking, especially in the spring when the trees and shrubs in yards and parkways are exploding in white and pink blossoms.

At a nursery she bought two pots of red geraniums which she wedged into the shoe box. Using a discarded venetian blind cord found in the motel laundry room, she tied her colorful "window box" to the wrought iron railing on the balcony outside her room.

Even on a dollhouse scale, Ginny needed something bright, alive, and growing to remind her of the garden she had left at home.

She borrowed the white Chevy of the young woman who was the motel's afternoon desk clerk to drive to the shopping mall on the western border of town. There she bought pillows to replace the pancaked ones in her room, some heavy-duty bath towels, an extension cord for the telephone, an ironing board and iron, and a small electric fan. To her dismay, she discovered at the mall that the borrowed car—which the owner called "The Bomber"—had no reverse gear, an incumbrance when trying to back out of parking places. When I heard about it, I made Ginny promise never again to borrow "The Bomber," which, I was certain, had liability insurance that matched its missing reverse gear.

Judging from her subsequent reports of journeys around town, I suspect it was a vow she did not keep. While I would trust Ginny with my life—as the last few years amply demonstrated—I always could tell when she was not about to follow my advice on some matter, big or small. When she was determined to do things her way no matter what her worrywart husband said, she invariably would distract me by one of two ploys—depending on her mood, my level of indignation, or whether we were in public or private. She either would (1) charge at me and start tickling my ribs until I forgot what I was upset about (this tactic she most often used in public, knowing I would retreat in befuddled embarrassment); or (2) shift the subject so quickly and radically that I would be left sputtering over something outrageous that SHE just said, forgetting what I had been lecturing her about.

In the last few years I have come to realize that one reason Ginny and I have been successful in this difficult business of staying married is that both of us have learned when to take each other seriously and when not to.

To those friends who did not know that we were at Mayo Clinic and what we were doing there, Ginny mailed brief notes written on her "Robert Redford" cards. These dated from a night we had our picture taken with actor Robert Redford at a cocktail party to raise funds for research into Sudden Infant Death Syndrome. I made the mistake that every politician avoids—allowing myself to be caught at the end of a line when the photographer snapped the picture.

When Ginny got the negative, she cropped me off the end and had her friend Elaine Pittas, who worked for a printer, make a few hundred notecards featuring Robert Redford with his arm around a beaming Ginny. These were the cards she mailed to her friends, with the scribbled query under Redford's face: "Don't you think Frank has gotten better looking since he's been sick?"

Each morning Ginny rose at dawn so she could sit in the tiny lobby of the motel, talking to the men and women who gathered there to share ailments, coffee, and glazed donuts while waiting for the vans that would haul them to their appointments in the clinic buildings. She enjoyed the camaraderie of the lame and the ill, easily extracting intimacies that they probably had not even told their closest relatives. When she bounced into my hospital room before nine each morning, she always had one or two wonderful tales of eccentricity or reports of rare maladies endured by one or more of the Mayo pilgrims she had encountered.

Each day Ginny made new acquaintances from hamlets and cities all over the United States and a few foreign countries. Close to 300,000 persons come to the Rochester medical center each year, from every state and 150 foreign countries. Within days of our arrival, Ginny had collected a score of new names in her address book, some identified down to ZIP Code and telephone number, others known only by first name or by a nickname—like "Aunt Grace," who had moved to Rochester just to be close to the clinic.

On one of her daily walks through the neighborhoods near the clinic, Ginny was joined by a smiling middle-aged man from New Jersey, who volunteered that he was staying at a retreat house in Rochester for alcoholic priests. Walking was part of his therapy, and he and Ginny became strolling companions through the parks and residential neighborhoods, including the so-called Pill Hill area of stately old homes where many of the clinic's physicians live. What most amazed the priest was how open and friendly everyone in town was—even though he never wore his Roman collar or any clerical garb that might tip people off to his profession. "Maybe we live too close together and feel threatened," he offered in expiation of his flock back in New Jersey.

During what turned out to be a 110-day sojourn in town, Ginny and I both responded to this pervasive quality of friendliness among

Rochestertonians, a civic habit developed far beyond the openness that I had encountered over the years as a reporter visiting many midwestern cities.

So many people in Rochester are in the "healing business" or depend on it for their daily bread that being polite, friendly, and cheerful have become civic virtues that are taken for granted by everyone from waitresses to gas station attendants.

Although Mayo Clinic dominates the city, it is not the only big employer in town. The clinic and its two hospitals, Rochester Methodist and St. Mary's, are the city's economic mainstay with 16,000 people, most of them well paid and highly educated, on the payroll. But the city's vibrant economy also is enriched by IBM, which employs 7,400 in its 3.5-million-square-foot plant north of town, the biggest IBM facility in the world under one roof.

If you are in good enough physical condition to appreciate where you are, visiting the Mayo Clinic can be a relaxing and pleasant experience, sort of like going to a ball game. Nobody feels threatened, nobody is out to impress anybody else with who they are or what they do—though there is a bit of one-upmanship when it comes to comparing diseases. When you are sitting on a wooden bench awaiting a chest x-ray with a bunch of strangers in hospital gowns, all of you looking like nervous parachutists waiting to jump, nobody much cares if you are a pig farmer from Waterloo or a tycoon from Wall Street. Sickness is a great leveler.

On any given day there always are celebrities of some magnitude somewhere in the clinic maze. Despite Mayo's discreet shuffling of VIPs in special elevators and dark-windowed limos, everybody in town seems to know which show biz or political personalities are undergoing exams or surgery, long before the clinic's low-key public relations department acknowledges their presence.

But some of the best-known or notorious temporary residents of Rochester happen to reside, not at the Mayo complex, but at the medical center on the eastern outskirts of town operated by the Federal Bureau of Prisons. About 750 federal prisoners with chronic diseases or in need of medical care are held there, along with a service crew of nonviolent prisoners who maintain the grounds, mop the floors, and serve the meals. I knew of quite a few Chicago aldermen and mob flunkies who had vacationed there. (One of my transplanted friends, Jim Werneski, of Kenosha, Wisconsin, later told me about the lonesome Christmas Eve when he and his wife could find nowhere else open for dinner but the coffee shop in the Kahler Hotel. The only other diner in the place was Tammy Faye Bakker, in town to visit her fallen evangelist husband, Jim, at the federal prison-hospital.)

There is a predictable rhythmn of the week at Mayo Clinic. On Saturday and most of Sunday, downtown Rochester, where the clinic buildings are clustered, becomes a ghost town. By mid-afternoon Sunday, cars and campers with license plates from all over the country begin arriving. Taxies and hotel vans flit from the hotels, past the giant corncob water tower at the vegetable packing plant to the airport eight miles south of town, where they pick up the new arrivals, many of them balancing on canes, shuffling behind walkers, or being pushed in wheelchairs.

The luggage piled up in hotel lobbies reflects the economic spectrum of the thousands of pilgrims who come each week to the healing mecca in the hills of southern Minnesota. Some people arrive with only canvas tote bags or battered square-rigged suitcases, but others arrive like potentates at the head of retinues of family and retainers bearing mounds of designer luggage. Bib overalls are just as prevalant on the streets of Rochester as three-piece suits.

Monday the main clinic building with its 1,000 identically furnished examining rooms starts filling up with newcomers, many of them wan and weary from chronic pain, but others—those in town for annual physicals—in almost a holiday mood, eager to see what changes have occurred since their last visit and whether their favorite doctors are still in residence and their favorite restaurants still open. The underground walkways and—in good weather—the streets are a swirl of fast-moving, white-clad nurses, technicians, and medical clerks.

On Tuesday and Wednesday, the clinic buildings and restaurants become as crowded and bustling as commuter stations at rush hour. But on Thursday afternoon, the exodus begins. The healed and the hypochondriacal pull up stakes first, leaving behind the stragglers still awaiting appointments or the unfortunate ones requiring more tests, surgery, or hospitalization. By Friday afternoon, the waiting rooms are as deserted as bus stations at midnight, and the only crowds are at the billing windows on the first floor of the main clinic building where people settle their accounts before heading home. A few people actually count out hard cash or write checks, but most just sign insurance papers.

Before long, Ginny knew the names of many store clerks in the lower level of the hulking Kahler Hotel that sits regally and conveniently in the middle of the bustling medical complex. That first week Ginny also met with the staff in the business office to sign papers and arrange for them to talk directly with *Newsweek*'s benefits department in New York to guarantee my insurance coverage. Cynics call this procedure the "wallet biopsy"—a ritual that all potential transplant recipients must undergo along with the required physical tests and psychological interviews. To get on a liver transplant waiting list anywhere in the country, would-be organ recipients must show that they have insurance to cover most of the cost (which can range up to $250,000 for the basic liver transplant and hospitalization) or can raise a substantial good-faith down payment through a combination of fund-raising, borrowing, or begging.

Unlike many who accompany the ailing to the clinic, Ginny never seemed to have an idle moment in her day. Though she always had something on her agenda—someone to see or someplace to go—she never neglected me. In fact, often late at night I would have to nag her to go back to the motel and get some rest. One side benefit of being in a town like Rochester was that I never worried about Ginny walking back to her motel alone, no matter what time of night.

We also discovered that tradespeople in Rochester are quite casual in running their shops. One night after Ginny had enjoyed a pizza at a popular restaurant near the clinic, she discovered that it did not take credit cards. Since she usually walks around with about fifty-three cents in her purse, this presented a problem—not immediately, she found, but in ever paying the bill. The cashier said to pay it next time she was passing. She immediately cashed a check at the clinic business office and rushed back to settle the pizza account. But no one would accept her money because they had no record of the debt. Come back when the manager was around, they said. It took her four days and four trips to get them to accept— grudgingly—what she told them she owed.

After seeing a sign that said: "Every six minutes a patient in the Mayo Medical Center needs blood," Ginny went to the blood bank to donate, only to be turned down because her spouse suffered from chronic hepatitis.

The Mayo blood bank told her they would rather be cautious. It was the first time that Ginny, who regularly gave blood back home, had ever been rejected as a donor. With me already paranoid about the subject and facing the certainty of more transfusions if accepted for a transplant, this only reinforced our confidence in the purity of the Mayo blood supply.

To my amazement, Ginny also somehow found time and opportunity in her dawn-to-midnight schedule to meet a number of other patients who were at the clinic for evaluation for liver transplants— and to talk with some recipients who were recuperating after their transplants. How she met them was a mystery to me; I hardly knew anyone. My days were filled with endless trips by wheelchair to various examining rooms in the hospital or to nearby clinic buildings, where I was poked, punctured, or scanned by either machine or technician. In between the physical tests, I was constantly questioned by men and women on the transplant team or by various consultants whose names I never could quite catch. They kept grilling me about my physical history, family background, and attitude toward life.

As someone who had made my living by asking questions, I tried to fathom what each of my inquisitors was trying to learn about me. Obviously, some of them were trying to uncover everything possible about my physical ailments and medical history. I remember one young woman cardiologist who grilled me relentlessly about my childhood ailments, particularly the two bouts of rheumatic fever that had damaged my heart valves when I was a teenager and the episode on St. Patrick's Day when my heart slowed to a stop. Even in my often confused state, it did not take me long to realize that the biggest roadblock between me and getting accepted for a liver transplant was the doctors' concern over the condition of my heart— whether that damaged fist-shaped pump could stand up to the rigors of such grueling surgery.

But other inquisitors seemed to be probing another flank—trying to determine if I had the commitment and family support to undergo the trauma of the high-risk surgery. Just as important, did I have the discipline to cope with the potent antirejection drugs, life-style changes, and susceptibility to diseases that transplant patients must face for the rest of their lives?

In those early days, I still was something less than a sincere applicant for an organ transplant. I remained unconvinced about the entire process—doubtful that the Mayo liver team would end up accepting me and unsure if I really wanted to undergo such an exotic and arduous surgery when the outcome appeared so tenuous.

But the more involved I became in the tests and interrogations, the more a dim hope started glowing deep inside me. When I sensed that my examiners seemed to be taking me seriously as a candidate, I started to get serious too. In a way, I was frightened by this emerging hope. Without hope, I had nothing to lose. With hope, I became vulnerable again—just like everybody else.

Despite these doubts, like a schoolboy I began to worry about passing my exams. I found myself wanting to impress the doctors, nurses, and social workers with my positive attitude.

One way Ginny came to know so many members of the sixty-member liver transplant team and the half dozen other prospective transplant patients then being evaluated was by attending the twice-a-week support group sessions conducted by the social workers in the patient lounge at Station 53, the liver transplant unit. The first week I was in the hospital, I never made any of these sessions because I always was undergoing a test for something, from routine dental checks to echocardiograms and more risky procedures, like still another biopsy of my liver or endoscopic examination of my battle-worn esophagus.

I also was learning what it was like to be a patient in a hospital that is connected to a medical school. (Mayo's small but prestigious school graduates about forty new doctors a year.) One morning a young doctor popped into my room and asked if I would mind being examined by two of her students. The doctor herself did not look much older than my daughter Katie, who was in her late twenties, and the solemn young man and woman accompanying her looked like two nervous kids on a blind date for the junior prom.

As she began using me as her teaching dummy, I felt like a bit player in an episode of "St. Elsewhere." I tried to hold perfectly still as she demonstrated how to locate the boundaries of my liver, thumping her way across my rib cage and chest. With a glance of apology my way, she commented that my liver appeared to be shrunken and harder than a healthy one. Then she told each of the students to try their luck at locating my liver and "feeling" its texture. Both of them looked at her in horror, as if she had asked them to hit me in the jaw. I decided to help out: "Go ahead, just start poking," I encouraged them.

On the way out, the doctor-professor thanked me for my patience in playing guinea pig. I thanked her for breaking the boredom of my day. Another time I was interviewed by a medical student who was doing a study on the psychological effects of chronic illness. All in all, despite the anxiety of not knowing if I was on the verge of dying or experiencing a medical miracle, I thoroughly enjoyed being observed—and observing—what was going on in Rochester Methodist Hospital. My only regret was that I was not on top of my game so I could make better notes and save the material for use in a story.

This holiday mood evaporated with my first "scary" procedure. Late one afternoon, Dr. Perrella appeared at my bedside and announced casually that he was going to tap a few hundred cubic centimeters of ascitic fluid from my bulging belly. I was alarmed that he intended to do it right there in my bed without the benefit of any anesthetic. By this time in my illness I no longer was overly sensitive to pain. But anxiety is a harder companion to shake than pain. If a doctor was going to cut me open and insert a drain line into my abdomen, I would just as soon be knocked out while the work was in progress. I did not even like the impersonal name he used for the procedure—"abdominal paracentesis." It sounded a bit too much like major surgery to be done outside the sterile confines of an operating room.

Since my stretched belly was making it hard for me to breathe, I realized they had to do something. Lasix, a strong diuretic they had prescribed from my first day in the hospital, did not seem to be having much success in reducing the ascites. (I was amused when they put me on Lasix because I recalled that horse trainers also use it to control pulmonary bleeding in thoroughbreds. One thing about being a general assignment reporter: you become an expert in trivia.)

After a nurse spent five minutes scrubbing my abdomen with the purple-brown antiseptic Betadine, the doctor made a quick nip with a scalpel and inserted what looked like a plastic tube or catheter into the incision. While the golden colored fluid slowly collected in the drainage bag, the nurse periodically took my blood pressure to make sure I was not going into shock from the sudden loss of fluid. About forty-five minutes later, Dr. Perrella returned, popped out the tube, stitched the small incision, and held up the container of ascitic fluid like a brewmeister inspecting a stein of beer. "Nice and clear," he said. Since I was by then trying hard to pass my tests, I was quite pleased with his assessment of my output. It also felt good to have a flatter belly—even though I knew it was only temporary.

That same night I expected Ginny to join me for dinner in my room, a homey practice that the hospital encouraged. She either could bring in her own carryout meal from the outside, or place an order with the dieticians who were charged with my daily diet. But to my dismay, Ginny informed me that she had a date for dinner with some man she had met named "Art." They were going to a fancy restaurant atop the Kahler Hotel.

Dying or not, I was hurt and jealous—until she explained that Art was eighty-three years old, had been born in a mining camp in Alaska, had buried two wives, lost two fortunes, and was at the clinic for treatment of a multitude of ailments.

"He probably is looking for his third wife," I warned Ginny. "Wait until he finds out you can't cook."

Art was one of many wounded or lonesome folk Ginny befriended during our Mayo days. It was another example of her native empathy for people who cannot possibly do her the slightest material good. As much as she focused on me during my sickness, she still found time to get involved in other people's lives, a habit that came naturally to her, but something I was only beginning to learn—at a very late hour.

She and Art often had coffee together or just sat and talked about his multiple health problems and the tests he was facing. Then one day he simply disappeared and she never saw him again. Because of the confidentiality of patient records, she never could find out if Art went back to Alaska or what happened to him.

But, to this day, she tells our friends about the meals and conversation she shared at a very dark time in her life with this crusty old gentleman from Alaska. And I am certain that Art—wherever he is—has fond memories of the lively little woman who got such a kick out of explaining to him such mysteries as why the lemon accompanying his fish in that fancy restaurant was wrapped in gauze.

16

VISITING MISS MOONEY

It didn't happen all at once. But sometime during the course of dying I began to regress to my childhood. I became a little boy again. Or at least I began to spend more of my time drifting through the backwaters of my memories. Maybe it was because childhood had been a happy time for me, and I needed to get back to the days when problems and joys were smaller and simpler. Or perhaps it was because, no longer able do things for myself, I felt more like a child than an adult.

In the year that I thought would be my last, Ginny often had to bathe me like a little baby and help me dress. There were times when I could not even pull my socks on. Friends and family started to address me with the slow gentle tones that one uses when talking to a child. People whispered outside my hearing, like they do when a child is not supposed to know something.

Unable to work, often unable to read or write, I drifted into the passive daydreaming world of a child. I fretted about the trivialities of life, what food was served to me, where my possessions were stowed. I remember one time getting furious with Ginny for moving a newspaper from one spot to another on my hospital bedside tray. I needed to have everything in its place. Like a child, I became protective of my territory and my "toys." Above all else, as my hold on life became more tenuous, I began spending more and more time in the world of my memory.

I recall one night, shortly after arriving at Rochester Methodist Hospital for my pretransplant tests, when a torrent of sadness overwhelmed me and I heard myself praying aloud to God, "Please remember me. I'm just a little kid."

Immediately I felt embarrassed for making such a pathetic appeal, actually shuddering like a dog trying to shake water from his back. I was ashamed to think that a mature man and father of four grown children would feel so sorry for himself that he would try to bluff God into special paternal or maternal care.

At the time, I never told anyone about my trips back to childhood. I was not sure even Ginny would understand, particularly since she is by disposition more pragmatic in facing problems than I ever have been, even when healthy. She always copes with obstacles by attacking them head-on. I usually try to ignore or zig-zag around them.

Months later, back at home, Dr. John McGillen told me that regression is fairly common among the seriously ill, and in some cases it can be a major obstacle in their treatment. Some chronically ill patients revert to such childlike behavior that it becomes nearly impossible for their doctors to communicate with them about even such simple matters as their medications.

Externally, I never showed any evidence of my regressive behavior—if indeed that was what I was experiencing. All I know is that the flight to childhood started during the year of my multiple hemorrhages and increased during the period of my testing at Mayo Clinic. I can detect it in many of the entries in my journal. Increasingly I drifted back to boyhood, usually to the time when I was about ten years old. I was like Ebenezer Scrooge peeping through the frosted window at his younger, happier self. I never deliberately went back to that land to find that little boy. The boy always came seeking me.

This boy who visited me always wore gray corduroy knickers with black high-top boots. The right boot had a tiny pocket that held a red-handled jack-knife. He wore a leather aviator cap like Charles Lindberg on his flight across the Atlantic.

The little boy and I climbed up into the old elm in Kelly's lot that had been split one night by a lightning bolt. There was a "V" crotch high in the tree, which became the cockpit of our B-17. Somehow the boy merged into me and I was flying a mission over Japanese territory—just like the old days. At my side was my regular copilot, who looked like Van Johnson in the movie *Thirty Seconds Over Tokyo.* I called him Biff because it sounded somehow manly and loyal. On occasion, our plane would be so decimated by attacking swarms of Japanese zeros that Biff and I would be forced to bail out of our crippled aircraft. Being the pilot, I would order the rest of the crew to jump first. Then, after making sure the doomed plane was not pointed at any churches or playgrounds, I would climb out on a branch, hang for a few deliciously scary seconds, and then let go, plunging twenty feet down through the black smoke and enemy gunfire. Biff and I must have hit the silk hundreds of times, but I only turned my ankle once during all of World War Two.

My father, who had died at age eighty-six, just four years before my transplant, often became a partner in the daydreaming of my ten-year-old self. Unlike my heroic battles against the Japanese warlords, the adventures with my father all really once happened, though they had faded from my consciousness long ago. Now they reappeared before my glazed eyes as vivid and distinct as players on a stage.

It was a Saturday afternoon right before Christmas. Dad was at the wheel of our gray Chevrolet. There was a "C" gas rationing sticker on the windshield in front of me. Dad got the high-priority sticker because it was a company-owned car, though I'm not sure why a wholesale lumber saleman's car was essential enough to the war effort to merit a "C."

We were driving east on Washington Boulevard past rows of red brick apartment buildings. Many of them had tiny white flags with blue stars in the window, designating the homes of servicemen. Occasionally we would pass a flag with a gold star, the home of a martyred hero. Being a bomber pilot myself, if only in imagination, I was familiar with the risks of combat and would nod reverently like a monk passing a tabernacle each time I saw a gold star in a window.

My father belonged to the St. Vincent De Paul Society, actually six men in our parish who helped out families or individuals who were down on their luck because of illness or unemployment. On this trip we were headed for Cook County Hospital, the gray rock of tears that still struggles to treat the wounds and illnesses of the poor in Chicago's inner city. Two weeks before, my father—accompanied only by my little brother, Joe, who was six—literally had carried an old spinster lady named Miss Mooney into the hospital's emergency room after he had found her dehydrated and uncared for in her boarding house room.

Now Dad and I were making a Christmas visit to Miss Mooney, and I clutched a box of candy that my mother had wrapped in white tissue paper with snowman stickers.

Though faded by the mist of four decades, Miss Mooney in her faded gray hospital gown seemed as real to me as if I had just seen her down the hall in my own hospital. Her bed was in a long aqua-green ward that smelled of urine, disinfectant, and stale tomato soup. Her skin was brittle as dried parchment, her hair tousled and stiff, like grass after an ice storm. Her neck was scrawny, with an egg-sized goiter on the right side that gave her an unbalanced look. I feared she would try to kiss me, but she didn't. Dad sat down in a chair, took her hand, and started talking about whatever popped into his head. Normally not a chatty person, he became almost garrulous around someone like Miss Mooney, someone who didn't get any visitors, someone who wasn't very important.

"Frank wants to be a newspaper reporter when he grows up," my father said, one hand nudging me closer to Miss Mooney's bed. "How nice," squeaked Miss Mooney. "Won't you be proud of him, Walter?"

Dad also told her that I was taking clarinet lessons, which made me feel awful. I knew what Dad didn't: that I never practiced.

"It's nice to have another musician in the family," said Miss Mooney, heaping coals on my guilt.

Later, driving home, I felt I had failed my father because I had been unable to think of a single word to say to Miss Mooney; and I don't think I smiled much to cheer her up. I felt like crying because it was so sad that Miss Mooney would be spending Christmas in that terrible smelling, lonesome place, her only gift the box of Fannie May candy from my mother.

Then Dad gave me one of the few direct messages I can ever recall him conveying to any of us. "You know why it was good for you to go with me today, don't you?" I didn't understand. "Miss Mooney never sees children any more. It made her very happy to see you."

Getting to go on any mission with my father was always a treat for me or my three sisters, Bunny, Patti, and Susan, and brother, Joe. Even when something disturbing happened, Dad always took it in stride. I remember once when I was driving with him "to call on the customers," he suddenly swerved the car to the curb and jumped out. It was a snowy day and he had spotted a disheveled man flat on his back on the icy sidewalk. The obviously inebriated man was twirling like a turtle on his shell, unable to get up. Dad helped him scramble into a wobbly stance, held him for a second to make sure he was in balance, and came back to the car.

Dad never said anything to me about what just happened. He never said anything like, "That's how we all should treat our fellow man, Son," or "See what drink can lead to?" Not Dad. He just saw this poor guy in trouble and went to help him get up. No judgments for the man—and no platitudes for me.

Dad not only liked people, he also liked animals, both domestic and wild. As a Depression-era family, we were big on going to the zoo. It seemed we were either at the Brookfield Zoo, the Museum of Science and Industry, or a picnic in the forest preserve every Sunday afternoon.

He liked stray dogs, particularly if they were scrawny and slightly out of kilter. We owned a series of eccentric dogs, including a tiny one named Ambercrombie, who persistently nipped family members, as if we all were intruders, and Leiderkrantz, a yelping three-legged mutt, which Dad particularly fancied. Neighbors admonished him that he should put the tri-legged dog to sleep, but Dad delighted in the little beast's pluck in chasing after us kids or the mailman and refused to have the animal executed.

Dad liked to tell us stories about growing up in a small town in northern Wisconsin and working as an assistant cook in a lumber camp in the summer. He talked about the wonderful eccentrics he had met in the north woods and such family characters as his Uncle Max Unflad, with the huge walrus moustache and limited English vocabulary, whose only known employment was to milk the family cow—inexplicably called Jacob—and to fetch a pail of beer from the corner saloon each afternoon at precisely four o'clock.

My father was the oldest of eight children and the first to work his way through college. After his death, I found a small notebook in which he recorded his weekly expenses as a student at the University of Wisconsin at Madison. There were days near the end of the month when money was so short that he lived on a single bowl of soup and glasses of water filled with sugar lifted from a soda fountain. But he never told us how spartan college life had been, he only talked about the torchlight homecoming parades and the heroics of the football players of his day. To hear him tell it, he might have been a rich fraternity boy on a scholarship—he certainly enjoyed his years in college.

Until he died, he remained a devoted, albeit disappointed, University of Wisconsin football fan. In the innocent days before collegiate football recruiting was professionalized, my dad was an unofficial scout for Harry Stuhldreher, quarterback of the famed Four Horsemen of Notre Dame who was the Wisconsin football coach for many unfruitful seasons.

Try as he might, Dad never had much success luring Chicago-area high school prospects to the Madison campus for a visit, much less for enrollment. But he truly worked at it. Many a night he spent helping some hulking high school lineman or speedy running back with his algebra homework. Often he would take me along to the home of a budding "student-athlete" for these tutoring sessions. I was awed to be in the presence of some all-state player, dense as some of them were.

I suppose he would have been proud if Joe or I had become football players at his beloved alma mater, but he was never one to push his children along any particular path in life. (We both ended up going to Notre Dame, which he accepted with equanimity.) If throwing a ball with your dad was all it took, both Joe and I would have become all-Americans in some sport. I remember how Dad would throw me long passes with a football for a half hour before dinner almost every night in the fall. He did the same for Joe when he got bigger.

I relived those practices with my dad as I lay in my hospital bed some forty years later. I could hear him chanting like a quarterback as I crouched into a three-point stance a few yards to his right. "Hup . . . hup . . . hup," he barked. I lunged forward ten yards, threw a head fake to the right, and then took off toward that lightning-struck elm at the end of the vacant lot. When I looked back, Dad was faking a handoff, then pumping the ball several times, finally letting her rip far into the darkening sky. I strained with all my might, my ears popping as I reached for the blurred outline of the spiraling football. Then the sharp sting of the ball in my fingers and Dad shouting, "Touchdown!"

I remember that Dad had to replace two broken windows at Mrs. Gare's house on the far side of the vacant lot. One time I smashed one of his baseball pitches into a basement window; the other time Dad punted a football right into her kitchen. Mrs. Gare, a nervous widow, put up with a lot from Dad and me.

Several times when reliving my practices with Dad, I know I actually yelled or made real head fakes. If any of the nurses in Rochester Methodist Hospital noticed my strange antics, they never mentioned it to me. Maybe they thought I suffered from a neurological disorder as well as a failed liver.

Despite having an inflexible streak on some matters, Dad usually was the most jovial of men. He made us squeal with delight when he abruptly would interrupt whatever he was doing at the time—hanging storm windows or carelessly mowing uneven rows in the lawn—to explode with a cheer from his old high school: "Ish-kee wee-wee; osh-kee wow wow; holy sockey-eye; mockey-eye; mellen high; wow!"

He was seldom solemn—though he enjoyed reading serious books (history and philosophy, but never novels). He had graduated from the business school at Madison, so all his life he tried to make up for his lack of liberal arts courses by reading during his lunch hours and going to community lectures at the library. When I was in college, he had me send him my reading lists so he could sample the books on them. Often he read books that I never got around to checking out of the library.

His favorite book, the one he read to each of us and to each grandchild in turn, was *The Wizard of Oz,* which he appreciated both as a morality play about our common journey through life, but also as just a good story. I remember how he enunciated the heroine's name, "Dore-ah-thee," when reading it to us. My son Danny slipped a copy of *The Wizard of Oz* into Dad's casket just before they closed the lid.

He also had a favorite admonition when urging his children and later his grandchildren to do their best at something—whether a piano recital or a school exam: "Remember," he would say, shaking a finger in mock seriousness. "Lay the milk on the back porch!" None of us ever knew the origin of this paternal directive, just its import, until one day, not long before he died, I asked him where he picked it up. It came, he explained, from a sport columnist named Roundy Coughlin, who had written decades before about a University of Wisconsin quarterback who was so precise in executing his passes that it was like "laying the milk on the back porch."

My dad liked to take us children with him whenever he could, whether on a business trip to a sawmill in Canada or a few blocks to the post office. We never felt we were getting in his way. Just the opposite; he seemed to like the complications of our presence.

During the Depression, Dad took a 50 percent cut in salary from the lumber company, but our family life never seemed to change. We lived in a rented, four-bedroom, red-brick house in south Oak Park: Dad and Mom, five kids, Grandpa and Grandma Mitchell, and my Uncle Jadie, my mother's older brother (whose real name was James), who was a music teacher and director of a church choir.

For Sunday dinner we not only had that entire crew around the table, but always some guests, maybe a friend of Uncle Jadie's or some hungry bachelor that my dad met in his work. Knowing what I do now about trying to support a family and save something for the future, I am amazed at the seeming ease with which my parents steered our family through those Depression years.

Though we were ordinary children with the usual talent for mischief, Dad never spanked us. My mother—the soprano—was the reluctant disciplinarian. When we acted up, she would send us to the bushes between our house and Kelly's lot to select a proper "switch." We learned to pick a branch that was nasty in appearance but weak in structure, then to hop and howl in agony at mother's first tentative stroke. She seldom landed more than one or two stinging caresses.

When I was dying, I tried to model my behavior after the way my father had died only a few years before. It did not come naturally to me. I could master the stoic, stout-hearted part easily enough; but his genuine good cheer in the face of pain was hard to imitate.

It was a difficult act to follow. He suffered a broken leg in a car accident, broke the other one in a fall, then was diagnosed with acute leukemia. During his last months, he never once complained or talked about his illness. When I visited him we talked about my work, books he had read, or characters he had met in the "old days." If he experienced any pain in those final months, he never let any of us know it.

I wanted to die with the same dignity, grace, and good humor that my dad did. That would be my last gift to my children—maybe the only thing of real value I would leave them.

The last time I saw my father alive he was working a crossword puzzle in his hospital bed. The last thing he said to me was to make sure one of my sisters bought a new set of tires for her car; he was worried that she might have an accident.

Mother came from a kissing and hugging family. She often told us that she loved us. But Dad, who sprang from a handshaking German family, never told my brother or sisters or me that he loved us. He never had to.

Part Three

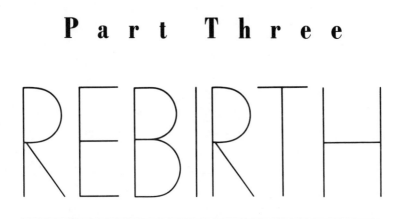

REBIRTH

17

THE
TRANSPLANTERS

on't get the idea that I spent entire days and nights wandering through the forests of my childhood. Most of the time I was living in the present just like everybody else. Actually, I was functioning better than I had in weeks because of the medication controlling my hepatic encephalopathy. I could write in my journal and even read a bit, though not without effort. Despite the fatigue, itching, and nausea that no medication could erase, I was more comfortable after the fluid tapping, and regular doses of strong diuretics had reduced my swollen belly.

Between tests and interviews, Ginny and I tried to get a basic education in organ transplantation—a subject about which we knew next to nothing. For one thing, we had no idea what life would be like for us if I survived a liver replacement—which everyone seemed all too eager to remind us was the most complex single-organ transplant being performed on the frontiers of medicine.

Could I return to work as a journalist, or would I be restricted in what I could do? Would my new life consist of perpetual vegetation before a television set? Or would I be able to throw a ball and fly a kite with that grandchild I might now have an outside chance of living to see? Would I have the same life expectancy as other men my age? Or was this expensive and agonizing ordeal only meant to prolong my life for a few more months or years? Was I only a guinea pig to help surgeons find answers that could help others down the road? Or had liver transplants become, like kidney replacements had been for two decades, realistic treatment for end-stage organ failure?

Until my talk with Dr. Vern Kerchberger a few weeks before, the last thing on my mind was something as exotic as an organ transplant. Now I was starting to feel like a sailor who rashly had signed aboard a vessel before he even knew where the ship was headed and who the captain was. Indeed, Ginny and I had a lot to learn.

In trying to understand what lay ahead, I had an advantage over other patients facing the sudden prospect of undergoing a transplant. As a reporter, I knew how and where to get information quickly. With Ginny's help, that's what I set out to do.

First, I asked *Newsweek*'s library in New York to search for recent newspaper or magazine articles on liver transplantation. Within days, the librarians air-expressed me a thick packet of reading material, some from scientific journals and some from the popular press. This gave us background on what we faced if I were selected for transplant.

The energetic Ginny also copied material on transplantation from journals and medical textbooks in the clinic's own library, some of which we could decifer only with the help of a medical dictionary and determined questioning of any doctor or nurse we could enlist for help.

In asking questions, Ginny far outperformed me, who had earned a living at it. She was determined and aggressive in extracting information from medical professionals. For my part, I still treated my healers with exaggerated respect, worrying more about inconveniencing or annoying them than satisfying my curiosity about my condition or treatment. Habits are difficult to break—even when you are dealing with your very life.

In fact, early in my illness Ginny had made up her mind that she would deal with doctors as she dealt with other adults—on an equal footing. For some physicians, this is a philosophy as foreign and unwelcome as psychic surgery. But Ginny was convinced that the basic responsibility for my treatment and care belonged with us; that the doctors worked for us, were paid by us (or our insurer), and should make a sincere effort to communicate with us. And, when it came to communication, that meant they should be patient in answering our questions.

As a minor part of Ginny's campaign against medical pomposity, she began to address my doctors by their first names—if they called her by her first name. This annoyed some, though not all of them. "If they can call me by my first name, I can call them by theirs," she said logically. "I'm not a little girl and you're not a little boy." (I wonder how she might have modified the last half of that sentence had she known of my imaginary trips back to Kelly's vacant lot.) It was one small way of putting herself on equal footing with medical authority figures. Without being overly conscious of it, Ginny was an early convert to the consumerism movement that belatedly has begun to creep into the patient-physician relationship. It was a stance that just came naturally to her.

Over the course of my illness, I adopted more of a compromise position in the doctors' first-name debate. I began to call them "Doctor John" or "Doctor Mark," or whatever—coating the formal title with the thinnest layer of familiarity. That was about as far as I felt comfortable in moving; I still was more intimidated by doctors than one would suspect of a "hard-bitten," cynical journalist. Much later I did start calling doctors by their first names, but only those with whom I had developed a personal, not just professional, relationship.

In addition to the "homework" Ginny and I assigned ourselves on transplantation, we found that the Mayo transplant team had its own indoctrination program. All patients were expected to participate, provided it did not conflict with their scheduled tests. Any spouses or family members who were in town also were urged to come to these twice-a-week meetings. The group sessions—part educational and part "support" therapy—were run by the transplant team's two social workers as part of the overall "psychosocial assessment" that each prospective transplant candidate was undergoing.

My assigned social worker was Jurine Schellberg, an Iowa-born mother of five grown children who had been with the liver transplant team since its start in March of 1985. (Mayo's first liver transplant recipient was a forty-three-year-old nun from South Dakota, whose identity the clinic has kept secret at her request.) The daughter of immigrants from Norway, Jurine reminded me of the good-humored, competent women portrayed in the movies by actress Barbara Stanwyck, the kind of woman who knows how to run the ranch without losing her feminity in the process.

"Jurine is going to be the answer to a lot of our problems," Ginny accurately predicted after our first short visit with the social worker.

At first I viewed Jurine as just one more face among my growing list of inquisitors, though her cheerful competence did remind me of Terry Schott, the hospital chaplain back in Arlington Heights who had been so instrumental in yanking me back from the brink of self-pity. As with all of my interviewers, I kept trying to figure out why Jurine was asking certain questions about my family, childhood, fundamental beliefs, and attitudes toward life.

As a reporter I was fascinated with the questioning process, trying to understand what they were trying to dig up. Much later, after we had become friends, Jurine confessed to being nervous during our first interview session because she knew my background as a reporter. "How do you interview a professional interviewer?" she asked. During that first interview, I was not nervous; I was acutely curious. "Why is she asking that? What strength or weakness is she probing for with that question?"

I was to learn that the evaluation by the social worker is as important in the selection process as is a patient's medical condition and nearness to death. Transplanters deal in the most precious of natural commodities—a human organ. Before investing the enormous amount of talent, time, and treasure on a patient, they want to make certain that a potential recipient has the commitment, emotional stability, self-discipline, and the support of family and friends to handle the grueling surgery and its life-long consequences.

As the senior social worker on the team, Jurine was responsible for scheduling the twice-weekly group sessions, which were held in the patients' lounge at Station 53, the restricted circular ward where liver and kidney patients recuperated after transplant. As a potential candidate, I was still bedded in a nearby station that did not have the tight visitor restrictions and sterile isolation of Station 53.

During the Tuesday afternoon sessions, Jurine encouraged us to speak openly and frankly about our anxieties and fears. At first, I was reluctant to get involved in any show-and-tell session with strangers, even though I could recognize from their jaundiced, weary faces that I had more in common with the men and women in that room than I did with some people I had known for years. In my first exposure to Jurine Schellberg's group sessions, I reverted to old tactics, hiding my fears and anguish behind jaunty palaver and one-liners. Rather than letting it all hang out, I was more comfortable providing comic relief for the rather heavy and emotional discussions.

Jurine gently prodded each of us to talk about our illness, our families, and our hopes. She also began to weave into the therapy sessions little packets of practical advice on such matters as controlling stress, coping with changes in life-style and employment, or how to add humor and positive thinking to our arsenal of weapons in fighting chronic illness.

I soon recognized that one of Jurine's strengths as a counselor of the afflicted was her ability to focus her full attention on whoever was speaking, no matter how convoluted, emotional, or irrational any of our comments might sound. When anyone spoke, Jurine locked on him or her like a radar operator, eyes alive with expectation, as if she were hearing for the first time some sparkling fresh insight.

After two sessions I began to drop my self-conscious defenses and started to feel more comfortable with these other men and women who had come to Mayo Clinic with their last measure of hope. Many of them had been seriously ill much longer and were carrying their burdens with much more grace than I. I began to feel—not competitiveness—but a genuine *esprit de corps* with my fellow patients.

My "class" at Mayo in the spring of 1987 consisted of Dorothy Hadden, a tiny retired schoolteacher from Topeka, Kansas; Robert Slaughter, a giant of a man the size of a football tackle who was a school principal from Waynesville, Missouri; Robert Bell, who worked for United Parcel Service and lived near Fort Wayne, Indiana; the Rev. Bert Schmidt, a Lutheran minister who pastored two flocks in tiny Mountain, Wisconsin; Rachel Olerud, who lived in Spring Grove, only a few miles from Rochester: Linda Sentner, who came all the way from Santa Anna, California; Don Wesley, a construction equipment operator from Florida; Kay Dodds, a soft-spoken schoolteacher from a small town in Mississippi, and Don Anderson, who ran a baby diaper service in Spokane, Washington. Both Wesley and Anderson were among those unfortunate people who had been stricken with sudden liver failure, not the usual long drawn-out illness that most of us had experienced. Only a few weeks before, Wesley had been working full-time and Anderson had been playing golf.

Of the group, Bob Bell and Rachel Olerud had just been transplanted, the others—like me—were nervously hoping to be accepted and put on the waiting list.

The ever-curious Ginny got her first look at a liver transplant scar by asking Rachel for a peek at her incision. At that time, I was in no mood to see anyone's scar—so I never asked Bob Bell for a look.

Unlike Ginny, I was not keen on knowing everything that could happen to me. I was content to know that the pyramid-shaped scar would extend from side to side just under my chest. The surgeons described it as looking like "half a Mercedes emblem," not an unlikely image for a physician to conjure up. Ginny commented that, after paying for a liver transplant, the scar was as close as any of us would ever get to a Mercedes.

Besides those of us being evaluated and the newly transplanted patients, veterans back for their annual physicals also attended Jurine Schellberg's meetings. Just by showing up, these transplanted patients became role models for us jaundiced, swollen, exhausted, and dying recruits. They were living proof that there could be meaningful life after transplant.

One morning Jurine called me at our motel and said for me to come immediately to Station 53 to meet someone named Mike Kelly, who had been transplanted the previous fall and was back for his six-month checkup. Feeling tired and put-upon, I was in no mood to walk to the hospital to meet a stranger, no matter what good the social worker thought it would do me. But Ginny literally pushed me out the door.

As it turned out, Jurine was right on target in introducing me to Mike Kelly, an extroverted veterinarian from the unpronounceable town of Waxahachie in northeast Texas. Meeting someone as full of life and energy as Kelly was an instant confidence-builder for me.

His biggest problem posttransplant was trying to keep his weight down. Prednisone, he explained, is an appetite stimulator that can cause all sorts of weight problems for those who must take it daily. He had to go on a special diet to take off thirty pounds that he had put on in the six months after his surgery.

He was back working full-time in his veterinary practice and was playing eighteen holes of golf regularly. In our conversation, I did not ask him for any specific advice—just looking at him was a tonic for me. Nonetheless, I remember him saying that one lesson he had learned was that "every day is a good day." Don't worry about what might happen tommorrow. "Enjoy the people you meet and whatever you're doing today."

He had one added nugget of practical advice—get a very short haircut before the transplant because it would be a long time before I would be able to shower afterwards. That afternoon I went to a barber in downtown Rochester, who reluctantly gave me a skin-top haircut that would have impressed a Marine Corps drill sergeant. When I looked in the mirror that night, I saw a bald, yellow-skinned face that might have belonged to an emaciated prisoner of war.

In addition to providing encouragement, these "alums" also presented us with some sobering realities. I remember one man who had been among Mayo's first transplants two years earlier, who said that people still treated him strangely, just as some people have phobias about being near the seriously ill or dying.

"You feel like you should wear a bell around your neck like lepers used to do," he told me.

Some who had a type of liver disease with the side effect of bone deterioration reported numerous fractures after transplant and some had to have hip joints replaced. A few even had lost inches in height from spinal collapse caused by bone density complications.

Other transplanted patients told of being dismissed by their employers even after their strength returned. Finding replacement jobs was difficult, particularly for anyone who had done hard, manual work before transplant. No one wanted to hire them after learning they had undergone such extraordinary surgery. There is an employment stigma attached to transplanted men and women that only education of the public eventually might erase. Even those few employers who piously proclaim their willingness to hire persons who have been transplanted often back off, claiming their health insurance costs would jump with transplantees on the payroll.

Still other "alums" told us about their thousands of dollars in unpaid medical bills and their arduous—and often fruitless—efforts to raise funds. One couple from Long Island described how humiliating it had been trying to raise money for the wife's transplant. After they had passed out leaflets in their neighborhood asking for donations, someone began leaving pennies in their mailbox. They became so paranoid about what their neighbors might think that, after buying a new sewing machine, they left a large sign on the carton set out for the garbage men: "This not bought with donated money."

The father of one young woman trying to raise money for her transplant said the family stopped going to the movies or even fast food restaurants after getting angry glares and snide comments from people who knew they were asking for funds.

"The only ones who really get a sympathetic response are little children," he said. "For older people, forget it."

Listening to the economic woes of so many of the transplanted or those seeking a transplant, Ginny and I realized how fortunate we were in having good health insurance. Even today many private insurers do not pay for liver transplants, and many who do pay for the basic surgery will not cover the expensive immunosuppressive drug therapy which is necessary to keep a transplanted patient alive. Unlike kidney transplants, for which federal funds have been available since the early 1970s, liver replacements generally are not eligible for any government assistance.

The other regular meetings, always on Friday afternoon, were educational, not group therapy, sessions. At these meetings, members of the transplant staff, including the surgeons and hepatologists, lectured us about specifics: how the liver functions—or is supposed to function; the techniques of a liver transplant (or "plant," in the lingo of the trade); how organs are procured, preserved, and transported, often over long distances; and the nature of the drugs used to suppress the immune system so that the body does not reject a "foreign" organ.

Most important, we learned about the possible side effects of these powerful antirejection drugs that we would have to take for the rest of our lives and the infections and diseases, including cancers, that these medications made us vulnerable to.

Within a relatively short time, Ginny and I began to understand the awesome complications, both medical and personal, that faced us. We also came to appreciate that the Mayo system was designed to let potential transplant patients know exactly what they were getting into. They did not want us to be surprised by anything that might happen during the long surgery or the period of recovery. In setting up their program, they defined terminal illness and trans-plantation, not just as medical challenges for the surgeons and technicians, but as problems affecting a patient's entire life, includ-ing relations with family, friends, and employers. They did not want either our anxieties or our hopes to get out of hand.

I always will remember the basic axiom told to us by Dr. Ruud Krom, the chief surgeon and head of the transplant team, in a talk called, "Historical Overview of Liver Transplant Surgery."

"Liver transplant patients never are cured," he said in his hearty Dutch accent. "They just trade a terminal illness for a lifetime of medical management."

I do not know how that struck others in the room that afternoon, but to Ginny and me it sounded like a pretty decent trade-off, one that I could live with—literally.

Gradually, some of our basic questions were answered, including the most basic: what kind of life expectancy would I have if I were successfully transplanted? Only five years before, the answer would not have been overly optimstic. The one-year survival rate for liver plants then was running about 30 percent. But, after the introduc-tion of the antirejection drug, cyclosporine, the survival rate nation-ally climbed to near 70 percent. It was too early in the history of liver transplantation for the experts to predict how that survival rate would look five or ten years down the road.

As for activity, certainly I would not take up karate. And I probably would not be able to engage in strenuous sports, even handball. But, I probably could take up golf again—which I had not played for maybe six years—and I could play catch, shoot baskets, and generally engage in horseplay with any grandchildren that might come along.

The more I learned about organ transplantation, the more fascinated I became with the pioneer surgeon-scientists and laboratory researchers, who had endured ridicule, embarrassing failures, and, in the early years, the near-universal contempt of the conservative medical world because of their crazy dream that vital human organs could be transferred from one human being to another. Many of these early surgeon-researchers were viewed by their colleagues as demented dreamers at best and goulish grave robbers at worst.

The dream of transplanting body parts from one human being to another can be traced through clouds of myth and legend to ancient Greece and India. Later, in the second century after the birth of Christ, there even was a popular, apocryphal tale of the twin physicians, Saints Cosmas and Damian, who were said to have amputated a man's infected leg and replaced it with one from a man who had just died. During the sixteenth century, a controversial Italian doctor, Gaspare Tagliacozzi, was an early experimenter with skin grafts, rebuilding noses (often detached in swordplay or eroded by syphillis) with tissue from a patient's own arm.

A celebrated English surgeon of the eighteenth century, Dr. John Hunter, experimented with animal transplants and with grafting knocked out teeth back into people's mouths. His success as a tooth restorer resulted from a successful, but bizarre, experiment in which he transplanted a human tooth into the comb of a rooster.

I was fascinated—as a reporter and collector of coincidences—to discover during a physical examination that one of my attending hepatologists, young Dr. Ellen Hunter, was a direct descendant of this illustrious John Hunter. The shy Dr. Hunter was affectionately—and gratefully—called by us patients, "The Biopsy Queen," because of her gentle and painless technique in punching a hollow needle between the ribs to extract a sliver of liver for microscopic examination. Dr. Hunter, who would become a friend of Ginny's and mine, was in the middle of a three-year fellowship at Mayo in gastroenterology research and, at that time, was assigned to the transplant unit.

But, to get back to the history of organ transplants as Ginny and I learned it during those first weeks at Mayo: the first serious work on human transplantation began with surgeons in Europe about the start of this century. However, their attempts to use the kidneys of monkeys, pigs, and other animals to replace diseased human kidneys failed miserably. These early transplanters not only operated without the laboratory testing tools, preservation fluids, and infection-fighting drugs available to modern surgeons, they also had no real understanding of how the body's immune system works; how it dispatches its own militia of special white blood cells (called T-lymphocytes) to surround and destroy any foreign "invader," whether it be a deadly germ, a tiny splinter in the toe, or a transplanted organ or tissue that does not respond with the correct "password."

Animal-to-human transplantation (xenografting) has remained a theoretical, and controversial, answer for replacing a failed organ. But it has been mainly confined to laboratory experiments, while serious advances have been made in the last part of this century in human-to-human transplants.

Modern organ transplantation dates from 1954, when surgeons at Peter Bent Brigham Hospital in Boston successfully transplanted a kidney from a healthy young man into his dying identical twin, who lived eight years with the borrowed organ. Because the twin's donated kidney was so genetically similar to his brother's, it did not trigger an alarm in the recipient's immune system.

Most of the early transplant work benefited kidney patients for several reasons. The body has two kidneys but can live with only one, thereby allowing use of living donors. Also, scientists had developed artificial kidneys—or dialysis machines—that could keep persons with failed kidneys alive while they awaited a transplant. Finally, replacement of a kidney is relatively simple surgery. The diseased kidney is not even removed. The donated kidney is simply hung next to the failed organ, which eventually shrivels away.

In the 1940s, surgeons experimented with radiation to disable the immune system before transplanting an organ. But radiation proved so effective that it left recipients vulnerable to every passing infection. They died of infection long before rejection became a problem. In the early 1960s, researchers began using an immunosuppressant drug called azathioprine and a multipurpose steroid called prednisone (which had been developed at Mayo Clinic) to prevent organ rejection.

The use of this immunosuppressant "cocktail" was a significant breakthrough for the emerging science of transplantation. It made living-related kidney donation a procedure almost as routine as an appendectomy. But it also opened the door for the first successful human transplantation of other vital organs: the heart and the liver in 1967, the pancreas in 1978, and the heart-lungs package in 1981.

In the expanding world of transplant medicine, many pioneers in Europe and the United States made significant contributions, some in the laboratory with animal experiments, others with human patients, and some in both lab and surgery. But, as Ginny and I did our research—more like pretransplant cramming—we came across the names of two determined and bold men whose work was crucial in making transplantation a realistic solution to the age-old problem of human organ failure.

One was Dr. Thomas E. Starzl, the hyper-driven, surgeon-scientist and "godfather" of liver transplantation, who heads the world's largest liver transplant program at the University of Pittsburgh. The other was an obscure researcher in immunology for a Swiss pharmaceutical company, Jean-François Borel. There is an old expression of my grandmother's that reminded us of our indebtedness to others who went before us: "We all have drunk from wells we did not dig." As I learned about the pioneering work of these two men, I remembered those words of wisdom. Were it not for these daring pioneers, I would not have this second chance at life, this chance to be born again.

It was Thomas Starzl, then at the University of Colorado Medical Center, who achieved what his surgical colleagues almost to a man said was impossible—the successful transplantation of the liver— with its multiple blood connections and its 500 or so vital metabolic functions. He failed in his first attempt at a human liver transplant in 1963 when his patient, a three-year-old boy, died on the operating table. He tried again and again, only to meet with failure each time, many of the patients dying within days, some of rejection but most of massive infections. But in 1967, Starzl performed the first successful liver transplant on an eighteen-month-year old baby girl, who lived for thirteen months before dying of cancer.

Not only has Starzl been the main teacher of most second-generation liver transplant surgeons (including Dr. Krom, who heads Mayo's unit), since moving to the University of Pittsburgh he has remained in the forefront of both research and surgical innovations, performing the first combined heart-liver plant and the even more daring "cluster" transplant, during which the liver, pancreas, intestines, and related organs are replaced as a package, a radical "heroic" surgery for patients with massive cancers in several organs.

Despite the individual genius and boldness of pioneering liver transplanters like Starzl and the first heart transplanter, Christiaan Barnard of South Africa and Norman Shumway of Stanford, who did the first heart plant in the United States, organ transplantation would have remained largely a rare and modestly successful experiment had it not been for the dedication and nerve of researcher Jean-François Borel, an immunologist with the Swiss pharmaceutical firm of Sandoz Ltd.

Borel, now a senior scientist at Sandoz and a self-described "mouse doctor," single-handedly developed cyclosporine, the wonder drug that has become for transplant surgery what penicillen was in the fight against infection.

Cyclosporine, which is derived from a white mold found originally in 1972 in a sample of dirt picked up by a vacationing Sandoz scientist in Norway, flopped as an antibiotic, the original goal of researchers. But Borel persisted in studying the fungus, often working in secret after his bosses told him to stick to more promising projects. What Borel discovered in his laboratory experiments with animals was that cyclosporine—for whatever reason—has the power to dampen the effectiveness of the body's T-lymphocytes without killing them. In effect, cyclosporine is a highly selective drug that blocks the immune system's attack on a transplanted organ while leaving the body enough resistence to fight deadly infections. The drug also does not interfere with the blood-producing function of bone marrow, an important quality for an immunosuppressant.

Borel's dedication as a scientist extended beyond the normal call of duty. At a critical point in cyclosporine's development as an immunosuppressant, Borel showed the bravery of many heroic medical researchers throughout history. Before cyclosporine's toxicity was known for humans, he became the first person to inject the drug to see how quickly it was absorbed in the blood and to test its side effects.

Finally, after extensive clinical trials on kidney and heart transplant patients, cyclosporine was approved in 1983 by the Food and Drug Administration. The introduction of cyclosporine marked the beginning of the golden age of transplantation, an age that is still in its infancy.

By one estimate, some 200,000 transplant patients throughout the world—including me—probably would not be alive today had it not been for the courageous persistence of two individuals: the flamboyant, pioneering transplant surgeon, Thomas Starzl, and modest "mouse doctor" researcher, Jean-François Borel, the developer of cyclosporine.

18

ON THE
BEEPER

I n the end, the decision on whether I would live or die rested, not on the condition of my liver, but on my heart. Both of the young doctors who were charged with my daily examinations, Mark Perrella and Ellen Hunter, told me that the last obstacle standing in the way of my being "activated" for a transplant was the senior doctors' fears that my valve-damaged heart might fail on the operating table during surgery that could last ten hours or more. My history of heart disease from the rheumatic fever of my teen years, plus the stopping of my heart on St. Patrick's Day, left the evaluators with serious doubts about my acceptability for transplant.

During their regular Wednesday afternoon conference on the fifth floor of Rochester Methodist Hospital, team members decided that my acceptance for a transplant would depend on the results of a heart catheterization, a high-tech procedure that enables a cardiologist to look right into the pumping heart.

The night before my scheduled heart cath, a chipper young doctor I had never seen before appeared at my bedside with a clipboard. He proceeded to explain the procedure: the cardiologist first numbs an area in my right groin with local anesthetic, then inserts a thin flexible catheter (or tube) into an artery. He slowly pushes the catheter up the blood vessel while watching its progress on a video monitor. "You can watch too if you like," said the doctor. Since no pain sensors are inside an artery, there will not be any discomfort—at least not yet, he explained.

When the snaking tube reaches the heart, the cardiologist injects a dye through it. Looking at the video screen, he then can read and take pictures of the inside of the heart as if it were a road map, inspecting my leaky mitral and aortic valves, as well as checking for fatty deposits in arteries or abnormalities in the organ's four chambers.

The young doctor's brow furrowed in professional concern at this point: "When the dye is injected, you may feel a very warm, rushing sensation, but that's perfectly normal."

Consulting his clipboard, he then began to read a list of all the possible things that could go wrong during a heart catheterization. It was all part of modern medicine's ritual of informing patients what is about to happen to them. But the litany of woes sounded to me like pitches I had heard in the past from life insurance salesmen—"God forbid, Mr. Maier, that anything should happen to you, but . . ."

Instead of putting me at ease, the young doctor was beginning to make me dreadfully anxious about what tomorrow might bring. When he got to the part about there being a remote chance of my heart being punctured, I held up my hand and said: "Enough! Please don't read any more. I trust you guys or I wouldn't be here."

At five the next morning, the nurses began prepping me for the procedure with a transfusion of two units of blood plasma. I was supposed to be transferred in mid-morning across town by ambulance to St. Mary's Hospital, where all of Mayo's cardiac surgery is performed. While waiting, I was not allowed to eat or drink anything. As it turned out, I was not wheeled into the catheterization room at St. Mary's until almost three in the afternoon. By then, I could not tell whether my stomach ached from hunger or anxiety.

A nurse leaned over me and said: "Dr. Bresnahan will be here in a minute."

Bresnahan! The heart that they were about to poke a tube into jumped in recognition of a familiar sounding name. I knew the name Bresnahan from somewhere . . . then it all came back. Ginny's sister, Mary Rowley, had told us that two of the Bresnahan brothers from our hometown of Oak Park were doctors at the Mayo Clinic. I had ignored this bit of intelligence from Ginny's Irish network, except I remembered that the Bresnahan clan included eight brothers, all standing about six foot, six inches tall. Three of them had become doctors and another a dentist. They all had played basketball at my old school, Fenwick High, though after my time.

When the tall masked man stepped up to the table, I impulsively grabbed his gloved hand like he was the pope himself. "Bresnahan! Oak Park! Fenwick High School!" I was almost shouting. Since all I could see of his face was his raised eyebrows, I could not tell if he was surprised, annoyed, or pleased by my exuberant greeting.

It turned out that this was indeed one of the Oak Park Bresnahans—Dennis. After I expressed my gratitude in advance of his services, he seemed genuinely pleased to have me to work on. Before he got down to business, we spent several minutes recollecting stories of our old high school, resurrecting its eccentric coaches and teachers and revisiting the old neighborhood. All the anxiety flowed out of me as we reminisced. Nothing wrong could possibly happen to me with Bresnahan running the show. Thank God for Ginny's Irish Mafia. Bless them, every one.

I even screwed up enough courage to take a peak at the video screen as the catheter crept toward my heart like a snake sneaking up on a rabbit. When the dye was injected, it was like a hot wave rushing through my insides, ending with a crushing pain in my chest. When I told him about the chest pain, my old buddy Bresnahan—rather my new "old buddy"—suggested we take a few minutes break. Instead of walking away from the table, he stayed and we resumed our conversation. Later, I closed my eyes and nearly fell asleep while he finished the forty-five-minute catheterization. To paraphrase the insurance company ad: I was in good hands with Bresnahan.

Before they carried me out, we shook hands one last time and I asked him: "You don't do liver transplants do you?"

It was well after five in the afternoon when the ambulance attendants finally got me back to my room in Rochester Methodist Hospital, where Ginny patiently was waiting. Except for the hollow pain in my still-empty stomach and the tight pressure bandage around my right groin, I was feeling expansive as I told her about the amazing coincidence of having one of the Bresnahan brothers do my heart cath. I was sure that the results of the test would convince everyone that my heart was fit enough for me to undergo a liver plant. A guy from my own high school wouldn't let me down.

All I wanted now in life, I told Ginny, was some food and water. When a tray finally was brought, I wolfed down whatever was on it like someone who had not eaten in days—and promptly vomited it all up. After I was cleaned up, Ginny sat reading a magazine at my bedside while I drifted into an exhausted half-sleep.

Some time later I heard Ginny talking to someone: "What is that?" she asked.

Through half-shut eyes, I saw a nurse about to hang a drip bottle on the IV pole next to my bed.

"It's his seven o'clock medicine," the nurse answered.

Quite often at night they had been giving me albumin, a protein that helps draw fluids back from tissues into the bloodstream. The problem was that it caused heavy urination—and with my leg elevated and in a pressure bandage, I could not get out of bed to hop to the bathroom.

"Is it more albumin?" Ginny asked the nurse, who was busy hooking the bottle to my IV line.

Now I was getting interested too. The nurse stopped, twisted the container around, and squinted at the label.

"Oh," she said matter-of-factly. "It's for next door."

Without a word, she walked out with the bottle of whatever it was. Ginny and I just looked at each other, amazed.

"Don't go away," I finally said to her.

"I'm not going anywhere."

Just before I fell asleep again, I asked, "When will I ever get taken to Station 53?"

"Only after transplant," Ginny answered.

"That won't be too soon for me."

What makes the story of the wrong medication so alarming is that Mayo has developed a system of delivering drugs in its hospitals that supposedly is foolproof. It is called the single-unit dosage system. Every pill, bottle, or plastic pouch of drugs is sent up directly from the pharmacy, bagged, and labeled with the patient's room and name on it. There are no drug carts rolling from room to room, causing a tired or distracted nurse accidentally to dispense the wrong amount of drugs or give it to the wrong patient. Even a single tiny capsule comes to the patient's bedside in an individualized, clearly labeled, unopened plastic package.

But, as we found out when I first checked into the hospital and had the wrong records delivered to my first examining doctor, the best system in the world depends ultimately on the alertness of a human being somewhere along the line. In the case of the almost-wrongly administered drug, the system broke down because a nurse carelessly walked into the wrong room. Had Ginny not been there, she would have hooked up the wrong medication to my IV line while I slept.

I have no idea what fluid came close to draining into my vein that night. Considering my malfunctioning liver, the decaying condition of my other vital organs and the mixture of other drugs in my system, it well might have killed me. And if it had, I doubt anybody would have ever known what did me in. In my condition, a routine autopsy could have come up with sufficient reasons for my death without the pathologist bothering to search for a more obscure cause.

"Saturday, April 11, 1987. Finally Ginny and I received some good news. Doctor Russ Wiesner, the chief hepatologist—the one with the big moustache from Milwaukee, says they are thinking of sending me home for Easter. Sort of a long weekend pass. What a wonderful gift for us! It will give my battered body time to rest before some final tests."

Only two days later I wrote in my journal: "Good news seems to have as short a life span as tufts of dandelion cotton on a windy day. Now they aren't sure about letting me go home on 'leave.' The level of creatinine in my blood has jumped up, a sign that my kidneys aren't working too well. It must come down before I can go home. One thing after another. I am just a few days short of a month in hospital beds. I'm not certain I will know how to act outside of a hospital. My world is so limited now. For a month I have not made any decisions: when to get up, when and what to eat, should I go someplace or do something? In a hospital, all decisions are made for you—even what you eat (though the dieticians cleverly make you think you are making choices, when in reality you get to pick from a narrow range of possibilities). The biggest decisions I make each day is what TV channel to watch and how far to pace the corridors—ever mindful that I must be within roundup range when the doctors make their morning and afternoon calls."

To our delight, my creatinine level dropped, and I was allowed to go home. Once again my editors at *Newsweek* sent a private plane on the Wednesday before Easter. I felt like a prisoner of war returning to his hometown after a long absence. Everything looked the same, yet fresh—and somehow strange—to us.

Ginny immediately attacked the garden and yard, yanking weeds, raking up blown papers, and picking up fallen tree branches. I just sat for hours on our side screen porch, hypnotized by the cruising cars and excited at the sight of the neighborhood kids riding by on their bikes. After being confined so long in the hermetically sealed hospital, I had forgotten what outside noises sounded like—birds chattering and the wind rustling the trees, basketball players shouting and dribbling on the blacktop at the park down the street, jets roaring down runways at distant O'Hare Airport, and the staccato clacking of the commuter trains' wheels only a few blocks away. I basked in the rainbow of sounds like a beach lover basking in the rays of the sun, letting the noises break over me like refreshing, uneven waves.

Over Ginny's mild objections, I insisted on going downtown to the *Newsweek* bureau to clean out my office so John McCormick could move into it as bureau chief. Both John and a close friend, Paul Fullmer, had volunteered to do the job, but I wanted to do it myself. Not knowing what would happen to me in the next few weeks, I did not want to leave the detritus from seventeen years on the job for someone else to clean up. The office was closed Good Friday afternoon as Ginny and I boxed my papers, notes, old clippings, and personal pictures, bickering over what to trash and what to save. Ginny is a pitcher, I am a saver; much of the time we spent debating the value of my memorabilia. I had even saved copies of every expense account I had filed since joining *Newsweek* and wanted to keep them, so I told Ginny, "to show the kids how inflation affects us." She didn't even bother arguing about it, just dumped them all in the trash barrel.

I also went through the personnel file that contained copies of all my confidential memos and evaluations of the work of every correspondent and intern who had worked under me. I tore up any that were negative, leaving in the file only the ones that were glowing and upbeat. There was no reason to impose my opinions about someone on any future bureau chief who might idly fan through the file some day. Ginny had weeded and spruced up her garden at home; I did the same thing at the office.

Easter Saturday, Ginny and my daughters, Katie and Heidi, went to a bridal shower for our son Danny's future bride, Xiomara Santamarina, whom he had met in Washington where she worked as a congressional aide while pursuing a masters degree at Georgetown University. Her parents, who lived in Spain, were coming for the June wedding in the chapel at Georgetown, an event I knew I was not likely to attend—no matter what the outcome of my transplant.

While they were at the party, the pastor of our church, Father Peter Bowman, showed up unexpectedly for a visit. He had heard through the parish grapevine that we were home and stopped to see how everything was going. I recounted our adventures at the Mayo Clinic and told of our hopes and fears as we awaited a decision on my case. Our conversation generally was upbeat, as it usually was with Peter. I remember telling him that one spiritual side effect of being terminally ill was that I was gaining a better understanding and more sympathy for older folks now that my own body was decaying day by day.

Then he made an extraordinarily generous offer. Though Easter Sunday was the busiest working day of his year, a day when all the parish's services were jammed with the faithful and the not-so-faithful, he offered to come to our home in the afternoon and say a special Mass just for our family. Not only would it come at the end of an exhausting day for him, it also would deprive him of Easter visits with his own extended family of nephews and nieces, brothers and sisters who live in the area. I said thank you, but no. He suggested that I might not be able to handle the crowds at Mass. I said no again. Before he left, he gave me his blessing—just like the old days when I had been an altar boy.

On Monday, Dorothy Kaese, the nurse-coordinator for the liver transplant team, called to tell me that I had "passed" my heart exam and other tests and would be activated on the United Network for Organ Sharing (UNOS), the national computer network based in Richmond, Virginia—a system that matches donated organs with waiting patients throughout the country. When I was "activated," about 500 other Americans were awaiting liver transplants, though on any given day less than a half dozen livers might become available. Some people wait months; in cases of rare blood or body size, for years. Many die before their number comes up. For liver patients, the key data keyed into the computer are size of body, blood type, and nearness to death. Dorothy Kaese told me I would be listed with UNOS as soon as I could get back to Rochester. In the jargon of the transplant trade, I was "going on the beeper."

Bubbling with excitement, Ginny and I packed up the car and immediately drove back to Rochester, where we checked into a small motel to begin what could become a short or a long—or a final—vigil.

They gave me a "beeper" that allowed us to travel anywhere within twenty miles of Rochester. Each night I had to check in with the clinic switchboard operator before going to sleep. I was given more blood tests, had my teeth and sinuses checked for infections, and was put on daily doses of a foul-tasting bowel decontaminant that we called "Krom's Cocktail." Dr. Ruud Krom, the head of the transplant team, had devised the yellow concoction to prevent infections, a major complication facing people who undergo transplants. I could barely choke down the liquid until another patient on the waiting list, Dorothy Hadden, a schoolteacher from Kansas, told me to dilute it in chocolate milk.

Although I did not have much of an appetite left, I was put on a restricted diet—also a defense against bacterial infections. Off limits were cheeses or fresh fruits, except if peeled, and no fresh vegetables of any kind. Instantly, I developed an irrational yearning for pizza and tossed salad.

Unable to sleep, I spent most nights in our motel room, watching old movies on TV and trying not to think about the obvious: for me to have a chance to keep living, some other human being in this country or Canada had to die.

One advantage of having to wait patiently at a major medical center like Mayo is that you are surrounded by people of all ages who are in much worse shape than you are ever likely to be. A person would have to be terribly self-absorbed not to notice all of the suffering men, women, and children on the streets and in the waiting rooms of the main clinic building.

I remember sitting in a waiting room next to a pale young man in his wheelchair, who was in obvious discomfort as he tried to chat cheerfully with his pretty wife. Then an elderly woman rocked, not walked, into the waiting room, pushing the wheelchair of her frail old husband, who was dressed in bib overalls and heavy work boots. Both of them looked exhausted and confused as the nurse at the desk checked their appointment book. Then I heard the young man next to me whisper to his wife: "Poor old folks. Wish I could help them."

All I could think was: "Poor young man, who only wants to help poor old folks, how I wish I could help you too."

While we were waiting as patiently as we could for the news that a liver had been matched for me, Ginny received heartbreaking news. Once again, it forced us to look beyond the boundaries of our own predicament and share in the pain of others.

A phone call brought word that the oldest son of one of Ginny's college roommates, an army helicopter pilot, had been killed during a training mission off an aircraft carrier—just weeks before he was to leave the service to enroll as a graduate student at Northwestern University. The body of Dee Ellison's son, Ken Maddock, a West Point graduate, never was recovered from the sea, adding to the heartbreak for his mother and family.

Ginny, who by now was near emotional exhaustion, because the sands were quickly running out on my life, immediately went looking for our social worker Jurine Schellberg. Jurine took Ginny to the small "crisis" room near Station 53 and just let her cry her heart out. The worst part, Ginny sobbed to Jurine, was that the young man was taken so suddenly, so finally. It seemed so unfair. At least Ginny and I had been given time to say good-bye. But not this young man and his family.

Jurine did what Jurine does best—listen. She offered no platitudes, no explanations for the sadness that inevitably shadows human existence. Jurine was "there" for Ginny—that's all that was needed at that dark moment when Ginny was steeling herself so she could in turn offer comfort to her afflicted friend.

Only later did Ginny learn that one of Jurine's own children was in the military service. He was a navy helicopter pilot operating off an aircraft carrier.

19

DEATH BY CHICKEN SOUP

At 1:30 in the afternoon on Thursday, May 7, 1987, fourteen days after my name went into the United Network for Organ Sharing computers, my beeper went off. I switched off the television set and turned to Ginny, who was frozen in the doorway to the kitchenette in our motel. My face flushed hot, and my stomach started to ache; my heart pounded until my eardrums hurt.

"I knew this was the day," Ginny said.

I gave her a blank look as I picked up the phone to call the transplant coordinator, Dorothy Kaese.

"I met Dr. Krom in front of the Kahler Hotel this morning," she explained. "He told me they had a line on a possible liver for you and would know for sure later."

We knew that Dr. Krom was scheduled to leave that Saturday to visit his parents in the Netherlands. When Ginny spotted him on the street that morning, she had told him: "I know two people who would be very happy if somehow you located a liver before you left town."

That's when he told her that a possible donor had been matched with me that very morning, a brain dead man or woman who was being kept "alive" somewhere in the country while tests were done at Mayo's request. The potential donor matched my blood type, was within 20 percent of my weight, and apparently was free of any malignancies or infection. Tests were ordered to make certain the donor did not have hepatitis, AIDS, any sexually transmitted disease, or any history of drug abuse.

"We should know something later today," Dr. Krom told Ginny.

Because she did not want to get my hopes up and because we had been told that "false alarms" do occur in transplant medicine, Ginny decided to keep the news to herself. Late that morning when I made my scheduled checkup visit to the nineteenth floor of the clinic building, no one hinted anything to me about a possible donor. When Ginny cornered one of the coordinator-nurses outside of my hearing, she only would say, "Things are looking good."

After my beeper went off, I mildly rebuked Ginny for not sharing the news with me, but I knew she had done the prudent thing. I would have been a basket case had I known what was going on. This way, if the donor were rejected, I would never have been the wiser, and would have been spared many hours of anxious waiting. Early in my illness, Ginny had adopted a "need-to-know" approach to dispensing information. If someone had no way of helping, there was no reason to inform anyone of the latest crisis in our life. It only spread anxiety without helping the situation.

When I reached Dorothy Kaese on the phone, she told me to come to the hospital at four o'clock with only a robe, slippers, toothbrush and any of Dr. Krom's special bowel decontaminants I had left in my refrigerator. Two surgeons, a nurse-coordinator, and a young woman resident, who was going along as an observer, already were heading for the airport to board a jet that Mayo leases for organ retrieval runs. Meanwhile, Dr. Krom and the surgeon who would assist him, Dr. Dan Hayes, were catching some sleep in anticipation of the night-long surgery facing them after the procurement team returned with the donated liver. Because of the privacy protocols followed by all transplant centers, I would not be told the identity of the donor and or even the destination of the procurement team.

As we were going out the door, the phone rang. It was Jim Griffin, my old college friend calling from Chicago to see how Ginny and I were doing. We had a standing joke: whenever Griffin called, something unusual, funny, or momentous would happen to us that day.

"You won't believe this, but I just got called," I said. "They have a liver for me."

"See, there I go again," he said. "Whenever I call, something happens to you."

"From now on," I told him. "Don't call us; we'll call you."

We walked the few blocks to the hospital, stopping at a Catholic church where we said a prayer for the generous strangers who, at a time of shock and sadness, had given permission for their loved one's organs to be used to keep me and probably several other dying people alive. Most of the brain-dead persons whose organs are transplanted each year are multiple donors, some of them giving both of their kidneys and corneas, plus heart, liver, pancreas, bone and skin. That means that only about 4,000 donors account for the 13,000 or so organs that are transplanted in the United States each year.

Because Station 53, the liver transplant unit, was filled, I was "prepped" for the surgery at an almost-deserted nursing station on the same floor. First they did all the basics—blood pressure, temperature, pulse and weight checks. Then in quick fashion—which kept my mind off what was about to happen—they took chest x-rays, gave me an electrocardiogram, drew what seemed to me gallons of blood, took urine samples and throat cultures, gave me three consecutive enemas and made me choke down two doses of the awful tasting "Krom Cocktail" bowel decontaminant. At some point, I also was given antibiotics and my first antirejection drugs, azathioprine and a steroid called Solu-Medrol.

As I lay on my bed between tests, staring blankly at the flickering, soundless television screen, members of the transplant team and several other liver patients stopped to wish me and Ginny well. Word always spread quickly through the tight-knit network when someone was being prepped for a transplant. As I shook hands or gave the thumbs-up sign to my string of visitors, I began to feel like a commando about to parachute alone into enemy territory—scared but exhilarated.

True to her "need-to-know" philosophy, Ginny decided not to call even our children until after my transplant was over. She reasoned that there was nothing any of them could do but stay awake worrying all night. The only person she called was her sister, Martha

Maddock, who insisted on flying from Chicago to be with her during the long vigil. Although Ginny warned her that there still was a chance that the transplant could be aborted, Martha decided to come, though it meant flying to Minneapolis and taking a shuttle to Rochester.

After Ginny left to get some food and prepare to meet Martha at the airport, the nurses told me that the retrieval team's coordinator had called to say that they would arrive with the donated liver about one in the morning. The liver would be submerged in a preserving electrolyte solution and packed in a plastic ice chest. Until it was time for me to be taken to surgery, I was told to watch television or try to sleep. Instead, as the hospital settled into silence and the hall lights dimmed, I flicked on the night light over my bed, took my journal from my toiletry kit and very slowly wrote:

"If I shouldn't survive the surgery, I want these to be my last words. I love Ginny with all my heart; and I love and give thanks for my family. God has blessed me beyond all my understanding. I wish I could give back all that love and beauty."

I was tempted to write more, to leave some final words of advice for my children, to mention special friends, maybe say a kind word about someone who never got much of my attention. Instead, I closed the journal, turned off the light, and lay, arms folded across my chest, staring at the ceiling, wondering if I would be alive at this time tommorrow.

Just after midnight a nurse came to say that the estimated time of arrival of the organ procurers had been moved back to two in the morning. A half hour later she returned with a plastic bottle of antiseptic soap and told me to go down the corridor and take a long hot shower. I stood in the shower, scrubbing and singing every old song I could remember, until Ginny finally came to fetch me. "Everybody thought you had drowned," she said, briskly drying my back with a towel.

At 1:30 in the morning, Dr. Dan Hayes, the young assistant surgeon, came by himself to take me down to the second floor surgery. He seemed awfully relaxed and well rested. To my amazement, the nurses had not given me any medication to quell my anxiety, not even a mild sedative. "We want you cold sober going in there," one of them told me.

As Dr. Hayes pushed my gurney toward the elevator, chatting amiably with Ginny, I suddenly felt like someone who had been goaded into boarding a roller coaster and now had second thoughts as it started creeping up the first rise.

"Hey," I said. "I haven't signed any release yet."

The doctor just laughed. "We don't use them. It's just a piece of paper that really doesn't mean anything. You know we're going to do our very best."

I certainly wanted to encourage that kind of positive thinking. "And you WILL do your best!" I said, raising my right fist in a pregame salute.

The only permission form I signed for Mayo Clinic was when a photographer wanted a release before taking my picture. But the transplant surgeons—the hotshots who were about to slice me open for ten hours or more of high-risk cutting, stitching, and customized fitting of a stranger's liver into a gaping canyon where the largest organ of my body had just been tediously removed—they didn't ask me to sign anything. If they felt that much self-confidence, I certainly wasn't about to plant any doubts in their minds.

Ginny kissed me good-bye, and Dr. Hayes handed my cart off to a nurse outside the surgical waiting area. "See you later," he said breezily.

After a short wait in a holding area, my cart started moving toward the surgery doors, pushed by some unseen hands behind my head. Having never been in an operating room before, I was stunned by the glaring lights and the cold. I had been told to expect to see a number of nurses and technicians in the room, but still I was surprised by how many people awaited my arrival. From my horizontal view on the gurney, the masked men and women in blue gowns seemed to be gliding around the room like robots on wheels.

As my gurney pulled up to the narrow operating table, one of the masked men greeted me with the effusiveness of a head waiter.

"Hello there. What's your name?"

"Frank Maier."

"What are you here for?"

"What am I here for?"

"Right. What are you here for?"

I was tempted to answer something like, "If you don't know, get

195

me the hell out of here!" Instead, I started laughing and said, "You guys are going to give me a brand new liver."

"Right," he said, sounding like a teacher who had finally gotten through to a likable, but rather dense, student.

With that, hands reached down on all sides, lifted me quickly into the air, and deposited me on the operating table. While I was still trying to orient myself, the masked men and women lashed me down like I was being crucified and began to attach monitoring and intravenous lines to my body.

I know they were moving briskly and efficiently—I had been told beforehand that was the drill—but to me everything seemed to slip into slow gear. I had experienced this sensation twice before in my life: in the hospital emergency room during my first bleed and once when I witnessed a car leaping a barricade into oncoming traffic of an expressway. Time did not stop; it just took longer to pass.

They spoke quietly among themselves, but every so often brought me into the conversation—of course asking me the inevitable Mayo question: "Where you from?" When I told them Chicago, they began to tease me about being a closet Cubs fan. They were all Minnesota Twins fans and were riding high because that was the year the Twins were to win the World Series.

I kept defending the honor—slight as it was—of Chicago baseball while they prepared me for what should have been the most terrifying experience of my life. I am certain that it was all part of the protocol for reducing anxiety and putting a patient at ease. All I can say is it worked for me. Instead of thinking about what was about to happen and all the things that could go wrong, I was enjoying the good-natured banter about my erstwhile Cubs and their vaunted Twins.

I was beginning to wonder when Doctors Krom and Hayes would make an appearance, when a nurse bent down and whispered brightly, "Think of something nice to dream about."

My last words before I went under were a mumbled: "The Cubs will win the pennant."

Ginny took a sleeping pill and, because all the sofas and chairs in the intensive care unit waiting room were occupied, she and Martha "bedded" down on pillows on the floor of a nearby room. Two hours after I had been taken into surgery, the door to this room opened. Someone flipped on the lights. It was Dr. Krom, still in surgical garb.

Knowing that my transplant should have lasted for at least ten hours, Ginny saw Krom and immediately thought the worst.

"Frank's dead," she said.

He reassured her that I was still among the living. The donated liver had not looked just right after it had been flushed. At the last minute before they were to slice me open to begin the tedious removal of my diseased liver, the surgeons aborted the transplant.

"We will give him nothing less than a perfect liver," Dr. Krom told Ginny.

The next thirty-six hours remain blank pages for me. What I know comes from Ginny and others. I remember trying to feel the staples that were supposed to be shaped like half a Mercedes emblem. "Boy, can those guys stitch," I thought. Slowly, as if through a fog, I began to perceive that something had gone wrong. I still had my old liver and I still was waiting to die. Because my impaired liver had to struggle to flush the anesthetic from my system, I remained in a stupor, demanding large quantities of food and babbling nonsense.

When Dr. Ellen Hunter stopped to see me the next morning, she found me sound asleep, my face only inches from a bowl of chicken soup on the tray across my bed.

"He was about to drown in it," she laughingly told Ginny.

The image of me drowning in soup broke the tension for poor Ginny.

"I could just see the headline in the paper," Ginny told me later. "*Newsweek* Reporter Drowns in Chicken Soup Awaiting Transplant."

I agreed that would have been a challenge for the Mayo Clinic public relations department.

Three days after being put to sleep, I "woke up" in a restaurant eating a waffle.

"Where's your sister Martha?" I asked Ginny.

"Back in Chicago at a wedding," she answered. "What's new with you?"

20

GINNY'S STORY

ess than a week after my aborted transplant, we were having chocolate milkshakes and hamburgers at Del's Cafe in nearby St. Charles, Minnesota, when my beeper went off again. From then on, it was like seeing a movie a second time. Only this time Dr. James Perkins, the soft-spoken number-two liver transplant surgeon, substituted for Dr. Krom, who was in the Netherlands. And this time, I underwent ten hours of surgery, starting in the early hours of Tuesday, May 12, 1987.

When I slowly floated back to consciousness, I was on a respirator, an endotracheal tube keeping me from speaking. A cold, wet cloth covered my eyes, preventing me from seeing anything. Every so often I could hear the low hum of voices, but could not understand what they were saying. Though my mind was scrambled, I had enough sense about me to realize that this time the surgeons had planted a new liver in me, that I was still alive, and that people were ministering to me.

Without any reference points to determine time or place, I wandered through a twilight world of confusion and fantasy. For a time, I became convinced that a nurse was trying to murder me with a suction pump. (Much later I figured out the nurses were clearing the area around the throat tube with a suctioning device.) I also thought that they had installed a small drainpipe behind my left ear (maybe

I had a pain there) and that miniature fire hoses were squirting liquid from both my sides. I learned later that I had four wound drains, two on each side, plus a bile tube protruding from my chest, a nasogastric tube up my nose, a catheter draining my urine, and the usual tangle of IV and monitoring lines hooked to my body.

My weirdest fantasy during the first hours after transplant was my suspicion that Dr. Perkins and Dr. Hayes were involved in a black-market scheme to sell spare parts of Disneyland characters to theme parks.

We had been told during Jurine Schellberg's weekly preparation sessions to expect posttransplant hallucinations because of the shock of long surgery and the sudden injection into our systems of the powerful immunosuppressant drugs. I remember her telling about one man who came out of surgery convinced that he had been cut into three parts. As I gingerly fingered the fifty-four metal staples across my own body, I wondered if the surgeons had used a chain saw on me.

In talking with other patients after their transplants, I discovered that my fantasies and hallucinations, strange as they were, were common aftereffects. For several days after his plant, Jim Werneski, of Kenosha, Wisconsin, watched foot-high chocolate soldiers marching upside down on the ceiling. He also was convinced that the surgeons had spirited him away to a remote castle in the North Woods. Dorothy Hadden, the Kansas schoolteacher, watched a funeral procession for the child of a Far East potentate parading through her room for several nights running.

What I suggest is that I am not the best-positioned observer to tell this part of Ginny's and my medical adventure. From the time I was put to sleep for the surgery until some time after its completion, I was either totally unconscious or totally confused.

Rather than me reconstructing the events of those hours and days, I step aside and let Ginny take over as narrator for awhile. I will be back later—if she will let me.

As we waited in the dark room after all Frank's tests had been completed, it was eerie quiet. It reminded me of Jimmy Cagney sitting in his cell waiting for the warden and the priest to come and walk him to the chair. In this case, it wouldn't be a chair—it would be an operating table; and it wouldn't be a priest and warden, but Danny Hayes who would come.

Earlier, I made just two phone calls—one to my sister Martha, telling her not to come this time. I would be just fine. I also called my good friend and neighbor, Barbara Dress—just because I needed to tell somebody. I asked them not to call anybody, at least not till I could let our children know in the morning that their dad was out of surgery. Based on what I learned from Frank's aborted transplant, I decided not to stay at the hospital this time, but to take his beeper and go back to the motel and try to sleep. I realized I needed to be bright-eyed for a long day ahead of me—no matter what the outcome.

About midnight, Danny Hayes arrived with the gurney—along with a smiling young friend, Bob Arensman, a pediatric surgeon who had flown from New Orleans to witness his first liver transplant. As they were pushing Frank's gurney into the elevator, Dr. Arensman asked, "Does he know where his liver is coming from? Can we tell him?"

"No," said Dr. Hayes. "The policy is not to tell."

I thought—oh damn—I almost found out.

After kissing Frank and saying, "I'll be with you," I walked across the street to the Kahler Hotel and sat in the empty lobby, sipping machine coffee from a plastic cup and trying to collect my thoughts. All I accomplished was that somewhere that night I lost my wallet. My first thought was—Frank will kill me when he finds out.

Back at the motel, I took half a sleeping pill and fell asleep until about four in the morning, when I called the intensive care unit where Frank was scheduled to go after surgery. They told me that the operating room had just reported that his old liver was out and they were beginning to put the new one in. I knew this was a critical time. There is no fallback if a new liver doesn't kick in after being connected. They were past the point of no return. But, if I had learned anything in the last two years, it was not to worry about what could go wrong—think only about what could go right.

Amazingly, I fell back to sleep for two more hours. When I called the next time, the duty nurse in ICU gave me good news—that the new liver was in and functioning, the doctors were checking for bleeding—a big problem in liver transplants—and getting ready to close him up. They said not to expect to see him until after eight o'clock.

When I reached the hospital, Frank was still in surgery, which alarmed me. Jurine Schellberg, who found me in the eleventh floor ICU waiting room, called the operating room directly and was told that all was still going well—that they were holding Frank to make sure there was no internal bleeding. With that, I felt it was safe to call my "switchboard" operators back home, so they could call their list of family and friends.

Within a half hour, our youngest daughter, Heidi, who was starting her first day on her summer job with the park district, managed to call me in the waiting room to say she was flying right up. She couldn't stand just waiting, but had to come right away.

They finally let me in to see Frank about ten in the morning. Believe me, I had seen a lot of ICUs in the last two years, and— being a mother of four and having worked in an emergency room way back in high school—I have never been squeamish. But I was not prepared for a sight quite like this.

It was a long narrow room, with a large picture window at the far end overlooking downtown Rochester. One wall was glass so a patient could be observed at all times. Two nurses were on duty inside the room for the first twenty-four hours.

Frank lay on a bed in the center of the room, with bright spotlights shining down on him like he was a piece of marble sculpture. He was like a pasty-white statue, absolutely frozen. Attached to the ceiling was an oval track—like a child's toy train track—from which all sorts of bottles and blood pouches were hung. At the foot of the bed was a machine that was pumping warm air into the mattress to gradually bring his body temperature back up to normal. At the head of the bed was the respirator and suctioning machine, going clack, clack, hiss, hiss. Hanging down on either side of the bed were the wound drains that collected blood in plastic jars shaped like canteens.

One of the nurses explained that the cloth was covering his eyes in case he woke up and became startled by the bright overhead lights. I agreed that we wouldn't want him to think he was walking through the Pearly Gates.

I was just becoming accustomed to the scene, when I noticed that his right arm was suspended in a blue sling from the overhead track. "What's with his arm?" I asked her. She said that he had a "bad plant" during surgery. That satisfied me because Frank had experienced several problems with his abused veins; when that happened, I knew you elevated the arm.

Just then an unfamiliar doctor entered the room, introduced himself and said, "I'm from Plastics." I thought, What's he talking about? Frank's new liver isn't made of plastic.

I asked, "Plastics?' "

He said: "Oh, you don't know."

"I don't know what?"

"Your husband was burned during surgery."

I already had gotten a verbal report from the surgeons and nobody had said anything about Frank being burned. So I was confused and, frankly, concerned. I knew enough about medicine to know that the biggest risk for a normal burn victim was infection. A burned victim with a suppressed immune system could be in extra big trouble.

It happened when his blood pressure dropped suddenly during the operation. He suffered a second degree chemical burn when an IV implant leaked as the anesthesiologist was pumping calcium chloride into one of those overworked veins in the back of his right hand.

When the plastic surgeon unwrapped the bandages, I saw that his skin was charred black from just below the wrist to about five inches up his arm. As we watched, the last black crater took shape like an ugly ink blot.

The "plastics man" told me that they would treat the burn with peroxide and silver sulfadiazine, an antibacterial cream. If the burn did not heal properly, they might have to resort to skin grafts. With Frank already listed in "critical" condition following the liver transplant, the news that he had an open burn wound on his arm and might need skin grafts left me devastated. After a year of battling an unrelenting enemy, just when I thought we might be near a victory, here we found ourselves facing still another crisis.

I had to leave the room to regain control of myself and let this latest setback sink in. As I reached the narrow corridor leaving ICU,

I met another woman, about my age, whom I had seen earlier in the waiting room. I knew only that she was from LaCrosse, Wisconsin, and that her daughter was gravely ill with complications from leukemia. She looked at me and I looked at her. The next thing I knew, she had her arms around me and I had mine around her, and we just stood there sobbing.

Whatever we said to each other, I cannot remember. To this day, I do not even know her name or whatever happened to her daughter. But for a brief moment, two perfect strangers shared a closeness that even good friends seldom know. I will never forget her.

Late that afternoon I picked up Heidi at the Rochester airport and, on the drive to the hospital, I tried to prepare her for the shock of seeing her father. It would not be like the times she had seen him in ICU back home.

When we entered Frank's room, Heidi hung back, not sure if she wanted to approach his bed. One of the nurses looked at her and said: "Sweetheart. I think you are going to pass out. Why don't you sit down in the chair?" Later, Heidi said she was stunned because her father did not look like himself with his face so swollen and his hair cut so short. "He looked like a bloated old marine," she said.

About six hours after completion of the surgery, Frank finally started to stir. He obviously was agitated because he was confused and could not speak with the respirator tube in his throat. One of the nurses brought a board on which we printed the letters of the alphabet. With Heidi's help, I painstakingly pointed to letters, noting each time Frank would nod his head. After many frustrating minutes, we finally deciphered what he was trying to say: "Call office."

I assured him that I already had called John McCormick at *Newsweek*'s Chicago bureau. After that, he seemed to relax and soon drifted off to sleep.

Some patients stay for weeks or even months in ICU following their liver transplants. Fortunately, other than the burn on his arm, Frank did not have any immediate complications—the internal bleeding had stopped on its own without further surgery, his kidneys were working and, most important, the new liver was pumping out rich quantities of bile through the tube stuck in his chest.

The throat tube came out twenty-four hours after completion of surgery, and, by the time our pregnant daughter, Katie, arrived the next day, they had him sitting in a chair, with all the bile and drain tubes dangling at his sides.

Frank looked pale but almost buoyant. He had good news—they were getting ready to shift him downstairs to the sterile environs of Station 53. By the time the girls and I returned after lunch, he had slightly different news. The isolated room they were preparing for him at Station 53 had been filled by two kidney transplant patients. He was going to be sent to an "overflow" station on the same floor.

I told Frank I had a phone call to make and immediately went looking for the head ICU nurse to protest. No way, I told her, were they going to send him to a regular nursing station in his immune-suppressed state with a second degree burn on his arm. I got nowhere with my protest, except she finally called the head nurse of Station 53, Joyce Overman, hoping I would accept her assurances that Frank would be well cared for and safe in the overflow unit.

Joyce and I sat down in the small "crisis" room where I had cried with Jurine only a few weeks before. All hospitals have these rooms for private meetings with relatives of patients. I had always tried to avoid getting maneuvered into them because I associate them in my mind with bad news and tears. Joyce Overman, a tall, peppy nurse with an air of confidence about her, tried to calm me down, saying she could not understand my panic about Frank not going to Station 53. He would be well cared for no matter what station he was at.

Finally I burst into tears and blurted out: "With the burn, he needs all the protection from infection he can get."

Joyce looked surprised and asked: "Burn?"

I felt like I was reliving the confusion with the plastic surgeon the day before. She had not been told that he had suffered a burn.

With that, she jumped up and said, "Don't leave. I'll be right back."

Within five minutes she was back with news that they were moving a patient who was four weeks out of transplant into the overflow unit and, as soon as his room was sterilized, Frank would be moved into it.

By the time I got back up to ICU, Frank had "good news" for me. "Guess what? I'm going to Station 53 after all."

I smiled and said, "That's terrific."

He looked at me like his old self and asked, "Did you have something to do with that?"

"Yes I did."

"Thank you," was all he said.

Maybe they all thought I was being paranoid and shouldn't have gotten so worked up over the burn and where they were putting Frank. But I remembered the terrible infection he caught back in the hospital at home and all the misery it caused us.

No way was I going to take chances—not after we had come this far. It was our fight to win or lose. And I knew that we still could lose.

21

REJECTION

A husky nurse who told me he once had been a Chicago schoolteacher lifted me from my bed in the intensive care unit and onto the gurney for a fast trip down corridors and elevator to Station 53. The whirlwind ride was like a journey back to life for me. For the first time since being put to sleep in the operating room, I began to focus, both with my eyes and with my mind, on what was happening around me.

With a sudden jolt of joy, I realized that I was alive—really alive; that I no longer had to die; that I had been reborn. Like Lazarus in the Bible, I had died and had been brought back to life.

Growing up, I had always wondered about Lazarus. Where had he been those four days before his friend Jesus arrived to raise him from the dead? Did he remember? What did he tell his sisters, Mary and Martha? (For some reason, I found it serendipitous that Ginny's sisters are named Mary and Martha.) And what did Lazarus's pals in Bethany think about his story? Did they treat him like a celebrity? Or a weirdo? If it happened today, I'm sure Geraldo, Phil, and Oprah would be throwing elbows like hockey players to get him first. "Tommorrow—The Resurrected Man!" Imagine the headlines on the tabloids at the supermarket checkout counter: "Lazarus Says Elvis Not There!"

All this was percolating merrily inside my head as my gurney arrived at Station 53, the sanctum where, I had been taught, I would begin my restoration.

When I saw a smiling Ginny waiting for me inside my private room, I felt like a groom greeting his bride at the altar. Tears filled my eyes and, despite the bandaged burn on my arm, the metal staples tacked across my body, the dark purple bruises from rib cage to thigh, and the tangles of drainage and IV lines that made me look like a battered octopus, I hugged her with all the strength I could muster. The more it hurt to hug her, the happier I felt. Pain—which I had come to accept as a dull and inevitable companion—now felt as good and God-given as any pleasure could be. Strange as it may sound, experiencing physical pain once more was another sign that I was alive again!

I was kept in "strict isolation" for two weeks after my transplant, the immunosuppressant drugs having left me with no defenses against infections. I was not allowed to leave my closed room and unable to have any visitors except Ginny and daughters, Katie and Heidi. Anyone entering my room, including nurses and doctors, had to scrub their hands and then don a clean cloth gown over their street clothes. The windows of the room, like all Station 53 windows, were sealed with duct tape. No flowers or children were allowed in the circular nursing station at any time. Relatives of patients were allowed for visits, but were not supposed to circulate into other patients' rooms.

Station 53 and a few other nursing stations in Rochester Methodist Hospital operate with a "primary care" nursing system. I was assigned one nurse with total responsibility and accountability for my care, from admission until discharge. From the patient's viewpoint, it is like having a nervous, first-time mother watching over you at all times. It solves one of the worst problems hospitalized patients face: the lack of continuity of treatment, the feeling that each new face appearing at your bedside really has no idea who you are or why you are there. From the nurses' viewpoint, the primary care system enhances job satisfaction, gives them more of a say in treatment and also a more personal relationship with their patients.

My primary care nurse was Mary Larson, a tall native Minnesotan, who had been with the team right from the start and had, in fact, been the primary care nurse for Mayo's very first liver transplant patient.

Though I had four wound drains in my sides and a bile tube protruding from my chest, Mary goaded me into faltering steps around my room before I could even settle into my bed. She taught me how to change all my bandages, including the dressing on the bile tube. This maneuver, which took me several days to master, involved applying antiseptic with a cotton swab, holding down the plastic tube so it did not "kink," and then taping the dressing to my skin so it would not slip. All of this tape-tangling exercise had to be done with my chin tucked down to my chest and my eyes focusing on a spot only inches below my nose. The bulky bandage protecting the burn on my right arm only complicated my maneuvers. To me, changing the bile tube dressing was the medical equivalent of trying to light a cigar in a tornado.

Mary and the other nurses who cared for me when she was off duty were patient with my klutziness. But they were firm in forcing me to start taking care of myself. They would not do anything for me that they felt I could do for myself. I complained to Ginny that they were like "benevolent prison guards."

Even as my body was sputtering back to life, Mary Larson brought in a small plastic basket filled with my daily medications, which I was expected to administer to myself and chart in a notebook, along with my morning and nightly weight, temperature, and blood pressure.

"I can't do that yet, Mary," I sighed, hoping that she would take pity on me and baby me for just a few more days.

"Sure you can," she said. "You've got to get used to taking care of yourself again."

Like a schoolteacher, Mary took every opportunity to drill me on my medications, explaining what they were for and their side effects. Before my transplant, when I was not really convinced that I would survive, I accepted in the manner of an indifferent student the general warning that the drugs I would have to take after transplant would have serious side effects and leave me vulnerable to cancers, pneumonia, and just about any stray microbe looking for a target. But, until Mary started educating me about the drugs, I did not really understand how potent they were—and how my life would be changed by having to take them.

First came the wonder drug, cyclosporine—the "golden bullet" that I would have to take twice a day for the rest of my life. The major threat from taking cyclosporine over the course of time was that it damages the kidneys. As one of the hepatologists, Dr. Rolland Dickson, explained to me, it was not a question of whether cyclosporine would harm the kidneys, it was only a question of how much it would hurt the kidneys. For that reason, Dr. Dickson explained, the search for a less toxic replacement for cyclosporine is one of the number one priorities of transplant researchers. A newly developed drug, called FK 506, recently has been used on patients who cannot take cyclosporine for one reason or another.

Dr. Dickson explained that the challenge for the doctors overseeing my recovery was to find the proper balance point where I would have enough cyclosporine in my system at all times to prevent rejection, but not so much as to leave me an easy target for infections.

Cyclosporine also can cause hand tremors, high blood pressure, overgrowth of the gums, and increased hair growth. This last property of the drug can be particularly annoying for women patients, who often find it causes embarrassing hair growth on their faces. In my case, my hair started growing so quickly that I now need a weekly cut to keep it trim—and it has changed in texture from straight to thick and wavy.

Azathioprine, known by the brand name Imuran, is a potent immunosuppressant that can leave the body vulnerable to all sorts of infections. It also causes general malaise in many patients.

Prednisone, a synthetic corticosteroid that has been used for more than three decades to fight a variety of inflammatory diseases, can cause all sorts of problems, particularly when taken in high doses. It can cause ulcers, fluid retention, vulnerability to skin cancers, wild mood swings, and, most annoying to those taking it, a puffiness in the face—which the medical professionals call "cushionoid," but which most patients call the "chipmunk look."

Although prednisone is a powerful appetite stimulator that causes many patients to gain weight, the transplant unit's dieticians at first did not seem worried about any weight gain. On the contrary, they seemed to be fattening me up for slaughter. As soon as I could start taking solid food, they began to calorie pack me like an athlete before the Olympics. I was encouraged to eat as much food as I could choke down. The regimen was designed to rebuild the wasted bodies that liver transplant patients universally bring to their surgery.

To my amazement, only a few mornings after arriving at Station 53, I downed a breakfast of orange juice, dry cereal, three pancakes, a scrambled egg, three strips of bacon, a pint of milk, and a cup of coffee, along with syrup and real butter. I couldn't wait for lunch, when I would be served a peanut butter and grape jelly sandwich, along with chocolate milk and apple pie à la mode. I half-complained to the dietician, Sara DiCecco, that I had not eaten that much food since I was a teenager.

"Enjoy it while you can," she said. "The day's coming when we'll cut you off and go just the opposite direction to hold your weight down.

While my body struggled to regain strength, my mind immediately started functioning on all cylinders as soon as I left the intensive care unit. For the first time, I grasped how brain-dead I had been for the last two years. Partly because of the powerful new drugs stimulating my system, but mainly because my new liver was detoxing my system so efficiently, my mind was racing. Like a freshly minted college graduate, I was bubbling with ideas, dreams, and plans.

Except when I was undergoing tests or watching the Iran-Contra hearings on television, I spent most days and nights furiously writing in my journal. Recalling the words of Dr. Vern Kerchberger back home about writing of my transplant experience, I started outlining in a notebook the skeleton of an article which I hoped *Newsweek* might one day publish. I couldn't wait to get started on it.

I remember dictating a hyperbolic memo to John McCormick that included my ideas for a transplant story, but also gushing out my gratitude to my editors and coworkers for all their support. Despite assuring me that he would transmit my message to New York as dictated, John wisely edited the ornate buncombe out of it before passing it along in a less frantic and more professional format.

For the first time in our life together, Ginny actually had to talk me down—I was that hyperactive. Usually she was the active, antsy one, while I was the put-it-off, laid-back partner in our marriage. But now, I was like the mild-mannered accountant in the movies who suddenly experiences a personality change and concocts a plan to embezzle a hundred grand and run off with a cocktail waitress. My usual lethargic manner faded—at least temporarily—and I turned into a frantic Type-A tiger. Not only was I neurotically anxious about starting to write again, I also had turned into a nonstop talker. When Mary Larson told Ginny that this was still another side effect of the prednisone, I remember Ginny telling her, "I married Gary Cooper and now he sounds like Daffy Duck."

About a week after I came under the care of the "Gentle Persuader," as Mary Larson was known in the unit, my body started to show early signs of rejecting the new liver. Though my mind was clearer than it had been in years and my legs and arms were starting slowly to regain strength, an army of white blood cells in my body had detected a "foreign" invader. The alarm had been sounded and an advance patrol was rushing to attack the stranger's liver that was keeping me alive.

My doctors detected the mild rejection, a phenomenon experienced by about half of all liver transplant patients, by daily blood samples and a biopsy performed by Dr. Ellen Hunter. Though they explained that mild rejection was not an uncommon experience, Ginny and I had read enough to know that, once started and untreated, any rejection can easily get out of control and be difficult to reverse once the immune system's army is fully mobilized. We also knew that two discharged patients were back in the hospital because their bodies were rejecting their first transplants.

To battle the first wave of rejection, the doctors put me on a drug called Solu-Medrol, a synthetic corticosteroid with the tongue-tangling generic name, "methylprednisolone." It normally was used to suppress allergic reactions, but had been found also to dampen the enthusiasm of the immune system's most aggressive storm troopers. In prescribing Solu-Medrol, one of the attending hepatologists, Dr. Jack Gross, warned me that the drug "just might have the side effect of mild euphoria."

That turned out to be a "mild" understatement. The first night after receiving a dose of the antirejection drug, at three in the morning I managed to get out of bed and shuffle, with all my drainage tubes in tow, to the patients' lounge where I plopped down on a straight-backed chair next to the refrigerator and blissfully made myself a root beer float. I remember having a dickens of a time spooning the ice cream into the overflowing paper cup of root beer; my hand-eye coordination was on a par with the town drunk.

Then I put my feet up on a nearby chair and in my mind began to compose a book that would explain how to eradicate all of the world's evils—hunger, war, television game shows, the whole works. It was to be a slim fifty-page volume that I would publish under the *nom de plume,* Frank Troll. In my benevolent state, I did not want any personal glory from my magnum opus, thus the pseudonym "Troll," which had been my nickname in college.

You have to believe me that it was a wonderful, incisive book—though written only on swirling golden sunbeams in my medicated mind. Barely able to concoct a root beer float, I was in no shape to handle paper and pen.

When I explained my behavior to Dr. Gross the next morning and asked if I had experienced euphoria, he rubbed his beard and smiled as if humoring me, "Sounds like it to me."

Ginny as always was most practical when I told her about my middle-of-the-night "composition."

"Did you take any notes?" she asked.

Two weeks after transplant my tests showed acute rejection of my new liver. If that happens to kidney patients, they can be put onto dialysis until a new organ is located. In an emergency, heart patients can live for a time on a temporary artificial heart. But, with the liver, there is no fallback. Unless reversed, acute rejection means death or a second transplant, an ordeal that I was unwilling to face. I was not about to go through all that trauma and anxiety again.

Dr. Hunter brought me the news that my body was going into acute rejection only hours after Ginny had departed for Chicago for some well-deserved home leave and to pick up her mother-of-the-groom dress for our son Danny's approaching wedding in George-town. Since our daughters had driven our car home when they left,

Ginny ended up hitching a ride to Chicago with a couple she had met at her motel.

"You're not hitching a ride with perfect strangers," I lectured her.

"But they're Catholic," she said, doing her best imitation of Gracie Allen.

"So was Al Capone and Adolf Hitler," I snapped, knowing perfectly well that she would get to Chicago her own way, no matter what my reservations.

Dr. Hunter called Ginny from my bedside phone to explain that I was experiencing "acute rejection," that everything was under control and she need not rush back. The transplant team had decided to give me a fourteen-day treatment of an experimental drug, Orthoclone OKT3, a space-age sounding "monoclonal antibody" produced in mice that battles the special white blood cells causing the rejection.

When Dr. Hunter handed me the phone, I jauntily told Ginny that I was feeling terrific, that I might go dancing with Dr. Hunter and some of the nurses that night and that she should not worry.

"Whatever you do, get your wedding dress, get your hair done, and don't come back until you feel like it," I told her.

Without telling me her plans, Ginny and her sister, Martha, drove to Rochester the very next morning, stopping only for gas on the way. Either Dr. Hunter told her something outside my hearing or Ginny instinctively sensed that we faced still another crisis and that she had better be on hand to help me deal with it.

I think patients should try to learn as much as possible about what's happening to them. But there are times when a bit of ignorance can be a blessing. That was true for me in the case of my rejection. I really did not need to know about all the possible things that could start happening once my body went into serious rejection of the new organ. In fact, I did not realize until later how grave my situation was. Since I was feeling better each day, my mind was functioning, and my strength returning, I did not sense that the agents of my own body were succeeding in their mission of killing my new liver.

Dr. Hunter told me that OKT3, which was approved "salvage"

therapy for kidney transplants, still had not been approved by the federal government for liver transplant emergencies. Since it was being given to me as part of a medical research study, I had to sign a permission form—not for Mayo Clinic, which does not use them—but for the federal government.

Before starting me on OKT3, they temporarily stopped my cyclosporine, which I still was taking intravenously, not by mouth. This gave me six added hours of freedom daily to walk around my room without dragging the infusion pump and IV lines behind me. It also stopped the hallucinations and "mind-racing" that the doctors blamed on "main-lining" cyclosporine. Up till then, I still was experiencing a nightly slide show, a series of strange faces, most of them comic and some looking like me, projected on the ceiling or walls of my room.

The first two days I was injected with OKT3, Dr. Hunter sat at my bedside doing paperwork, just in case I suffered any side effects from the experimental drug. Chills and fever were the most common reactions, but on rare occasions, patients had suffered pulmonary edema, which—if not quickly treated—can cause death.

In my case, I experienced bone-rattling chills the first time they injected me with the drug, forcing the nurses to pile blanket after blanket atop my shaking body. My jaws trembled so violently that I feared I might severely bite my tongue. The next day—with blankets piled on a chair in anticipation of the same reaction—the opposite side effect kicked in. I developed a soaring fever that left me feeling and looking like an actor in a jungle film. By the third day, my body adjusted to this strange antibody that had been produced in mice, and I experienced no further side effects for the rest of the two-week therapy.

All we could do was wait to see if OKT3 would work its magic and stop my rejection. At night, as I lay looking at the ceiling and wishing for the dawn, all I could keep thinking was: Ginny has fought so long and so hard for me, I can't let her down, not when we're so close to winning.

22

MR. UPTIGHT
GOES TO
WASHINGTON

idnight. Today is June 1, 1987. My fifty-fourth birthday, the exact number of metal staples I still have
in me. It's spooky knowing that my body has raised
a defense army that is trying to kill the stranger's
liver that is keeping me alive."

That's what I wrote in my journal at the start
of what seemed destined to be the dreariest day of my life. About
the only good news that had come our way since the start of the
rejection was the plastic surgeons' tentative decision that I would
not need any skin grafting for the burn on my arm. I also was
removed from strict isolation and allowed to shuffle around the
nursing station. But the buoyant mood that had filled me immediately after transplant had faded. I wasn't depressed. I wasn't discouraged. I was just flat.

Then, before dawn, I fell while trying to walk in my room for
exercise. My legs turned to rubber, and I went down. Try as I might,
I could not get up from my knees or reach the nurse's call button.
After so many days in a hospital bed and so many months dying,
the muscles in my arms, legs, and back had atrophied. I was like
a hundred-year-old man trying to get up after falling on a deserted,
icy roadway. I remember shouting to nobody in particular, "Don't
leave me in this ditch!"

Finally, I crawled to a chair, slowly pulled myself up, then lunged for the side rail on my bed, grabbing it like a trapeze. I stood, wobbling like a scarecrow, until a nurse came for my morning temperature and blood pressure checks and boosted me into bed. I was learning to have much more sympathy for old folks whose aging bodies no longer respond to commands from their still-active minds.

I never was big on celebrating birthdays—even as a small boy. Christmas was the day I looked forward to all year long, that and the Fourth of July. Early in our marriage I made Ginny promise, after we had endured a disastrous birthday celebration for an acquaintance, that she never would throw a surprise birthday party for me, no matter what the provocation. Despite that promise, Ginny decided that a birthday observance of some sort was just the ticket to lift my sagging spirits. So she went to work on the day's events.

To start the day, I received a phone call from Margaret Kennedy Moser from back home. Ginny had arranged the call so Margaret could read me a few upbeat passages from the Bible and then "chat" me up, as she put it.

Ginny suggested to Margaret that we say a special prayer of thanksgiving for the family of my donor. Until then, I had not thought much about my donor and his or her family. In my wonderment at being alive again, I had ignored my unknown benefactors. All we had been told by Mayo's procurement coordinators was that my donor had lived about 1,000 miles from Rochester and, in addition to giving me a lifesaving liver, he or she had also provided two kidneys and bone to other strangers. (Much later, Ginny brought me a map on which I roughly drew a 1,000-mile circle radiating from Rochester. It took in so much of the United States and Canada that I was left with no useful information about where my liver might have come from.)

Now that Ginny had brought up the donor family in our telephone conversation with Margaret, I felt ashamed that I had given so little thought to them since coming back to my senses after transplant. In my exuberance at finding myself alive again, I had forgotten the enormous debt that I owed—and never could repay—to people who had freely given me such a priceless gift.

In late morning, a "pink lady" volunteer arrived with an armful of mail, including get well cards from some of the boys and girls in my SPRED group back home. They were simple, beautiful cards that I never will throw away. Also in the bundle of mail were individual notes from people at *Newsweek*'s offices in New York who had given blood in my name. In all, the *Newsweek* employees donated 121 pints. Amazingly, according to Ginny's count in her notebook, that was precisely the number of units of blood that I had received up to that point in my illness and recovery.

In late afternoon Ginny showed up at my room all bubbly and decked out like she was going dancing. Over my protests, she pulled me out of bed, stuffed me into my blue bathrobe, and said, "We're going to a party, big boy."

I continued to protest, saying I was in no mood to go anywhere, least of all to some party. She pushed and pulled me to the patients' lounge, which was filled with nurses, doctors, patients, and their families. "Surprise," everyone shouted as the flashbulbs popped. Our social worker, Jurine Schellberg, who had become the main stabilizer of my shaky emotions, cut the sheet cake that Ginny had ordered from the Kahler Hotel's catering service. The inscription on the icing, which Ginny had lifted from a greeting card she had seen that morning, read: "The Best Is Yet To Come."

Despite my initial grouchiness, I was overwhelmed at the warmth generated by the people who had come to my party—all of them strangers to Ginny and me such a short time before. Yet each of the men and women in that room, whether medical professional or fellow sufferer, had held out a hand to us in this last desperate part of our journey. They had been there for us when we most needed help and encouragement.

I kept from crying by nonstop babbling—maybe the prednisone was driving my tongue again. I ended my hyperbolic thank-you remarks by declaring, "Don't let the doctors near the cake!" After spending so much time in hospitals, I knew enough to stay on the good side of the nurses.

At the dinner hour, I received a long-distance call from members of my Thirteen-Thirteen Investment Club, who were meeting that night in a Chicago restaurant. The jist of their joshing was that they wanted me to stay away for a bit longer because the investment portfolio had grown rapidly in my absence. A sad irony: two of the men who got on the phone to laugh and encourage me that night

217

have since died. At the time, they seemed in the peak of good health.

Later, a nurse brought me a sheet of pink paper with white hearts from Jennifer Hoce, a plucky sixteen-year-old who was two rooms from me. Jennifer, who lived in Jacksonville, Florida, had been Mayo's fifth liver transplant two years before. She was hospitalized for treatment of recurring, painful kidney stones. Because I only recently had been let out of the strict isolation of my room, I had talked to Jennifer briefly one time, though Ginny had spent time with her and her parents. But I knew of Jennifer mainly from hearing her singing sweetly in the morning and teasing a visiting Dr. Krom about his golf game. Everybody knew that Dr. Krom had a soft spot in his heart for Jennifer, one of the few children Mayo has transplanted.

"Frank," her note said, "here's a poem I remember that's one of my favorites. I didn't write it, but it's still very special to me. 'You can't see the rainbow till after the rain / And you can't share the joy till you've weathered the pain / For life is a blending of laughter and tears that brings love and meaning to all of our years.' © Love, Jennifer. P.S. Hope you like it. Happy Birthday."

The warm glow from the party did not last long. It began to fade just like the sunset I watched from my hospital bed that evening. I had every reason to be discouraged—at least I gave myself permission to think so. At fifty-four I was supposed to be in my most productive years. But I didn't know if I ever would be able to work again—least of all in a strenuous trade like journalism. I faced medical bills already over $200,000, with the meter still running and no clear idea how much eventually would be covered by insurance. For the rest of my life I would have to take antirejection drugs that themselves were a threat to my health and life.

My still-feeble body was rejecting the liver that the generous family of some innocent soul had given to me, and there was nothing in all my power that I could do to turn the process around. My sides were bruised purple from rib cage to hip, like I had been stomped by a gang of Hell's Angels. The burn on my arm throbbed and sweated under the bandage. The metal staples felt like someone was pulling a chain tightly across my body. A tube still drained coffee-colored bile out of my chest into a clumsy collection container. I had not showered since the morning of my transplant three weeks before.

Then, without any conscious effort on my part, a litany of names started running through my mind, names of people—some friends and some near-strangers—who had helped Ginny and me at different junctions in our journey. I began to recite the names quietly, almost like saying a private prayer. As I said each name, the appropriate face appeared, as vivid as if that person were standing at the foot of my bed. It was like the numinous experiences that had exploded on me during the weeks prior to my transplant. Only this experience was deeper and more ineffable, like the biblical "peace that surpasses all understanding."

In the fading light I reread Jennifer's note. Then I called the motel to say goodnight to Ginny and tell her how happy she had made me on my birthday. She was so exhausted that she fell asleep while we were talking. But I stayed awake most of that night—out of simple joy at being alive.

The fourteen-day treatment with OKT3 worked. My "numbers"—the various enzyme counts in my daily blood samples—slowly turned in the right direction, and another biopsy by Dr. Hunter showed that the rejection had been stopped. In my mind I envisioned a group of cartoonlike white mice waving a flag and holding a victory celebration over the fallen bodies of the bully-boy lymphocytes who had been sent out by King Immunity to kill my precious new liver. Admittedly, the image was a bit confused since normally you think of mice or rats as bad guys and your immune system as the friendly local police department. But life, I was learning, was not simple for people who had undergone organ transplants.

I began to settle comfortably into the daily routine of life at Station 53 under the observant eye of Mary Larson and her fellow nurses. Not only did I slowly begin to regain my strength, but I began to feel a deep attachment to the place. It was my safe harbor, a warm and friendly place where I could write in my journal, begin to enjoy reading and eating again, and generally bask in a languid world of little stress and minimal responsibility.

One month after my transplant, the transplant team decided it was time to make me flap my wings and try to fly on my own. It came as quite a surprise and shock when they kicked me out of the nest.

Two days before Ginny was to fly to Washington, D.C., for Danny and Xiomara's wedding, Dr. Russell Wiesner, the big friendly chief hepatologist of the transplant program, stopped by for what I presumed was just a visit.

"I hear you've got a big weekend coming up," he said.

That's right, I told him. Ginny was flying to the wedding, which would be in the chapel at Georgetown University.

"I hear you're going too," he said with a big grin.

I figured he was pulling my leg.

"I've got a tape recorder and I'm sending a message with Ginny," I said.

"No," he said. "We think you should go. Matter of fact, you're going."

My stomach went cold. Was he kidding? I was in no shape to go across the street let alone on a long airplane trip. My staples had been plucked out, but I still had a bile tube in my chest. My arm was still heavily bandaged to prevent infection. I could barely walk twenty-five steps without stopping to catch my breath. The nurses had drummed into me that I was fair game for every passing microbe. Surely they were not going to risk sending me back into the world before my time.

Over my very real protests, Ginny escorted me to a nearby men's store where she picked out a dress shirt and tie, underwear, and socks for me like I was a ten-year-old going to boarding school. I had a kelly green blazer and a pair of khaki slacks that would be "passable" for the wedding ceremony, she said. She changed her airline ticket and bought me one, and arranged for us to ride a van to Minneapolis for a direct flight to Dulles Airport.

They "capped" my bile tube so I would not have to drag around a collection container and handed me over to Ginny to take me to the motel for the night. I felt like a prisoner who had just gotten comfortable with his life sentence and now found himself shoved out the gate without a hearing.

The night before our departure for Washington, Ginny took me on a "date" to wean me from my dependence on Station 53. We sat in the mezzanine of the Kahler Hotel listening to a pianist play show tunes and then had dinner at the restaurant atop the hotel—the place where Ginny and her "boyfriend" Art had dined on that night that now seemed so long ago.

As we waited in the hotel lobby for the airport van the next afternoon, I felt panic churning in my stomach. I had not been out of a hospital for two months and was almost in a state of shock. I had been so indoctrinated by the nurses about avoiding crowds, people with coughs, small kids with the sniffles, that I had turned into a neurotic hypochondriac.

I suddenly said to Ginny: "When the van comes and I say I'm not going, don't argue with me. It may happen. I'm not sure I can go."

"Of course you're going."

"Seriously. If I can't get into that van, you've got to go without me."

When the van came, I climbed sheepishly into the back seat—as far as possible from the driver and two other passengers. Ginny immediately fell asleep. I stared out the window at the passing farm fields, clutching an "emergency" survival kit that contained two rolls of tape, a small box of bandages for my bile-tube changes, packaged antiseptic sticks, a roll of gauze for my arm, a notebook and two fiber-tip pens, and a three-day supply of granola bars, peanut butter packets, and crackers. I also had two dozen wrapped alcohol swabs that I had gotten from Mary Larson. They would come in handy for cleaning doorknobs at the motel and sterilizing my hands after touching anything—especially after shaking hands at the wedding.

I was ready for anything. When the driver of the van sneezed, I covered up like a boxer on the ropes and immediately unwrapped my first alcohol swab. I looked at Ginny who was watching me through half-closed eyes, smiling. I started to tell her that this was no joking matter—but decided against it. If she didn't understand the jeopardy that the doctors and she had placed me in, who could? I just stared out the window, pouting, for the rest of the ride to the airport.

Ginny told no one in advance that I was coming to the wedding. She figured—correctly—that the decision on my coming would only be made at the last minute. She did not want to raise anyone's hopes.

So when Danny met her at the airport—only to find he was meeting "us"—he broke down and cried like a baby. Seeing how glad he was to see me, I realized how selfish and outright goofy I had been acting. Ginny immediately sought out her mother and my mother to tell them that I was a surprise guest at the wedding. "I don't want them to come around the corner and see you and think you're a vision," she explained.

Though I realized I was acting goofy, I could not change my bizarre behavior. By present insights, my paranoia at Danny and Xiomara's wedding seems embarrassing and hilarious. At the time, when I was just beginning to regain a measure of control over my life and getting used to being forever a "transplant" recipient, it seemed perfectly reasonable to me.

That weekend in Washington I acted like a classic compulsive neurotic, constantly washing my hands, fleeing from every coughing passerby, and even posting "Do Not Touch" signs on all of my possessions in our motel room—to the amusement of our relatives and friends. I even drew a skull and crossbones symbol on the signs. As soon as I would post a sign, Ginny would take it down. "What is this? A poison control center?" she asked. It was like a child's game. Even as I was taping the hand-drawn signs all over the room, I knew that I was acting crazy—but I kept right on doing it. I couldn't help myself.

I also learned that weekend that real people need money—something I had not had to worry about for months. It happened the morning before the wedding when Ginny and others went to visit the White House, a tour that Danny had arranged for his mother. I wandered around the motel, mixing with the wedding guests who had virtually taken over an entire floor. Relishing my new-found freedom and gaining confidence in my ability to function in the real world again, I entered the gift shop off the lobby and picked up more bandages, tape, and candy bars for my emergency kit.

When the clerk said, "That will be $7.45," I just stared at her. It was as if she were speaking in some strange dialect. Then I realized that I was being asked to pay for the collection of goods she had just put into the brown paper sack. And I realized that I had not a cent in my pockets—and that I had not had a cent in my pockets for months.

As it turned out, she was a kindly lady who was very interested in my tale of chronic illness and fascinated to meet someone who had undergone a transplant. She then shared with me each and every illness that she had ever experienced in her life. We were like two veterans exchanging war stories. Instead of holding my purchases until I could get the money from Ginny, the woman insisted on my taking them with me and paying her whenever I was passing.

Rather than embarrass myself further by asking Ginny for money and having to explain my stupid behavior, I hit upon a plan. All that afternoon as I wandered around the motel, whenever I encountered a relative or friend—and the place was filled with people arriving for the wedding—I would casually ask, "Say, do you happen to have a spare quarter?" Like a crafty street urchin, in this beggarly fashion I not only accumulated enough money to pay my bill at the gift shop, but ended up with $2.25 of "walking around" money. I was smugly pleased with the survival instincts that had prompted me to ask for a quarter from many people rather than the entire $7.45 from one person. Crafty Frank figured that nobody expected to be paid back a loan of a quarter, whereas they certainly would expect to get repaid a larger sum.

Late that afternoon, I also hit upon a plan to improve my appearance for the next day's wedding. I knew that my green jacket looked more suitable for a golf outing than a wedding, no matter how much Ginny tried to reassure me that "it looks just fine." I was determined to buy a more sedate navy blue blazer to wear to the church and reception.

Because Ginny was not around to veto my plans, I badgered our youngest daughter, Heidi, who had a credit card, into accompanying me to a shopping mall a few blocks from the motel. Not only did I pick out a blue blazer that, Heidi informed me later, was two sizes too large and of tissue-paper material, I bought a box of 100 rubber surgical gloves and two more rolls of tape. Because Heidi controlled the credit card, she had the leverage to block the jacket purchase, though she did humor me by letting me keep the gloves and tape.

As we walked back to the motel, I felt compelled to confess to her, "I know I'm acting nuts, Heidi."

"That you are," she said. "But we all love you anyway."

That didn't stop Heidi from telling Ginny and everybody else about our hilarious trip to the shopping mall and my near-purchase of the gaudy blue jacket. I got the impression that I was the clown prince of the wedding party—providing comic relief for the guests until the big event itself.

My craziness was benign and, I was told later, greatly appreciated by family and friends, always eager to store up anecdotes to tell at reunions and parties. "Do you remember when crazy Frank . . .?" or "Then Dad insisted on buying this really wierd polyester jacket . . ." Even as I was living through that wedding weekend, I could appreciate that I was generating mounds of new material for family folklore.

My bizarre trip to Washington concluded on a frightening note that left me shaken and more paranoid than ever. Even now, it makes me wonder about my sanity during Danny and Xiomara's wedding weekend. The actual wedding and the reception afterward at a country inn in Virginia went off beautifully. I even relaxed to the point of eating a dinner roll at the reception—along with one of my granola bars. (I was afraid that I might catch something from the prepared meal.)

Later there was a casual backyard party in Arlington, Virginia, for the bride and groom, but I was too exhausted to attend. I stayed in my motel room, sitting in the dark for hours because a sudden electrical storm had blown all the electricity for miles around. My college roommate, Frank Lolli, and his wife, Diane, who had been Ginny's friend since high school, kept me company until I insisted that they leave and go have fun at the outdoor party. After repeatedly asking if I would be okay, they finally agreed to go. Frank left me a flashlight in the unlikely event that I wanted to take the stairs down to the lobby.

After they left, sitting in the dark in the motel, I suddenly felt vulnerable and terribly alone. I realized that I did not even have a telephone number to reach Ginny. I could not even turn on the television to distract my thoughts. Using the flashlight, I located my emergency kit and compulsively cleaned the area around my capped bile tube and covered it with a well-taped fresh bandage. Then I applied antiseptic to the scar across my body, slowly so as not to miss a spot. After that I ate some of my rations of crackers and peanut butter—and felt as alone and dejected as an explorer abandoned by his friends at the end of the Earth.

I awoke in the middle of the night to sense Ginny in the bed beside me. She had not disturbed me when she returned from the party. When I flicked the switch to discover if the lights were working, I not only learned that the power failure was over but that daughter Heidi was missing. Because of the allocation of people to rooms, Heidi was supposed to sleep in the other queen-sized bed in our room. I looked at the clock and saw that it was almost three in the morning.

I immediately woke Ginny from a sound sleep to tell her the horrible news: our youngest daughter had met with an accident or had fallen into the clutches of murderous Washingtonians! There was no other explanation for her being missing at three in the morning.

In my agitated state, I never thought that she and some friends might do what young folk do after a wedding, go to an after-hours joint in Georgetown. At first, Ginny tried unsuccessfully to calm me down, offering all sorts of logical explanations for Heidi being out so late. But, as I became ever more anxious, even Ginny started to half-believe my imaginings.

She woke our oldest son, Mike, to see if he knew where Heidi had gone after the party. Soon, we had all of the family and many of our closest friends assembled in their nightclothes. Someone called the police, someone else called local hospitals. People paced, not sure if they should be more concerned about Heidi or me. I kept bewailing my own close escape from death only to have our youngest daughter taken in the prime of life. Even poor Danny and Xiomara, the bride and groom, ended up down in the lobby with the anxious mob. Her parents, who had come all the way from Spain for the wedding, also were awake and alarmed.

About four in the morning, convinced that Heidi was indeed beyond help, I went up to our room and began packing my bag. When Ginny protested, I kept saying that I had to get back to Station 53. That's where I had to be when we got news of Heidi's fate. I never was so convinced of anything in my entire life as I was that something terrible had happened to Heidi—who never would stay out all night without calling.

Heidi and her fellow revellers, including Xiomara's brother, Everard, appeared at dawn's early light. They were amazed at the large reception committee waiting for them in the lobby.

By then I was so shaken that I insisted on catching the next plane back to Minnesota. I could not take the real world just yet. I had to get "home" to my protectors at the Mayo Clinic.

Once you have reconciled yourself to the fact that you are a dead man, it's surprising how vexing it is to be yanked back to life. Not many people will ever experience it—but, in some ways, coming back to life can be tougher than dying.

23

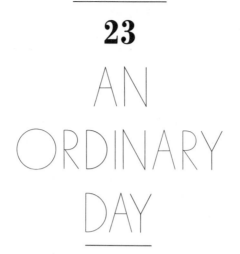

AN
ORDINARY
DAY

our days after returning from the wedding, I was yanked back into Rochester Methodist Hospital because my skin and eyes had turned jaundiced. Blood tests showed that my cyclosporine level was down and my bilirubin count was up.

This meant one of two things: either I was back in rejection again or my main bile duct was blocked.

Bilirubin levels are monitored closely in patients with liver disease. It is a reddish pigment formed in the blood by the breakdown of hemoglobin. Normally the liver removes bilirubin from the blood and flushes it from the body in bile. When the liver is not performing efficiently, excess bilirubin builds up in the body and a person's skin and eyes turn greenish-yellow, or jaundiced.

The low cyclosporine level was equally disturbing to the doctors. If my body was not properly absorbing my daily doses of cyclosporine, my immune system would encounter no opposition in attacking my new liver.

Ginny and I were terribly discouraged. We had been warned that the road to recovery would be rough and uncertain, but we felt that determination and a positive attitude could get us around any obstacles. Two of my fellow patients also were back in the hospital because of recurring problems, and this added to our anxiety: Rachel Olerud had rejected her first liver and had to be retransplanted.

Bob Bell, who had been sent home to Indiana and was to have been married on the same day as our Danny, instead was back at Station 53 for treatment of an abscess behind his new liver.

In a rare display of weariness, Ginny said to me one night as she left to return to the motel: "All I want in life is an ordinary day. Do you think we'll ever see an ordinary day again?"

After she had gone, I wrote in my journal: "My illness seems like a ball of string that keeps tangling as it unwinds. One thing leads to another. Just when we thought life was getting easier, another snarl develops. We thought after the transplant my job would be to take my medicines religiously, watch my health, and regain my strength. It's not that simple. Each time Ginny and I mount a hill, we find still another hill ahead of us. When will we ever reach a downward slope?"

Using ultrasound and other tests, the hepatologists and surgeons discovered that my problem was caused by a blockage in the main duct that drains bile into the intestines. This meant surgery to remove the block. Dr. James Perkins, the surgeon for my transplant, did this second operation, which lasted four hours. He explained to Ginny later that it took longer than expected because he had to cut through the scar tissue from my original transplant.

This time the incision was not as long and only twenty-four staples were needed to close it up. But the residual pain from this second surgery was more intense than from the transplant. Even a shallow breath was agonizing because of the fresh incision. Adding to my discomfort, the nurses kept forcing me to cough and breathe deeply to clear my lungs and prevent a fluid buildup called "atelectasis," a hazard for all surgical patients, especially those in run-down condition. For the first time, I asked for and received a small amount of morphine at night so I could sleep.

I was discharged from the hospital following the second surgery just in time for the mid-summer Rochester Days festival, which featured a big parade with marching bands, floats, clowns, and horses. There also was a band concert, an outdoor food fair by the town's restauranteurs, an old-fashioned ice cream social, and other red-white-and-blue Americana right out of *The Music Man*.

I became as excited as a little boy on the Fourth of July, nagging Ginny to walk me from our motel to as many events as we could make. The Sunday afternoon antique auto parade almost was my undoing. It proved that I was not ready for prime-time action just yet.

Ginny left me sitting on a curb watching the parade of old cars while she went to buy us hotdogs at an outdoor stand a few blocks away. For someone who has absolutely no interest in automobiles—antique or modern—I thoroughly enjoyed watching the vintage cars chugging through town.

When the parade of cars was over, families collected their kids, collapsed their folding chairs, and went home. City workers came with a truck and picked up the wooden horses blocking the intersections. I found myself sitting on the curb with the sun sinking behind me—wondering what could be keeping Ginny with our hotdogs. That's when I realized that I could not get up. My legs were like floppy tree branches; the staples in my body burned like hot rivets when I tried to use my arms to push up.

After sitting on the curb like the town drunk for maybe half an hour, I became seriously distressed. No pedestrians were strolling along the Sunday evening streets; living room lights were flicking on all over town. That old paranoia returned to hover over me like a dark cloud; Ginny never would have abandoned me unless something had happened to her. Could she have been run over by an antique auto on the way to get our hotdogs?

Finally, I flopped back on the grass and rolled over and over until I hit the metal pole of a no-parking sign. Using the pole, I managed to pull myself to my feet. Exhausted from the effort and anxious about Ginny, I wobbled back to our motel, arriving just as she pulled up in a taxi. Finding the hotdog stand closed and not wanting to disappoint me, she had wandered all over downtown looking for a sandwich vendor. In desperation, she had gone all the way to the hospital to buy two packaged tuna fish salad sandwiches in the employee cafeteria. She looked so tired, and I was so relieved to see her in one piece, that I didn't tell her about my own street corner adventure—not until we finished the tuna fish sandwiches. They weren't half bad.

In mid-July, 110 days after we first arrived at Mayo Clinic for evaluation for transplant, I was sent home. My brother Joe's wife, Colleen, drove up in a dense heat wave to bring us home. Before leaving, I was given a black loose-leaf notebook with specific instructions on how to keep myself alive and how to ease back into seminormal life.

Some of the instructions were obvious, but some were not. For one thing, I was never to take aspirin because it can cause internal bleeding. Blood clotting always is a problem for liver patients. Nor could I take erythromycin or tetracycline, two commonly prescribed antibiotics, because of complications when mixed with the immunosuppressant drugs. Because patients who are immunosuppressed are at risk of skin cancers, I was to use a sun screen when in direct sunlight.

"Avoid contact with persons known to have contagious illnesses such as chicken pox, shingles, hepatitis, influenza, etc." In my hypochondriacal state, this warning seemed unnecessary. I was directed to inspect inside my mouth daily for any white spots that might indicate a fungal growth. At the first sign of any problems, I was to telephone a special number at Mayo Clinic. I was never to take any medication—even if prescribed by my local doctor—without getting an okay from the transplant coordinator on duty.

During recovery I was told to refrain from driving a car for at least four weeks and should lift nothing heavier than fifteen pounds for six months. Given my general sedentary home life prior to transplant, Ginny was amused by this warning: "Do not participate in contact sports such as football and karate."

Once home I was exhausted from the second surgery so soon after the trauma of the transplant, and I was enervated by the oppressive heat of that summer. Now that the crisis had passed, Ginny was psychologically and physically drained. For the first time, she slipped into a shell, not sure if she wanted to be alone or among friends. Not used to seeing her so quiet and withdrawn, I was totally inept in trying to lift her spirits. I was still too wounded to take over her duties as family cheerleader.

We experienced other conflicts that strained our homecoming. In my efforts to regain control over my life, I began to butt into everybody's business, most particularly Ginny's. I remember spending one afternoon rearranging everything in the kitchen cabinets—for no particular reason except that I was bored and it did not involve any heavy hauling. Unwilling to take any more of my bossiness, she told me one day in no uncertain terms: "Buzz off, buster."

I also became overly possessive about our joint checking account—something that never had been a problem in our marriage. Needing the independence that money in the pocket provides, I became obsessive about carrying the checkbook and wanting to take over all of our check writing.

For two years Ginny had become used to making unilateral decisions and managing our affairs. It was not easy for either of us to regain the balance in duties and responsibilities that had developed more or less naturally in our marriage prior to my illness.

There were other, less tangible, experiences that added to our malaise and disappointment in those first weeks back home. When you go through a long, frightening ordeal, you assume that other people appreciate and know something about what has happened to you. To our dismay, we learned that some acquaintances and many neighbors did not have any conception of what we had gone through for the last two years. This came across one day soon after our return when a neighbor from around the block stopped upon seeing Ginny working in the garden and idly asked, "Have you been away on vacation?"

I'm not sure what we expected, but it certainly was not indifference on the part of so many people who, while not close friends, should have shown some interest in what's happening to people they know. Ginny compared our disappointment to what soldiers who fought in Vietnam must have felt upon returning to an indifferent reception. In one sense, we wanted to put it all behind us. In another, we wanted people to understand what hell we had been through. Perhaps we were seeking validation in the wrong place— some sort of a psychic victory parade.

The other annoyance, for me at least, in the immediate days after our return from Rochester came, not from indifferent acquaintances, but from relatives and friends who would not—or could not— understand that I was not "cured," but would have to live with severe restrictions and specific health hazards for the rest of my life. Organ transplantation is not like having a successful operation that once and for all clears up your problem and makes you whole.

"It's a miracle," one friend said, hugging me. "You're all well again."

231

One side of me did not want to play the martyr and ignore the positive results of what truly was a "miracle" of medical science. But I wanted to explain to people that Ginny and I faced recurring battles ahead; that whatever victory we achieved would always be a partial one.

Late one afternoon about two weeks after we were home, Ginny and I went to see Dr. Vern Kerchberger, the young doctor who had, more than any single person, convinced me to try for the transplant. Not only did we want to thank him for what he had done for us, we wanted to tell him what we had learned about transplantation and, not least of all, show him that I was on the road to recovery.

He took us into his office and just stood smiling at me, like someone who was seeing a real, live movie star up close. "I can't believe what I'm looking at," he said, rubbing his hands. "You look so good!" Then I realized that Kerchberger and his partner, John McGillen, never had seen me except with the green pallor of death on my face. They had become our main doctors after I already was in end-stage liver failure.

When I thanked him for convincing me to try for the transplant, he shook his head, "I sure would have felt terrible if you had died up there."

I reminded him of what he already knew: that I was out of options and was going to die whether I went to Mayo Clinic or stayed home.

Dr. McGillen was not in the office that afternoon, so we only saw young Kerchberger. But we sat talking to him for ninety minutes after his last patient was gone. Near the end, Ginny began telling him about her problems in adjusting to normal life after so many months being my nursemaid and living like a gypsy in motels. In one sense, she said, she felt more at home and secure in Rochester than she did in her own hometown.

"At least people there understand what we went through," she said.

Kerchberger, an internist forced into the role of psychologist, listened patiently, then looked at Ginny with a boyish smile and said: "The trouble with you, Ginny, is that you're suffering from Mayo withdrawal."

Ginny denied it vehemently. But a few days later she said to me, "You know, Vern is absolutely right about Mayo withdrawal."

That night she got on the telephone to Jurine Schellberg's home in Rochester for an hour of spousal counseling. It may not have been in Jurine's official job description as social worker for the transplant team, but holding the hands of patients and their spouses long after they had been sent home to heal was part of how she viewed her job.

Meeting with Dr. Kerchberger reminded me of the promise I had made to Ginny and myself about trying to repay the enormous debt we owed to people who had helped us. I remembered him saying that, should I survive the transplant, I could do something many others could not—write about it. Ever since regaining my senses after the transplant, I had been scribbling notes for a possible article and book. Now was the time to do something more than make notes and harangue Ginny about my plans. Also, both of us knew I needed to regain my confidence that I could write and work again.

In the first week of October—less than five months after my transplant—we flew to New York so I could try to sell *Newsweek*'s editors on my idea for a story on the emerging science of organ transplantation. While Ginny went shopping, I had lunch in a small dining room at the magazine's headquarters on Madison Avenue with five editors, including editor-in-chief, Rick Smith, and editor, Maynard Parker. Though I knew each of the men in the room well—three of them for almost twenty years—I was so nervous and hyped-up that I could not eat a single bite of lunch. Like an overeager job applicant, I babbled out my proposal—which was to do an overview article on the science of transplantation and the critical shortage of organ donors, along with a short personal "sidebar" on my own experience.

No one spoke as I rambled nonstop, barely pausing to catch a breath. They quietly ate their lunch, occasionally nodding in a kindly, but noncommittal way. I could not tell if they were fascinated by my proposal or wondering what might be for dessert.

"So that's my idea," I concluded, as the waiter removed my untouched plate. "I know I'm strong enough to write the story—and the people in the Chicago bureau could help me out if needed."

No one spoke for some time after I finished. My stomach turned cold. All the confidence drained out of me. Maybe I had become so enmeshed in my own story that I had lost all judgment about its worth as a piece of journalism. After all, Vern Kerchberger was a doctor, not an editor. What did he know about satisfying the interests of readers of *Newsweek?* And why would these sophisticated New York editors care about my near-frantic desire to use *Newsweek* to repay a perceived debt to people who had helped me or to encourage more people to become organ donors? These might be proper motives for a letter to the local newspaper, but were they reasons for using up scarce column inches in an international newsmagazine?

At last Rick Smith spoke. He said, "No." My heart sank. I felt as defeated and empty as when John McGillen had told me that I only had a few months to live. As a journalist, I was losing the chance to write the best story of my career. In the entire history of the world I was the first professional writer to undergo a liver transplant, the most complex operation being done in this emerging medical science. Beyond that, I was losing the chance to give meaning to all that Ginny and I had gone through; to transform all the anxiety, pain, and fear we had experienced into a message of hope for others facing similar or worse ordeals.

I was so stunned that I did not realize at first that the editor-in-chief was still speaking—or that, far from rejecting my story, he was already performing as an editor—publishing my idea and giving it focus. The story would have the most impact, Smith said, if it was not done in the traditional newsmagazine format, but as a first-person narrative that showed all the pain, fear, and, yes, even humor of our experience.

"Do you think you can do that?" he asked.

"I'm your boy," I said eagerly.

By the time our plane landed at Chicago's O'Hare Airport, I already had written in my notebook a tentative opening—or "lead"—and a possible concluding paragraph—or "kicker"—for the story. I showed them to Ginny as we taxied to the gate.

"Now all you have to do is fill in the big blank in between," she said in her old way.

We were home at last. Tommorrow would be just another ordinary day.

24
HAPPILY
EVER
AFTER

I went to work on my story for *Newsweek,* often scribbling on a yellow pad in the middle of the night. I worked in short bursts, whenever my energy peaked for a few hours. My mind was far ahead of my body in coming back to life. Six months passed before I could walk up a flight of stairs. Liver transplant patients have no stomach support muscles and have to crawl up stairs for months after surgery. I could not even make the one low step outside our front door without help. A long walk was to the corner and back—slowly.

I also learned that the warnings of side effects from the antirejection drugs are not to be ignored. At my three-month checkup, Ginny pointed out to the doctors two raw lesions on my face that turned out to be cancerous. Fortunately, they were basal cell carcinoma, the least serious type of skin cancer. A dermatologist cut them out while I was in bed awaiting a liver biopsy. He asked Ginny to press gauze on the forehead incision to stop the bleeding while he sliced off the other growth on my cheek. "Now I can say I assisted in surgery at the Mayo Clinic," she told the young doctor. Thereafter I followed orders about using a sun block when outside.

For the first time I had problems after a biopsy. Dr. Hunter was working with white rats on a research project and was not available to do the job. It was no one's fault, but I began bleeding internally after the biopsy. I had to fight for each breath. Since I never experienced this before, I was alarmed. After checking with the doctors, Mary Larson gave me a shot of Demerol to smother the pain so I could take deep breaths. Eventually the bleeding stopped by itself.

I also had an angiogram, the insertion of a probe up an artery in my right leg. Unfortunately, the probe did not enter the vessel at the proper angle and the next day I had a lump the size of an ostrich egg in my groin. I was hospitalized for a week. At first, they put a heavy sandbag on the leg to stop the internal bleeding. It was like being trapped under a log all night. When that did not work, Dr. Krom took me to surgery, put me under general anesthetic, and closed the leak with two stitches. For the next month I hobbled around on a stiff leg that was bruised purple and yellow.

It was one more proof of what we had learned—that any invasive medical procedure is accompanied by risks, even when done by skilled professionals at one of the best medical centers in the world.

Things went smoothly at my six-month checkup, which seemed more like a reunion party for Ginny than a checkup for me. Not only did she get a chance to renew friendships while I was undergoing my tests, she also met a new group of men and women who were there for liver transplants. Jurine Schellberg recruited Ginny to encourage the newcomers, who—like us such a short time before—anxiously were waiting word on their chances for transplant or sitting "on the beeper" awaiting a lifesaving organ.

Neither of us realized it then, but those few days in Rochester marked a new beginning for Ginny and me. From then on, we became involved in the lives of men and women from all over the country. In this way, we came to understand a simple truth: that you never can repay the actual people who help you in your trip through life, whether they be parents, teachers, or friends. But you can "pass the payment on," looking for opportunities to share in the pain, the loneliness, and the fears of someone else.

This came more naturally to Ginny than to me. In my case, it took serious illness and a close brush with death to make me less indifferent to the troubles of others and more aware of our connectedness to one another.

At the Tuesday afternoon support meeting, Ginny met Michelle

Gersten of Miami, whose husband, Walter, had been transplanted two months before and was still hospitalized with multiple complications. Although their backgrounds were different—Michelle, Jewish and originally from New York, and Ginny, Irish "to the max" and from Chicago—they became instant friends. Not only did they share a love for gardening, they also had the same street-smart, no-nonsense way of facing problems.

Standing atop one another, Ginny and Michelle could not dunk a basketball. Together they didn't weigh as much as a second-string high school fullback. More than just in size, they were alike in their honesty in facing life head-on and not deceiving themselves.

At our motel Ginny also met Tom and Becky Ozbirn, from Belmont, Mississippi. Tom, a soft-spoken Baptist minister, and Becky, an ever-smiling southern beauty, needed all the encouragement people could offer. Tom had suffered from a delibitating liver disease for three years, with a bone-density complication that caused him constant pain when he walked. They faced one of the roughest roads of any couple we were to meet at Mayo, but they ended up inspiring the staff as well as other patients with their courage and good humor in the face of mounting troubles.

Besides answering people's specific questions about my transplant, Ginny tried to give them hope. It was the same encouragement that Mike Kelly, the Texas veterinarian, and other transplant recipients had given us in the anxious days before my own surgery.

One snowy night during my six-month checkup, Dr. Ellen Hunter invited Ginny and me and Becky Ozbirn to her small, rented house for a turkey dinner. Ginny, who had just met Michelle Gersten that afternoon, asked if we could bring her new friend. Both Michelle's and Becky's husbands were hospitalized, so I was the only man at the dinner. Two years before, I would have made any excuse to avoid being the only male at a party. But I had become more comfortable in the company of women during my illness. I could talk to them without having to pretend that I was witty or cool or tough—or any of the other "social" poses that men sometimes feel they must adopt in mixed company.

While I joined in the conversation, I felt somewhat an outsider when Michelle, Becky, and Ginny talked about how their lives had changed since their spouses became ill. I realized how different the caregiver's experience is from the patient's. In many ways, it is far easier to be the one who is ill than the one doing the nursing. You become passive when seriously ill, unable to do anything for yourself. But, if you are the one providing care, you take on burdens that at times seem superhuman.

During this six-month "oil and lube job" at Mayo, I realized how vain I could be. Maybe it was a sign that I was coming back to life, but I began to worry about my appearance again. I became self-conscious of my puffy jowls and pop-eyed look from taking prednisone. I kept waiting for this "chipmunk" face to diminish as my nurse Mary Larson had said would happen as my dosage gradually was lowered to a maintenance level. Ginny teased me about covering the lower part of my face with my hand, like a matron trying to hide a double chin.

With my scarred arm and cross-stitched body, I was not exactly a candidate for modeling watchbands or swim suits either. One time while sitting on a bench with other shirtless men awaiting chest x-rays, an old gentleman looked at my "half Mercedes" scar and clucked: "Looks like somebody took after you with a can opener, son." I folded my arms primly across my chest.

Six months after my transplant, I suffered another setback. It started with a dull, persistent pain behind my left ear and around my left eye. Reverting to my old paranoia, I immediately thought the worst. "Either I have a brain tumor or a leak in my head," I told Ginny. Long ago she had stopped getting excited over my self-diagnoses. But, after a few days of listening to my woes, she called the doctor.

Dr. John McGillen looked at the crusty red blisters forming on my forehead and around the eye and said, "You have to go to the hospital for a few days."

I had herpes zoster, better known as shingles. When he told me that I had shingles, I started laughing. Now I knew he was kidding about going to the hospital. Shingles are what your Aunt Tilly got—they itched and caused discomfort, but you didn't go to the hospital with them.

Wrong! In my immunosuppressed state I was in danger of all sorts of complications from shingles, not the least being blindness, if my eye became infected, and death, should my new liver be compromised.

The doctor explained that the shingles actually was an eruption of chicken pox virus that had lain dormant in my spinal root ganglia since I had it as a child. With my immune system dampened by the drugs, the virus "woke up" and migrated to the nerves around my left eye.

I ended up in the hospital for a week with an IV draining a drug called acyclovir into my arm. I remembered Mary Larson had given me acyclovir in pill form for several weeks after my transplant to fend off the herpes virus.

While hospitalized, I wrote the last section of my story for *Newsweek* on a yellow legal pad. The first week of 1988 I printed the story on clean, double-spaced paper and sent it to my editors in New York, confident that it would run as a feature in the Medical section of the magazine within the next few weeks.

After two decades at the magazine, I should have known better. The story idled in the editorial gizzards of *Newsweek* for nine months. During the wait I felt like an expectant mother, wondering whether I ever would see my story in print. When I saw Dr. Rudd Krom in the recovery room after my one-year biopsy that spring, he asked about my story. When I told him it was "in the works," he smiled: "I think it was easier for you to get a new liver than it is to get your story into *Newsweek.*" I was beginning to think the same thing.

During the one-year checkup, I gave Robert Saunders, Mayo's organ procurement coordinator, an anonymous thank-you letter to be forwarded to the family of my donor on the anniversary of my transplant. I had delayed sending it until I could tell the family, with some certainty, that my transplant was working and that their priceless gift had not been wasted. It was Bob Saunders who told us that my donor had lived about 1,000 miles from Rochester and also had provided two kidneys and bone. The family had turned down a specific request for the heart and corneas. I thought this puzzling until a medical ethicist later told me that some religious fundamentalists believe that a person's heart and eyes are central to one's being and needed in the afterlife.

Several circumstances melded to delay publication of my *News-week* story—one in my favor. The top editors decided that it would run as a cover story. That guaranteed it prominent display and plenty of space. On the other hand, the magazine can only run fifty-two cover stories a year. Without a "time peg," my story had to compete for one of those weekly cover spots against breaking news from all over the world. Since it also was a presidential election year, political stories were certain to knock competing news off the cover week after week.

After several cancellations, my story finally was scheduled to run the week after the Republican convention in August. The editors figured that the convention would be cut-and-dried, that readers would be bored with political news, and that a medical cover story would offer a nice change of pace to end the summer. What did George Bush do? He made unexpected news by naming Dan Quayle as his vice presidential running mate. My story was put on hold again. It looked as if candidate Bush had delivered the coup de grace to my transplant story. Magazine stories do not have unlimited shelf life. If they keep getting held, the editors get bored with seeing them on the weekly story lists and decide to "kill" them—even though they would still be fresh for readers.

The story finally appeared on Labor Day weekend, 1988, with the back of my head and Dr. John McGillen's face on the cover as he examined me with his stethoscope. In any given week, some 3.4 million people subscribe to *Newsweek*. But studies show that world-wide more than 18 million people read the magazine each week.

Knowing how many people would read the story—and how long magazines lay around doctors' offices and barber shops—I felt a sense of accomplishment that made the long, anxious wait seem worthwhile. As Ginny and I sat on our screen porch, not reading, just fanning the slick pages of the magazine and thinking of all the people in the world who would read our story, we both felt that our journey had ended. Publication of our story gave meaning to our experience, allowing us to offer hope to people who were hurting and repaying, if only in small coin, those who had helped us.

Actually, getting our story into the magazine marked, not the end, but the start of a new phase in our journey. Within days we began receiving letters and phone calls from all over the country—actually, it later turned out, from all over the world. Many were from people who were dying from a variety of diseases. Some had undergone transplants or had lost relatives following unsuccessful transplants. The most touching letters and calls came from families who had donated organs of their loved ones so people like me could keep living.

I even got a letter from "Dear Abby," in real life Mrs. Morton Phillips of Beverly Hills, California. She had mentioned my article to a young editor at the *Los Angeles Times,* John Brownell, who turned out to be a former student of mine when I taught a news writing course at Northwestern University. By coincidence, John's father owns the drug store across the street from Del's Cafe in St. Charles, Minnesota, where Ginny and I were having lunch when my "beeper" called me to transplant.

Ginny received a letter from the English wife of a man in Moscow who had undergone a liver transplant in London about the time I had mine at Mayo Clinic. "This is just a hand-squeeze across the ocean from one supportive wife to another," she wrote. Another coincidence: When I told my friend Bill Schmidt about this letter, it turned out that he had been a guest in this couple's home when he had been a correspondent for *Newsweek* in Moscow.

Soon our days and evenings were filled with answering letters and talking to people on the phone. I remember one Saturday night when Ginny was on the phone for two hours with a young mother from Kansas City who had been told she would die without a transplant. She was terribly frightened by the idea—with good cause, it turned out. Eighteen months later she never woke up after her liver transplant.

At first we were stimulated by the letters and phone calls asking for advice, encouragement, or information about transplantation. But, as with the young mother from Kansas City, we soon realized how many people were desperately seeking the smallest measure of hope and how limited was our capacity to provide it.

An Indianapolis business executive called me after learning he had terminal liver disease. I arranged through Jurine Schellberg for Mayo to evaluate him for a transplant. Ginny and I even met him there—for a brief pep talk between his tests. They told him his only hope was a transplant, but he wanted first to put his affairs in order

241

back home. The night before he was to return to Mayo, he called me because he was experiencing mind-blurring hepatic encephalopathy and was frightened. I told him to call his doctor immediately and not to drive anywhere by himself. Not hearing from him for a few days, I called his office and learned that he had died in an Indianapolis hospital from bleeding and kidney failure the day after he had called me.

Though I barely knew him, I was devastated—maybe because our stories had such parallel beginnings but such sadly divergent endings. His secretary later sent me an essay he had written about his illness. Ironically, he had submitted it a few months before to the My Turn section of *Newsweek,* which had politely rejected it "because one of our staff is writing a story on the same subject."

One night Ginny and I drove to a northern suburb of Chicago to meet Paul and Martha Flannery, a young couple from New Jersey who had written to us. He was dying of liver disease, and they were staying with relatives while he was evaluated at a Chicago transplant center. They had two little girls, then four and twenty-two months old. We tried to encourage them as best we could.

We did not hear from them for several months. Then we got a short note from Martha. I will never forget her opening sentence: "Paul and I have fallen upon some bad times." Indeed, they had. He had been accepted for transplant, only to be rejected at the last minute when cancer was found in his lungs during final tests. They went back to New Jersey where Paul died within two months. Ginny and I cried after reading her letter.

One of the first letters we received after the *Newsweek* story was from a woman who had found the magazine in a motel room while in Memphis with her thirty-eight-year-old daugther, who had suffered from chronic liver disease since birth. In an emotional five-page letter, the mother said that she and her daughter, Mary Ann, sat up until three in the morning rereading the article. "It could only be the hand of God that left it for us," the mother wrote.

That was how Mary Ann Mowery entered our lives. We began a long-distance phone and letter-writing friendship with her. In a picture she sent us, Mary Ann had the calm eyes and gentle smile of a fragile madonna.

The divorced mother of three young children, Mary Ann had no health insurance and needed to raise a $95,000 deposit to get on the waiting list for a liver transplant in Memphis. Her neighbors in Smyrna, Tennessee, did everything from holding bake sales to walk-a-thons to help raise the money. Then a man who said he owned a pest control business volunteered to handle her fund-raising. Later identified as a con man from St. Louis, he took off one day with all the money they had raised—an estimated $10,000.

A businessman from the nearby town of Lebanon read of Mary Ann's plight and came to her rescue. Jack Cato, a soft-spoken, "good-old-boy" who owns an appliance store, took it upon himself to become a legitimate fund-raiser for Mary Ann. He carried her cause to churches, civic groups, and newspaper editors throughout western Tennessee. He even lined me up to do some long-distance radio talk shows with Mary Ann.

Within a few weeks, one of Jack's friends, a local contractor named Eddie McCrary, decided that it would take too long to raise the money through public appeals. Mary Ann might not live that long. Incredibly, Eddie McCrary wrote a personal check for $75,000, the balance still needed for Mary Ann to be activated for transplant. He dropped it off at Jack Cato's store like it was the last payment on a television set.

Soon after that, Ginny and I returned from participating in a panel on "Death and Dying" at the University of Tennessee in Knoxville, at the other end of the state from Mary Ann Mowery, Jack Cato, and Eddie McCrary. There was a message on our answering machine from Jack. A donor liver had been found and Mary Ann had been taken to surgery for her transplant. She died on the operating table when surgeons could not stop her bleeding.

There were many sad endings to the stories we heard. But we also shared in many joyful and surprising stories.

Though it started out sadly, one happy tale belonged to young Jim and Judy Werneski of Kenosha, Wisconsin. They came to lunch on our porch one Sunday after Jurine Schellberg had recommended they talk to us. Their young lives had been devastated by the news that Jim, a big, friendly construction worker, was dying of the same form of hepatitis that had ravaged my liver. Jim first realized he should see a doctor while erecting a giant construction crane for a new medical education building at Mayo Clinic. "Do you realize where you are?" one of Jim's fellow hard hats asked when he complained of constant fatigue and itching. He decided to see what Mayo's experts could do for him. Their only answer was a transplant.

Not only did Jim's illness appear to destroy their hopes of having a family, it also threatened their economic future. Unable to work, he lost his job and his medical insurance. Even if he survived a transplant and figured out how to pay for it, he no longer would be able do the heavy construction labor for which he was trained.

We talked for four hours, answering question after question that Jim had written in a spiral notebook. For someone who had worked with his hands most of his life, he was extremely well spoken and studious in manner. They left at twilight to drive back to Kenosha. As I helped Ginny clear the table after they were gone, she said to me, "I really think we gave them some hope."

The glow from the young couple's visit was to remain with us long afterwards, lifting our spirits at other times when we wanted so much to help someone who called on us, but didn't know how.

Among the most touching letters we received after the *Newsweek* article were eighteen from parents or relatives of organ donors. To my surprise, one came from Reneé Panno, head of the intensive care nurses who had kept me alive through so many crises at our local hospital. Her brother-in-law had been a liver and kidney donor.

One letter, written on New Year's Eve, 1988, was from Jean and Gary Ales of St. Paul, Minnesota. Their eighteen-year-old son, Kevin, a handsome, talented high school senior who wanted to be a writer, had died two years earlier from a burst aneurysm in his brain that had gone undetected since birth. They had given permission for Kevin's organs to be donated. His heart saved the life of a fourteen-year-old girl from South Dakota who was dying of cardiomyopathy; his liver went to a Minnesota mother of two teenage boys. One kidney went to a thirty-seven-year-old woman at the Mayo Clinic, the other kidney to a thirty-seven-year old man from South Carolina. Kevin's lungs were used in research; his corneas restored the vision of two unknown people; some of his skin and bone went to an undetermined number of others.

While Jean and Gary Ales took comfort in knowing that many

people benefited from Kevin's priceless gifts, they expressed hurt over the impersonal way they and other donor families had been treated by the transplant community. They felt that they were the "unrecognized and unsung participants in the transplant process." Once they had given permission for Kevin's organs to be transplanted, they felt abandoned. Their letter told of their efforts to start a national support group for families of organ donors.

We were so touched by their letter that we drove to St. Paul to meet them. In a way, I was transferring my feelings for my own unknown donor family to this couple, who had shown extraordinary generosity at a time of intense grief. Experts say that sudden death and the death of a child are the hardest losses for survivors to cope with. That's what makes the families of organ donors so remarkable.

The protocols of transplant medicine, which are designed to protect the privacy of both donor and recipient, have the negative side effect of isolating donor families during their grieving—even from one another.

Another motive I had in visiting Jean and Gary Ales was to explore the possibility of writing about the problems and concerns of donor families, the "forgotten heroes" of transplantation. It would be another chance to pay a debt—not to my actual benefactors—but on behalf of all organ and tissue recipients to the kind strangers whose names we never would know.

Meeting the donor families made me ponder again the age-old question: Why do such good people have to suffer? One of the paradoxes of life is that the good seem to suffer even more than the rest of us. I will not venture an answer beyond the hopeful one I learned from my parents and grandparents—that God works in mysterious and wondrous ways.

But I offer one observation that slowly formed in my mind over the course of Ginny's and my ordeal. When people in trouble or pain cry out, "Why me, Lord?" they should not be dismissed as complainers or ingrates. They are asking precisely—precisely—the right question.

In every sadness lies a seed of promise. Like little Jennifer Hoce's poem put it: "You can't see the rainbow till after the rain." When you cry out "Why me?" you really are asking, "What can I become or what can I do for others because of my experience with suffering?"

People who stoically shoulder their pain without asking "Why Me?" are missing the chance to enrich their own lives and the lives of those around them. They are failing to look for the promise that lies hidden just beneath the surface of every heartbreak.

EPILOGUE: TRULY A GOOD KID

I just came home from romping in a field with two horses named "Thunder" and "Lightning." Before you start thinking that Ginny and I have retired to a ranch in Montana, let me explain. "Thunder" is our oldest grandson, Matthew VanEgeren, now three years old. "Lightning" is his little brother, Kevin, who is fourteen months and just beginning to toddle around. Two little fellows I never expected to see—much less play horse with.

Matthew decided to become a horse—and to transform me into "Grandpa Horse"—after we took him to the circus where he saw a white stallion dance on his hind legs. When his mother suggested that horses need names, he picked "Thunder." After his brother arrived, it was agreed all around that a fitting name for Thunder's stablemate would be "Lightning."

If I ever write a book on child rearing, I will devote a chapter to "Horsing Around." I have discovered a wonderful secret from playing with my pair of grandson-horses. When they are in their "horse mode," they will obey every command, whether it be to eat their cereal ("Have some more oats, Thunder."); go to bed ("Head for the barn. There's a storm coming!"); or share a toy ("Let the little horse do some of the work."). I have told their parents not to be in any hurry to rear them out of their horsehood. They will drop their whinnying and attention to orders soon enough.

One dark day when I was dying, I wrote in my journal that all I wanted was to live long enough to take a grandchild to Wrigley Field. That came true through the kindness of John Madigan, chief executive officer of the Tribune Company, owner of the Chicago Cubs baseball team. After reading in my *Newsweek* story about my affection for the Cubs, he sent me front-row seats behind the team dugout for Ginny and me, little Matthew, and his parents, Rick and Katie. Not only was it Matthew's first Cubs game, it also was Ginny's.

They even gave Matthew a baseball, which might spoil him for life if he thinks he will get one every time he goes to a game. More than anything, he liked watching a small airplane lazily pulling a beer sign over the park all afternoon. Ginny, an indifferent sports fan, enjoyed talking to a family behind us and watching the grounds-keeping crew—especially when they had to roll out the tarpaulin during a rain delay.

I can modestly say that I am more suited for being a grandpa than for anything else I have done in life. I am good at crawling around on all fours pretending to be a horse. I also like visiting fire stations, watching freight trains rumble through town, and teaching youngsters how to make all sorts of sounds by blowing across bottle tops. I am good at making up stories about frogs and trolls. When I read storybooks to little people, I can imitate any pitched voice, from monster to mouse.

Newsweek's editors and I agreed that I never again would have the stamina for day-to-day journalism. After doing a story on the shortage of doctors in rural America and a piece about economic development in a small Illinois town, I dropped my "comeback" and took early retirement to start a new career as a speaker on organ donation and a free-lance writer.

My first story as an independent writer was for *Ladies' Home Journal* about the family of Kevin Ales and eight other donor families. As for Gary and Jean Ales, who could pose for a Norman Rockwell portrait of an American dad and mom—he works with young people in his job as a high school guidance counselor and coach, and she has a new studio behind their St. Paul house for doing pottery and painting. They are helping other organ donor families cope with their unique type of grieving. When one of their daughters recently was married, among the guests was the Minneapolis woman who became a close friend after learning by accident that their son Kevin's liver is keeping her alive.

Ginny is a volunteer at Northwest Community Hospital where I spent so many days and nights during the early months of my illness. For two years she served as chairwoman of the Chicago Metropolitan Area Liver Transplant Support Group. Much of her time, especially evenings, is spent encouraging nervous patients facing transplants or advising their families how to cope with the changes serious illness makes in their lives.

Margaret Kennedy Moser, her two children now in college, has joined the staff of another large Catholic parish in our area, coordinating its "Caring Ministries" and seventy volunteers. In addition to still making her daily hospital and home visits—on weekends accompanied by her accountant husband, Ron—Margaret has started a support group for widows and widowers called "New Day."

By coincidence, Terry Schott, my other "spiritual adviser," also has started a support group for the widowed called "Transitions." She works mainly with men and women under forty who have lost their spouses and are dealing with grief at the same time they are struggling to raise young children.

The self-effacing Dr. John McGillen finally showed me a sample of his writing and asked for a critique. It was a nonfiction piece about his two sons playing football for their school. He called it "The Boys of Autumn." I spent a Sunday afternoon with a red editing pencil, taking apart every sentence like a watchmaker. I figured I owed him the same professional effort as an editor that he gave me as a doctor. I'm not sure how he took all my red pencil marks. Ginny said I was too negative in my criticism. Actually the piece was quite entertaining, and his writing showed potential if he ever decides to give up doctoring for a less hectic career.

Recently Ginny and I ran into his partner, Vern Kerchberger, and his wife at a local restaurant. With them were their two little sons. Watching those well-behaved little boys having dinner with their doctor parents, I thought about the impact one person can have on our lives. Were it not for those boys' daddy, I would not be alive; he was the one who persuaded me not to give up, to risk the transplant. Because this young doctor took a special interest in me,

I would be taking my own grandsons to see the bright red engines at the fire station the next morning. Do you understand why I no longer can look at another human being with indifference?

Jurine Schellberg has retired as social worker for Mayo Clinic's liver transplant team. She and her architect husband, Willis, have built their dream house overlooking the crystal cold waters of Lake Superior. Ginny and I still call her for motherly advice whenever we encounter troubled waters.

My primary care nurse Mary Larson, who had two dogs and a husband when she was caring for me, has added two children, a boy and a girl, to her household. She still is on the job at Station 53 under head nurse Joyce Overman, helping an ever-growing parade of new liver transplant patients make their first tentative steps back to life. Last fall we attended Joyce's wedding to a young man who works for IBM in Rochester.

Two of the people closest to Ginny during our sojourn at Mayo endured long battles, only to experience different outcomes. After seven months of fighting multiple posttransplant infections, Michelle Gersten's husband, Walter, died in Rochester Methodist Hospital from bacterial infection throughout his body. One night after we returned from a speech in Indianapolis, Ginny felt compelled to call Michelle at her motel in Rochester. She broke into tears when Michelle told her that Walter was dying. Their conversation consisted of Michelle comforting Ginny, not the other way around. We left at four in the morning to drive to Mayo to be with her, arriving thirty minutes before Walter died. Michelle now works as a librarian at her temple in Miami, loves her garden, and still has long late-night phone conversations with Ginny, who I'm convinced more than ever was born with a telephone in her hand.

We thought we also would lose another friend, Tom Ozbirn, who not only endured three liver transplants because of chronic rejection, but also had both hip joints replaced because of bone deterioration from his disease. After spending months in the cold and snow of Minnesota, Tom and Becky finally made it back home to Mississippi. Tom has decided not to resume a traditional pastorate, but to use his ministry to inform church groups about transplantation and the critical shortage of organ donors.

Another new close friend, Frieda Kohn, also had to have both hip joints replaced after her liver transplant, one of many of my fellow patients to have follow-up complications. Unlike some, who have not been able to return to work, Frieda is back teaching in a Chicago school classroom.

Close friendships develop among many transplant recipients. Like soldiers who fought side by side in the trenches, they share a special bond that even the most empathetic "outsiders" never will understand. Among the strangest, and strongest, new friendships formed at Mayo Clinic was that of Tom Jorgensen from Ames, Iowa, and Howard (Bud) Brown from Naperville, Illinois. Tom, a high school coach and devoted Iowa State football fan, awoke from a coma after his liver transplant to find himself staring at a bright red University of Nebraska sweatshirt tacked to the wall. It was put up by his roommate, Bud Brown, who grew up in Nebraska and is a rabid "Cornhusker" fan. Tom later recalled that drifting out of a coma and seeing the hated Nebraska shirt made him think he had died and "gone in the wrong direction." Today they telephone and visit one another regularly, constantly bickering and razzing each other to the point that the rest of us call them "the odd couple." They have a standing date each fall to attend the Iowa State–Nebraska football game, loser paying all expenses.

Jim Werneski, who survived a twelve-hour transplant two months after visiting us on our porch, is studying at a community college to become a draftsman or illustrator. He also is back playing low-handicap golf and experimenting with abstract airbrush paintings. Someday he would like to exhibit his work at an art show.

Jennifer Hoce, the tiny song bird whose encouraging poem brightened my fifty-fourth birthday, graduated with honors from high school in Jacksonville, Florida. A class leader and accomplished musician, Jennifer also showed her old surgeon, Dr. Krom, how to swing a golf club. Despite recurring hospitalizations and setbacks since her transplant in April of 1985, she was captain of her school golf team. She attends the University of North Florida on a scholarship and is working toward a double degree in elementary education and business management.

Ginny and I finally met Jack Cato, who invited us to a day of fund-raising in Tennessee for a nurse needing a heart-lung transplant. Jack and his wife, Ruth, now devote most of their substantial energies to raising money for people needing transplants, mainly children. Along with his friend, Eddie McCrary, Jack has started a "One Hour for Life" campaign throughout their part of the state. The idea is to have people donate just one hour's pay each year to a special fund for those who cannot afford a transplant. The money left over from Mary Ann Mowery's failed surgery went to pay for some childrens' transplants.

I pray that *People* magazine and talk show hosts keep stroking their celebrity philanthropists and never discover Jack, Eddie, and their friends, who quietly are helping their neighbors—not because it is trendy or because it is good for their careers or because it massages their egos—but out of the simple goodness of their hearts.

While in Tennessee, I spoke to first-year medical students at Vanderbilt University in Nashville. Standing in the back of the auditorium during my talk was Dr. Ellen Hunter, my examining doctor from Mayo, now on Vanderbilt's medical staff. She turned tomato red and nearly fled in embarrassment when I told the would-be doctors of her skills and reputation as the "Biopsy Queen" of Mayo Clinic. Ginny, a chronic matchmaker, was delighted to learn of her plans to marry a Nashville pediatrician she had known since med school.

After my *Newsweek* article, Ginny and I were invited to speak or participate in panels by many medical and civic groups. Two of the invitations were particularly welcome. They came from the surgeons who had done my transplant: Dr. James Perkins and Dr. Dan Hayes, both of whom had left the Mayo Clinic.

Dr. Perkins started the liver transplant program at the University of Washington Medical Center in Seattle. Dr. Hayes established the liver transplant program at the Ochsner Clinic in New Orleans. Not only did their invitations give us a chance to visit two premier vacation cities, they also gave us a chance to renew our friendship with the surgeons who literally brought me back to life on that long night in May of 1987.

Our trip to New Orleans also provided an unexpected ending to our story, one that I never could have concocted were I writing fiction. It would have been too contrived an ending to be believed.

At a cake-and-coffee reception before my short talk to mark the first-year anniversary of Dr. Hayes's transplant program, a doctor came up to me with a smiling young man at his side. He introduced him as Bruce Pinsonat with the Louisiana Organ Procurement Agency. As one does at a reception, I prepared to make some small talk with them.

But the doctor's serious expression did not seem suited for small talk. He looked me squarely in the eye as if to make sure I was paying attention, then cocked his head toward the young man at his side and said: "Bruce here is the one who got you your liver."

I was so stunned that I could not speak; I just stared at this smiling young man, a stranger who had acted as my proxy in asking a grieving family for a priceless gift of life for me. Other than having been told that my new liver came from about 1,000 miles from Rochester, I had no idea where my donor lived or anything about him or her.

Baffled by suddenly meeting someone who had done me such a great kindness, I was struck dumb. I remember reaching out and touching the lapel of his suit jacket and trying to say, "Thank you." I am not certain if anything came out of my mouth, but that's what I tried to say.

Then someone came to lead me to the front of the room where a photographer took pictures and I said a few words. Afterwards, I looked for Pinsonat, but he had left. Fortunately, Ginny had gotten his card.

Back home, I wrote to Bruce Pinsonat to thank him for what he had done for me. By now I knew enough about organ procurement to understand how stressful and emotionally draining it is for the men and women who must approach spouses, parents, brothers, and sisters to ask them to consider donating the organs of their loved ones. They must do this delicate negotiating at a time when a family has just learned of the death of their loved one, usually under tragic and sudden circumstances.

In addition to thanking Pinsonat, I also wanted to learn as much as he could tell me about this nameless person whose liver now kept me alive. I was curious simply as a reporter. As a human being, I was even more intent on learning what I could about my unknown benefactor.

Several weeks passed, and I began to think that I never would hear back from him. Then we received a handwritten, three-page letter from Metairie, Louisiana. First, Pinsonat thanked me for encouraging him and his coworkers, including another nurse-coordinator named Catherine Brunson, "who helped with your donor."

Then he went to the heart of the matter.

"Mr. and Mrs. Maier, I really can't give you a whole lot of information about your donor, and I hope you understand.

"He was a young teenager involved in an auto accident. I can tell you from what I gathered and witnessed at the time from family and friends, that he was very well liked by his peers and truly a good kid.

"I see his mother occasionally, and your letter has brought her great comfort and is much appreciated."

Truly a good kid. Having raised four kids of my own—and knowing their friends as they grew up—I always have had warm feelings for teenagers, those awkward half-children, half-adults whose lives swing like a pendulum between hope and despair. I knew what it meant to say someone was "truly a good kid." I was comforted in knowing that I was kept alive by an organ that once belonged to someone like him.

There is not much of a track record yet for liver transplant patients. I have no idea what awaits Ginny and me over the next hill. All I know is that I have been given a reprieve, a sweet reprieve, that has allowed me to enjoy a happy, productive life for a few more years. Only a decade ago, I would not have had that option.

The medical miracle has not been without cost. What Mayo's experts predicted at the time of my transplant has come to pass: the wonder drug cyclosporine has begun to damage my kidneys. As a result, my doctors recently began to wean me off the potent drug. After taking cyclosporine religiously twice a day for more than three years, I feel like a tightrope walker performing without a net. But given the toxic harm that long-term cyclosporine use is known to cause in the kidneys, I have no choice. Perhaps researchers will come up with a new drug that will suppress the immune system without the harsh side effects. Or maybe my body will make friends with the stranger's liver and no longer see it as an invader to be expelled. That would be the happiest outcome.

But Ginny and I have lost most of our anxieties about the medical uncertainties that face us. We accept the basic premise that the transplanters gave us when first we wandered into their unfamiliar land: transplant recipients never are cured, they just trade a terminal disease for a lifetime of medical management.

Often at night when I cannot sleep, I sit in the dark and think, not about my physical health or how many more years I might have to enjoy friends and family, but about all that has happened to Ginny and me because of my illness. I think about how we have grown and changed because of what we have experienced and who we have met on our journey; how our lives have been enriched by it all.

Quite often my thoughts keep drifting back to the great mystery, the unanswerable question: why did God grant me a few more years of life, rather than that "truly good kid" from Louisiana?

POSTSCRIPT

In the fall of 1990 Frank Maier caught a virus. He and Ginny returned to the Mayo Clinic on November 18, their thirty-fifth wedding anniversary. The virus gradually overwhelmed his immune system and on Christmas Eve, Frank and Ginny decided to return home. Frank Maier died there, with his family, on the afternoon of New Year's Eve 1990.

That night his family celebrated his life. They did not cry. His sweet reprieve had been a triumph.

(Frank received his gift graciously, held it tenderly, and returned it with gratitude and hope. Unable to donate for transplant, he left his organs to science for research, so that the road might be made smoother for those who will follow.)